# Learn Swift by Building Applications

Explore Swift programming through iOS app development

**Emil Atanasov**

**BIRMINGHAM - MUMBAI**

# Learn Swift by Building Applications

**Commissioning Editor:** Ashwin Nair
**Acquisition Editor:** Reshma Raman
**Content Development Editor:** Nikhil Borkar
**Technical Editor:** Madhunikita Sunil Chindarkar
**Copy Editor:** Safis Editing
**Project Coordinator:** Ulhas Kambali
**Proofreader:** Safis Editing
**Indexer:** Pratik Shirodkar
**Graphics:** Tania Dutta
**Production Coordinator:** Arvindkumar Gupta, Nilesh Mohite

First published: May 2018

Production reference: 1230518

Published by Packt Publishing Ltd.
Livery Place
35 Livery Street
Birmingham
B3 2PB, UK.

ISBN 978-1-78646-392-0

www.packtpub.com

`mapt.io`

Mapt is an online digital library that gives you full access to over 5,000 books and videos, as well as industry leading tools to help you plan your personal development and advance your career. For more information, please visit our website.

## Why subscribe?

- Spend less time learning and more time coding with practical eBooks and Videos from over 4,000 industry professionals

- Improve your learning with Skill Plans built especially for you

- Get a free eBook or video every month

- Mapt is fully searchable

- Copy and paste, print, and bookmark content

## PacktPub.com

Did you know that Packt offers eBook versions of every book published, with PDF and ePub files available? You can upgrade to the eBook version at `www.PacktPub.com` and as a print book customer, you are entitled to a discount on the eBook copy. Get in touch with us at `service@packtpub.com` for more details.

At `www.PacktPub.com`, you can also read a collection of free technical articles, sign up for a range of free newsletters, and receive exclusive discounts and offers on Packt books and eBooks.

# Contributors

## About the author

**Emil Atanasov** is an IT consultant who has extensive experience with mobile technologies. He started working in the field of mobile development in 2006. He runs his own contracting and consulting company, serving clients from around the world—Appose Studio Inc. He is an MSc graduate from RWTH Aachen University, Germany, and Sofia University "St. Kliment Ohridski", Bulgaria. He has been a contractor for several large companies in the US and UK, serving variously as team leader, project manager, iOS developer, and Android developer.

*I want to thank my wife Elena, my family, and my friends for being very supportive, really patient, and super cool. Thank you for keeping me motivated through the endless work days. I know that in your eyes I'm a bizarre geeky person, who is spending most of the time in the digital world. I appreciate your understanding.*

# About the reviewer

**Giordano Scalzo** is a developer with 20 years of programming experience, since the days of ZXSpectrum. He has worked in C++, Java, .Net, Ruby, Python, and in a ton of other languages that he has forgotten the names of. After years of backend development, over the past 5 years, Giordano has developed extensively for iOS, releasing more than 20 apps—apps that he wrote for clients, enterprise application, or on his own. Currently, he is a contractor in London where, he delivers code for iOS through his company, Effective Code Ltd, aiming at quality and reliability.

*I'd like to thank my better half, Valentina, who lovingly supports me in everything I do: without you, none of this would have been possible.*
*Thanks to my bright future, Mattia and Luca, for giving me lots of smiles and hugs when I needed them.*
*Finally, my gratitude goes to my mum and dad, who gave me curiosity and the support to follow my passions, which began one day when they bought me a ZXSpectrum.*

# Packt is searching for authors like you

If you're interested in becoming an author for Packt, please visit `authors.packtpub.com` and apply today. We have worked with thousands of developers and tech professionals, just like you, to help them share their insight with the global tech community. You can make a general application, apply for a specific hot topic that we are recruiting an author for, or submit your own idea.

# Table of Contents

# Preface

*Learning Swift 4 by Building Applications* is a book that teaches the basics of Swift in the context of iOS. If you finish the book, you should be able to develop small-to-medium mobile apps. You will know how to create the app UI in storyboard using Xcode, how to load and display images fetched from the cloud, how to save and load information between different sessions of the app, and how to share data between all users of the app using the cloud.

## Who this book is for

The book is designed for beginners who have little or no experience with Swift or any other programming language. The first couple of chapters introduce the Swift and the core programming principals, which are used throughout the process of software development. The rest of the book discusses the Swift development of iOS mobile applications. We will explain how to use open source libraries to achieve rapid software development and develop apps that are consuming information and images from the cloud.

## What this book covers

Chapter 1, *Swift Basics – Variables and Functions*, discusses the basics of the Swift language, starting from the A, B, and C.

Chapter 2, *Getting Familiar with Xcode and Playgrounds*, presents the Xcode—a free IDE that we will use when developing Swift. We shouldn't forget that Xcode is developed by Apple and that the playgrounds are the perfect place for learning Swift step by step.

Chapter 3, *Creating a Minimal Mobile App*, makes you examine the minimal mobile app and its structure. This is the basis of every iOS mobile app written in Swift.

Chapter 4, *Structures, Classes, and Inheritance*, covers the benefit of different data structures and how easily we can model a real-world problems.

Chapter 5, *Adding Interactivity to Your First App*, looks at the different ways to add interactivity to an app or how to interact with the user in the app.

Chapter 6, *How to Use Data Structures, OOP, and Protocols*, explores the data structures and different techniques to incorporate them in our solutions.

Chapter 7, *Developing a Simple Weather App*, focuses on how to build a real mobile app starting from the UI and displaying static data.

Chapter 8, *Introducing CocoaPods and Project Dependencies*, introduces the modern way of rapid development using various dependency managers of Swift libraries.

Chapter 9, *Improving a Version of a Weather App*, discusses about consuming information from the public API and displaying it in our *Weather* app.

Chapter 10, *Building an Instagram-Like App*, builds an app from the idea step by step starting with the design, defines the basic UI, and connects it with a real cloud service provider—Firebase.

Chapter 11, *Instagram-Like App Continued*, makes the app complete and functional so that it can look like a working product, ready to be shared with users.

Chapter 12, *Contributing to an Open Source Project*, takes you through the basics of contributing to an open source project.

# To get the most out of this book

You have to know what is a computer and have basic knowledge of how to use a Mac. You have to be curious about how things work. We will start from the basics of the Swift programming language and Xcode. Most of the book is related to iOS, and it would be nice to have an iOS device to see your mobile applications working on a real device.

You need enough time and patience to go through the book and to experiment with the code, which can be found on GitHub.

# Download the example code files

You can download the example code files for this book from your account at www.packtpub.com. If you purchased this book elsewhere, you can visit www.packtpub.com/support and register to have the files emailed directly to you.

You can download the code files by following these steps:

1. Log in or register at `www.packtpub.com`.
2. Select the **SUPPORT** tab.
3. Click on **Code Downloads & Errata**.
4. Enter the name of the book in the **Search** box and follow the onscreen instructions.

Once the file is downloaded, please make sure that you unzip or extract the folder using the latest version of:

- WinRAR/7-Zip for Windows
- Zipeg/iZip/UnRarX for Mac
- 7-Zip/PeaZip for Linux

The code bundle for the book is also hosted on GitHub at `https://github.com/PacktPublishing/Learn-Swift-by-Building-Applications`. In case there's an update to the code, it will be updated on the existing GitHub repository.

We also have other code bundles from our rich catalog of books and videos available at `https://github.com/PacktPublishing/`. Check them out!

# Download the color images

We also provide a PDF file that has color images of the screenshots/diagrams used in this book. You can download it from `http://www.packtpub.com/sites/default/files/downloads/LearnSwiftbyBuildingApplications_ColorImages.pdf`.

# Conventions used

There are a number of text conventions used throughout this book.

`CodeInText`: Indicates code words in text, database table names, folder names, filenames, file extensions, pathnames, dummy URLs, user input, and Twitter handles. Here is an example: "This code creates a place in the memory, called `text`, where we store the text, `Hello world!`."

A block of code is set as follows:

```
func generateGreeting(greet:String, thing:String = "world") -> String {
    return greet + thing + "!"
}
print(generateGreeting(greet: "Hello "))
print(generateGreeting(greet: "Hello ", thing: " Swift 4"))
```

When we wish to draw your attention to a particular part of a code block, the relevant lines or items are set in bold:

```
let number = 5
let divisor = 3
let remainder = number % divisor //remainder is again integer
let quotient = number / divisor // quotient is again integer
```

Any command-line input or output is written as follows:

```
swift package init --type library
```

**Bold**: Indicates a new term, an important word, or words that you see onscreen. For example, words in menus or dialog boxes appear in the text like this. Here is an example: "Also, add an action to the **Sign In With Email** button."

Warnings or important notes appear like this.

Tips and tricks appear like this.

# Get in touch

Feedback from our readers is always welcome.

**General feedback**: Email feedback@packtpub.com and mention the book title in the subject of your message. If you have questions about any aspect of this book, please email us at questions@packtpub.com.

**Errata**: Although we have taken every care to ensure the accuracy of our content, mistakes do happen. If you have found a mistake in this book, we would be grateful if you would report this to us. Please visit www.packtpub.com/submit-errata, selecting your book, clicking on the Errata Submission Form link, and entering the details.

**Piracy**: If you come across any illegal copies of our works in any form on the Internet, we would be grateful if you would provide us with the location address or website name. Please contact us at copyright@packtpub.com with a link to the material.

**If you are interested in becoming an author**: If there is a topic that you have expertise in and you are interested in either writing or contributing to a book, please visit authors.packtpub.com.

# Reviews

Please leave a review. Once you have read and used this book, why not leave a review on the site that you purchased it from? Potential readers can then see and use your unbiased opinion to make purchase decisions, we at Packt can understand what you think about our products, and our authors can see your feedback on their book. Thank you!

For more information about Packt, please visit packtpub.com.

# Swift Basics – Variables and Functions

**1**

In this chapter, we will present the basics of the Swift language, starting from square one: introducing the basic concepts. The code, which is part of the chapter, illustrates the topics under discussion. In the next chapter, we will learn how to execute code samples in Xcode.

Let's begin with a brief history of Swift. This is a brand new programming language, developed by Apple and announced in 2014. In 2016, Swift 3 was released as open source, and this is the first major version, which enables people interested in Swift to develop the language. This means only one thing: Swift will start spreading even faster, beyond Apple's ecosystem. In this book, we will give examples of Swift, and we will discuss most of our solutions related to iOS, but you should know that the knowledge here is applicable across all places where Swift code is used.

Before diving into real code, let's define some basic concepts that we can use later in the book.

What is a **computer program** or **application (app)**? Simply, we can think of an app as a set of computer instructions that can be executed. Each app has a source code, written in a language describing all actions that the program does. In our case, we will write mobile (iOS) apps in Swift.

There are many low-level computer instructions, but Swift helps us to write without hassle, without knowing much about the low-level organization. Now we will start with the basic concept of **variables**.

We will discuss the following topics:

- Constants and variables
- Initializing using expressions
- Basic types in Swift
- Optional types
- Enumeration types
- Code flow statements – `if`, `switch`, loops
- Functions
- Tuples
- The `guard` statement
- Top-down and bottom-up

We begin with the basic building blocks of all programs.

# Variables

What is a **variable**? This is a place in the memory where we can store some data and use it later in our program. A good example is if you want to take an action based on a user's input, then the input should be stored somewhere on the device (computer). Usually, this place is in the device's memory. To let our program know that we need such a place, we have to express that. A `var` statement is used.

In Swift, declaring a variable looks like this:

```
var text = "Hello world!"
```

This code creates a place in the memory, called `text`, where we store the text, `Hello world!`. Later, we can use it to carry out some meaningful actions.

An advantage of a variable is that it can be changed later to contain a different value. Here, we should be careful—Swift is pretty strict about types (this will be discussed later), and, thus, we can't mix different value types. There are strict rules that should be followed, and we will get familiar with these soon. So, in our case, we can do the following to change the text that is stored in our variable, named `text`:

```
text = "Hey, It's Swift!"
```

Now we know what a variable is and how to work with variables. Let's try to do some calculations using variables, with stored integer values:

```
var five = 5
var four = 4
var sum = four + five
```

In the preceding code, we have created three variables. The first two were initialized with literal expressions, or simply with exact values. In the code, we can use complex calculations, and the Swift compiler will handle this case easily as follows:

```
var five = 2 + 3
```

This is the same as the previous code snippet.

The last variable `sum` is initialized with the value of the expression `four + five`. To calculate this expression, the compiler uses the values stored in the previously declared variables (on the previous lines). The evaluation happens once the code is executed. What does this mean: *The evaluation happens once the code is executed?* In short, if `four` or `five` contain different values, then the `sum` variable will reflect this. The code is working with the names of the places in memory, but the actual result depends on the values stored there.

We could read the preceding code like this:

- Create a place in the memory, which we will call `five`, and store the value 5 in it

- Create a place in the memory, which we will call `four`, and store the value 4 in it

- Create another place in the memory, called `sum`, and store the value of the expression of what's stored in `four` plus what's stored in `five`

Usually, we use variables to allocate places in memory, which we will modify in the following code. But we don't always want to change the value of a variable once it is set. Thus, to simplify it, there is a special word in Swift, `let`, which denotes a place in the memory that won't be changed in the future. Its value is set initially and it can't be changed. (This is slightly different when we are working with objects, but this will become clear later in the book.)

The following code defines a place in memory that won't be updated. If we try to update it, then the Swift compiler will inform us that it is not possible. The value on the left is a constant and we are trying to change it:

```
let helloWorld = "Hello World!"
helloWorld = "Hello, Swift World!" //the compiler is complaining
```

The exact error is: `Cannot assign to value: 'helloWorld' is a 'let' constant,` which means that we are trying to set a new value to a constant.

Let's see how we can update our previous code snippets, once we know that there are `var` and `let` keywords.

The first code with the `text` variable should be the same, because we change the value of the variable `text`. The second code, with the sum of two integers, could be rewritten as follows:

```
let five = 5
let four = 4
let sum = four + five
```

A good practice is to keep using `let` whenever possible. The compiler gives us hints all the time. Of course, it's possible to keep something stored in a variable instead of a constant while developing, but if we want to squeeze out every single bit of performance, then we should stick to the best practice—replace all unmodified variables with constants.

Why do we gain performance when using `let`? The short answer is, the compiler knows that this place in the memory will be used only for reading from operations, and it cuts all the extra logic, which is needed to support modifications. The developers can reason locally and don't need to foresee any future changes of this value, because it is immutable.

Now we are familiar with variables, it's the perfect time to introduce the concept of a type. First, each variable has a type. The type defines the set of values which can be stored in a variable. Each type uses a different amount of the device's memory. Based on the type, the compiler knows how much space should be allocated when we declare a new variable.

In Swift, we define the type of a variable after the declaration of the variable itself. Our first code would look like this:

```
var text:String = "Hello World"
```

Is it mandatory to add a type declaration after each variable definition? No.

The Swift compiler is quite smart, and it infers the types based on the expressions on the right side. There are many examples which could illustrate how smart it is. But we should remember one: if the variable or constant is initialized, then we can simply omit the type. Of course, explicitly pointing to the type will make the code easier for other developers to understand. It's good to keep the same code style through all your code across every project. For some projects, it could be better if the type is omitted; for some, it may be worse.

Let's present all the basic types that Swift uses. The numbers are presented by several different types, based on the precision which is needed. The largest type takes extra memory, but it can store bigger values. The integer numbers can be stored in variables or constants from the following types: `Int`, `Int8`, `Int16`, `Int32`, `Int64`, `UInt`, `UInt32`, and `UInt64`. Floating-point numbers can be of the following types: `Float`, `Float32`, `Float64`, and `Double`. We are already familiar with the `String` type. It's used to store text in computer memory. Later, the text can be manipulated and presented to the user in different forms. The other quite popular data type is `Bool`, which takes exactly two values—`true` or `false`. We will discuss the need of boolean expressions later in this chapter, once we get familiar with conditional statements in Swift. We will define enumerable types and tuples. These are specific types that we can define, compared to the other ones, which are already defined for us.

Until now, we could declare variables or constants in one particular way. There are advanced ways to do this—one is to declare multiple variables on a single line, like this:

```
var a, b, sum: Double
```

All variables are from the same type, namely, `Double`.

We can specify a different type for each one, which gives us the freedom to declare variables/constants in a single shot on the same line.

The following code is an example of this:

```
var greeting: String, age:Int, money:Double
```

We can expand this even further by setting a default value, like in the following code:

```
var x:Double = 3.0, b:Bool = true
```

Of course, Swift is smart enough, so the following code has the very same meaning:

```
var x = 3.0, b = true
```

This automatic process is called **type inference** and greatly reduces the unnecessary boilerplate code which we would have to write.

Before diving into the details related to the different data types, we should know how to add comments to our code. Comments are blocks of text which are part of the source code, but they are removed when the source code is compiled.

The compilation is a complex process of transforming the code to machine code (in the case of Swift, it's something like this: *Swift* is converted to *BitCode* and this is converted to *assembler*, which is converted to *machine language*—low-level machine instructions which are understood by the hardware and are executed pretty quickly).

The comment's role is to clarify the code. There are two types of comments that we can use when we are developing a program in Swift. The first type is a single-row comment, which starts with // (double slash) and continues until the end of the row. Usually, developers prefer to start this comment on a new row or to add it to the end of a line, presenting a detail about the code, so it's easier for the reader to understand the encoded programming logic. The other type is a block comment, which starts with /* (slash and asterisk) and ends with */ (asterisk and slash). The comment can start anywhere, and continues until the matching ending sequence.

An interesting improvement from C++ or some other languages is that we can have several comment blocks which are nested in other comment blocks.

This is something new, which simplifies the process when we are adding comments.

When writing good code, try to add comments to make it easily understandable. In most cases, naming the variables with explicit names helps, but, usually, a brief comment is enough to clear the fog around a pretty complex sequence of your code.

# Optional types

We are familiar with basic types and their forms, but now it's time to introduce the **optional** type(s). This is a new concept, compared to what we have in Objective-C, which helps developers to avoid common mistakes when they are working with data. To explain the optional type(s), we should present the problem they are solving.

When we are developing a program, we can declare a variable, and we should set it an initial value. Later in the code, we can use it. But this is not applicable in general. There may be some cases when the default value is to have NO-VALUE, or simply nil. This means that when we want to work with a variable which has NO-VALUE, we should check that. But if we forget the check, then while our app is executed, we can reach this strange state with NO-VALUE, and the app usually crashes. Also, the code which checks whether a variable contains a value is reduced, and the programming style is concise.

To summarize: optionals enforce better programming style and improve the code checking when the compiler does its job.

Now let's meet the optional types in the following code snippet:

```
var fiveOrNothing: Int? = 5
//we will discuss the if-statement later in this chapter
if let five = fiveOrNothing {
    print(five);
} else {
    print("There is no value!");
}

fiveOrNothing = nil

//we will discuss the if-statement later in this chapter

if let five = fiveOrNothing {
    print(five);
} else {
    print("There is no value!");
}
```

Every type we know so far has an **optional version**, if we can call it that. Later in the book, you will understand the whole magic behind the optional types; namely, how they are created. Here are some of those: String?, Bool?, Double?, Float?, and so on.

Until now, we have learned how to store data, but we don't know what kind of actions we can do with it. This is why we should get familiar with basic operations with the data. The operations are denoted with operators such as +, −, *, and /. These operations work with particular data types, and we have to do the conversion ourselves.

Let's check this code:

```
let number = 5
let divisor = 3
let remainder = number % divisor //remainder is again integer
let quotient = number / divisor // quotient is again integer

let hey = "Hi"
let greetingSwift = hey + " Swift 4!" //operator + concatenates strings
```

# Enumeration types

In Swift, we can define simple types which have limited possible different values. These types are enumerations. We define them with the keyword `enum`. The following code is an example of this:

```
enum AnEnumeration {
    // the value definitions goes here
}
```

Here's another code that does this:

```
enum GameInputDevice
    case keyboard, joystick, mouse
}
```

The code has three different enumeration cases. All cases may appear on a single line, such as in the preceding code, or even one by one on a line.

We can meet the following notation, because Swift infers the missing part:

```
var input = GameInputDevice.mouse
//...
//later in the code
input = .joystick
```

The code bundle for the book is hosted on GitHub
at `https://github.com/PacktPublishing/Learn-Swift-by-Building-App`
`lications`. In case there's an update to the code, it will be updated on the
existing GitHub repository.

# Basic flow statements

What are basic flow statements? These are several statements which help you to structure
the program code in a way that allows you to do different action(s) based on the data stored
in particular variables. We will learn how to execute just part of the code if a certain
condition is met (the condition could be a pretty complex Boolean expression). Then, we
will find a way to execute different actions several times in a loop. The next thing will be to
learn how to repeat things until a condition is met and to stop executing statements once
the condition is not satisfied. Using flow-control statements, we can construct pretty
complex code chunks, similar to what we can express with regular text writing. To develop
a program, we should first create an algorithm (a sequence of steps) which leads to the
desired result, taking into account all external and internal conditions. Based on this
sequence, we can then develop a program, using all flow operators. But let's get familiar
with some forms of them.

# The if statements – how to control the code flow

This is how we can branch our code logic based on some data stored in a variable:

```
let num = 5
if num % 2 == 0 {
    print("The number \(num) is even.")
} else {
    print("The number \(num) is odd.")
}
```

The general pattern of an `if` statement is organized as follows:

```
var logicalCheck = 7 > 5
if (logicalCheck) {
    //code which will be executed if the logical check is evaluated to
true
} else {
    //code which will be executed if the logical check is evaluated to
false
}
```

We know that the `if` clause gives us huge freedom to shape the code that will be executed (evaluated). An application may handle many different cases, but only the code that fulfills the conditions encoded in our solution will be triggered.

# Loops

Let's learn how to implement repetitive tasks. There are several ways to do that, using different loops: `while`, `for...in`, and `repeat...while`. The most popular one is the `for...in` loop. Here is what the basic form looks like:

```
let collection = [1, 2, 3]
for variable in collection {
    //do some action
}
```

The code will be interpreted like this: the variable will be set to all possible values, which are stored in the collection. If the collection is empty, then no code will be executed. If there are some elements, then the body of the loop (the code in curly braces) will be executed for each element of the collection. The variable loops through every single element and can be used in code.

We need an example to illustrate this. Let's use the following code to print all numbers from 1 to 10, inclusive:

```
var sum = 0
for index in 1...10 {
    sum += index
    print("(index)")
}
print("Sum: \(sum)")
//sum is equal to 55
```

The sum of all numbers from 1 to 10 is stored in a separate variable and the code prints every single number on a new line. The sequence defined with 1...10 is converted to a collection (we can think of it as an array), which is fueling the `for...in` loop.

 We can use variables or constants to define custom ranges of numbers.

Take a look at the following code:

```
let threeTimes = 3
for _ in 1...threeTimes {
    print("Print this message.")
}
```

Using _ (underscore) we declare that the argument should ignore the values set in the variable, and it doesn't matter to the rest of the code. The code will print three times: Print this message.

# The while loops

The while loops execute the body of the loop (list of the statements in the body part) until the condition is evaluated to false.

There are two types of while loops. There is the classical while loop, which checks the condition, and, if it holds, then the code in the body is executed. Then the check is performed again and everything is repeated until the condition is evaluated to false. The other variant is the repeat...while loop, which first executes the body, and then does the check. The second type is executed at least once, compared to the first one, which could be completely skipped:

```
var i = 1
let max = 10
var sum = 0
while i <= max {
    sum += i
    i += 1
}
print("Sum: \(sum)")
```

The code sums all numbers from 1 to 10. The condition will be broken once i reaches 11.

We can use repeat...while to do the same:

```
var i = 1
let max = 10
var sum = 0
repeat {
    sum += i
    i += 1
} while i <= max
print("Sum: \(sum)")
```

We can use `while` to implement the `repeat...while` loops and the reverse, but with slight modifications. The best rule for picking the right type of loop is to know whether the sequence should be executed at least once. Executing once means that it's much easier to implement it using `repeat...while`; otherwise, the classical `while` loop is the best choice.

There are some special conditions which we should handle, but to do so, let's see what they are.

We can use the special words—`continue` and `break`—to trigger special behavior while we are in a loop. The `continue` statement is used when you want to stop the current iteration of the loop and start over. When using this, be careful that you change the value in the condition; otherwise, the loop could be an infinite one, which means that your program won't end.

The `break` statement is used once we want to stop the entire loop. Be careful when you have nested loops. The `break` statement stops the current iteration immediately, and then jumps to the very first line after the end of the innermost loop, which contains the `break` statement. If you want to break two or more nested loops, then you have to find an appropriate way to do so. To be explicit when breaking nested loops, you may use labeled statements. It is a convenient way to give a name of a loop and then to change the flow when using `break`. It's good to know that `break` may be used as part of a `switch` statement. This will be discussed in the next part.

There are a few other special words, such as `return`, `throw`, and `fallthrough` which change the default order of execution of the code. We will get familiar with these later.

# The switch statement

A `switch` statement is a concise way to describe a situation where we have several possible options to pick from and we don't want to write a lot of boilerplate code using the already familiar `if` statement.

Here is the general pattern of a `switch` statement (please note that this is not a valid Swift code):

```
switch a-variable-to-be-matched {
    case value-1:
        //code which will be executed, if variable has value-1
        //we need at least one valid executable statement here
          (comments are not an executable statement)
    case value-2,
        value-3:
```

```
        //code which will be executed, if variable has value-2 or value-3
    default:
        //code which will be executed, if variable has value different
          from all listed cases
}
```

What we see is that `switch` has many possible cases, each one starting with the special word `case`, and then a specific value. Swift supports specific value matching, but it supports more complex rules for pattern matching. Each case could be considered as a separate `if` statement. If one case is activated, then all others are skipped. The `default` case is a specific one and is triggered if there is no match with any other case. The `default` case appears at the end, and it's defined with the special word `default`.

We can use `break` to interrupt execution of the code in a `case` statement. If we want to have an empty `case` statement, it's good to add `break`.

We have some specifics with the implementation of `switch` in Swift, which are new when compared to the other programming languages, but they improve the readability of the code. First, there is now a way to have an empty body of a specific case. To be correct, we have to add at least one valid statement after the case. There is no implicit fallthrough after each case. This means that once the last executable statement in a `case` branch is triggered, we are continuing after the `switch` statement. Nothing else that is part of the `switch` statement will be executed. We could consider that every `case` statement has a hidden break at its very end. Next, we need the special word `fallthrough` to simulate the regular behavior of the switch. Another interesting thing is that we can have interval matching, tuples matching, and value bindings. Finally, we can use the `where` clause if we want to express some dependency between the data which should be matched. It's also possible to list several cases if they have to share the code which should be executed. They have to be separated with `,`.

Here is code that shows how easy and smart `switch` is:

```
let point = (1, 1)
switch point {
case let (x, y) where x == y:
    print("X is \(x). Y is \(y). They have the same value.");
case (1, let y):
    print("X is 1. Y is \(y). They could be different.");
case (let x, 1):
    print("X is \(x). Y is 1. They could be different.");
case let (x, y) where x > y:
    print("X is \(x). Y is \(y). X is greater than Y.");
default:
    print("Are you sure?")
```

```
}
```

# Functions

In this section, we will learn how to define functions and how to use them in our code. They help us to reuse sequences of statements with ease. We can define a general solution of a problem and then apply it, customized, to different parts of our app. This approach saves time, reduces the potential of bugs in the code, and simplifies huge problems to small ones.

The first function, which we already saw in use, is `print()`. It's used to display text on the screen. We will experiment with this in the next chapter, once we get our hands dirty with Xcode and Swift.

Now let's define our first function, which executes a sequence of statements in its body:

```
func printSum() {
    let a = 3
    let b = 4
    print("Sum \(a) + \(b) = \(a + b)")
}
```

When defining a function, we start with the special word `func`. Then the name of the function follows and the list of the arguments in brackets `( )` and its returned type. After that comes the body of the function in curly braces `{ }`.

 The name can start with any letter or underscore and can be followed by a letter, digit, underscore, or dollar sign. A function name shouldn't match any keyword from the Swift language.

This definition doesn't do anything if we don't call (execute) the function. How is this done?

We have to call the function using its own name as follows:

```
printSum()
```

Once a function is called, we may think that the same sequence of code is executed where the function call is made. It's not exactly the same, but we can think of having the body of the function executed line by line.

Now let's see the general form of a function:

```
func functionName(argumentLabel variableName:String) -> String {
    let returnedValue = variableName + " was passed"
    return returnedValue
}
//here is the function invocation and how the result is returned
let resultOfFunctionCall = functionName(argumentLabel: "Nothing")
```

Each function may have no arguments, one argument, or many arguments. Until now, we have seen some without arguments and with a single argument. Every argument has an argument label and a parameter name. The argument label is used when the function is called. This is really useful when we have many parameters. It gives us a clue what data should be passed to that specific parameter when using the function. The parameter name (variable name) is the name which will be used in the function body to refer to the passed value. All parameters should have unique parameter names; otherwise there is ambiguity, and we won't be able to say which one is which.

A function may return a value from a specific type, or it may be void (nothing will be returned). When we want to return something, we have to define that, and this is done with -> and the type of the result. In the preceding code, we see -> String, and this means that the function returns a value of the String type. This obliges/binds us to using the keyword return in the function body at least once. The return keyword immediately stops the execution of the function and returns the value passed. If a function doesn't return anything, we can still use return in its body, and it will work similarly to break in a loop.

We can use _ if we want to skip the label of an argument. Here is a simple piece of code that illustrates that:

```
func concatenateStrings(_ s1:String, _ s2:String) -> String {
    return s1 + s2
}
let helloSwift = concatenateStrings("Hello ", "Swift!")
// or
concatenateStrings("Hello ", "Swift!")
```

When we don't use the _ (underscore), then the argument name is the same as the parameter name (variable name).

Similar to what we have seen with the labels, we can ignore the returned value once the function is called.

What happens if we want to return multiple values? We can use tuples to return multiple values when executing a function. The following code is an example of this:

```
//define a function which finds the max element and its index in an
  array of integers
func maxItemIndex(numbers:[Int]) -> (item:Int, index:Int) {
    var index = -1
    var max = Int.min
    //use this fancy notation to attach an index to each item
    for (i, val) in numbers.enumerated() {
        if max < val {
            max = val
            index = i
        }
    }
    return (max, index)
}

let maxItemTuple = maxItemIndex(numbers: [12, 2, 6, 3, 4, 5, 2, 10])
if maxItemTuple.index >= 0 {
    print("Max item is \(maxItemTuple.item).")
}
//prints "Max item is 12."
```

# What is a tuple?

A tuple is a bundle of different types (they may be the same) which have short names. In the preceding code, we have a tuple of two Int statements. The first one is named item, and the second one is named index. After the execution of the function, we will store the maximum item and its index in the tuple. If there are no items in the array, then the index will be −1.

It's possible to return an optional tuple type if there is a chance to return nil in some cases. The previous function may return nil if there are no items, and a valid result otherwise.

Each parameter may have a default value set. To set a default value, you have to declare it and add it right after the parameter's type. The following code is an example of this:

```
func generateGreeting(greet:String, thing:String = "world") -> String {
    return greet + thing + "!"
}

print(generateGreeting(greet: "Hello "))
print(generateGreeting(greet: "Hello ", thing: " Swift 4"))
```

We can easily define a function which accepts zero or more variables of a specified type. This is called a **variadic parameter**. Each function definition could have, at most, one variadic parameter. It's denoted with . . . after its type. In the body of the function, the type of this parameter is converted to an array. This array contains all passed values:

```
func maxValue(_ numbers:Int...) -> Int {
    var max = Int.min
    for v in numbers {
        if max < v {
            max = v
        }
    }
    return max
}

print(maxValue(1, 2, 3, 4, 5))
//prints 5
```

One specific thing that we should know about function parameters is that they are constants. We can't mutate these by mistake. We should express this explicitly. To do so, we have to use the special word `inout` to mark the parameter. The `inout` parameters is added before the type of the parameter. We can pass variables to the `inout` parameters, but we can't pass constants. To pass a variable, we should mark this with `&` when calling the function. The `inout` parameters can't have default values. Also, variadic parameters can't be marked as such. In general, we can use the `inout` parameters to return values from a function, but this is not the same as returning values using `return`. This is an alternative way to let a function affect the outer world in the matrix. Check out the following code:

```
func updateVar(_ x: inout Int, newValue: Int = 5) {
    x = newValue
}

var ten = 10
print(ten)
updateVar(&ten, newValue: 15)
print(ten)
```

# What is the guard statement?

The `guard` statement has similar behavior to an `if` statement. This statement checks the condition, and if it's not met, then the `else` clause is triggered. In the `else` clause, the developer should finish the current function or program, because the prerequisites won't be met. Take a look at the following code:

```
func generateGreeting(_ greeting: String?) -> String {
    guard let greeting = greeting else {
        //there is no greeting, we return something and finish
        return "No greeting :("
    }
    //there is a greeting and we generate a greeting message
    return greeting + " Swift 4!"
}

print(generateGreeting(nil))
print(generateGreeting("Hey"))
```

This is a tiny example, showing us code that illustrates the regular usage of the `guard` statement. We can combine it with the `where` clause, or we can make the check really complex. Usually, it's used when the code depends on several `if...let` checks. The `guard` statement keeps the code concise.

# How to tackle huge problems – bottom-up versus top-down

Step-by-step through this book, we will start solving problems until we can write a fully-working mobile app. It's not an easy task, but we can take two different approaches when trying to solve a huge problem (such as writing a mobile app). The first one is **top-down**. This technique starts from the top with the main problem, and breaks it down into smaller problems and functions. Once we reach something unclear, something which is not well defined that we should implement, then we define a new function, but we won't continue developing the exact implementation of this part of the app immediately. Let's assume that we are trying to develop a mobile app with three screens. The first one displays a list of news. The second one renders specific news, and the last one shows information about our application.

If we apply the top-down approach, then we will have the following abstract process. We start from the biggest problem: how to develop an app with three screens. Then, we break this huge task down into three sub-tasks with their respective functions. Those functions are empty functions. The first one will be responsible for creating the first screen, the second one should create the detailed news presentation, and the third should define the last screen. By doing this, we have decomposed the main problem into three smaller ones. These new functions are empty, but at a later phase we will implement each one of them. We can start with the first one: we define another help function which creates the list of news, and another function which fetches the news from an internet address. Now it doesn't look really hard to define those functions. We will learn how to do this throughout the book, but the general idea is to break down each problem into smaller ones until you reach a state where you can solve them without any hassle. In the end, the main problem will be solved, because all parts that have been decomposed are already working, and the final result will be a fully-working mobile application.

The other approach is bottom-up, which does things in reverse. It's more like working with **Lego**, but you first go and build many small building blocks, which you combine together until you manage to build a solution to the whole problem; in our case, until you build a working mobile app. Abstractly, we develop simple enough functions that we can implement to solve small problems. Then we combine those into bigger chunks. Those bigger chunks are put together in even bigger and more complex functions or app parts, until we define the final working app.

Neither of these two approaches is the best. Every developer prefers to use a nice mixture of both techniques, which leads to the final result—a working app.

 If top-down, or bottom-up, is used on its own, it is not a silver bullet. Try to use top-down and bottom-up together and you will find the solution easier.

Just tweak your approach based on what you know at the moment, and what you have.

# Summary

In this chapter, we became familiar with Swift 4 basics. We now know what variables and constants are. We can use basic types, the `if` and `switch` statements, and loops, and we can define functions. These are the smallest key building blocks that we will need to start our adventure in **Swift 4** and the iOS/macOS/watchOS world.

In the next chapter, you will become familiar with Xcode—the development environment software that is really handy when we are writing code in Swift. You will develop your first playground, which is a nice tool to check and demo the code. You can use everything learned in this chapter, and, in the end, you will be familiar with how to add descriptions using a markup language to make your playgrounds and functions well documented. Don't spend a minute more—find a macOS and move to the next chapter to get your hands dirty with some real code.

# Getting Familiar with Xcode and Playgrounds

**2**

In this chapter, we will get familiar with Xcode, the **Integrated Development Environment (IDE)** that is used to develop iOS, macOS, tvOS, and watchOS apps. We will introduce a pretty neat way of playing with and exploring the Swift language called **playground**. We will see all the panels and the many different options that are available in Xcode. We will find an easy way to use templates and we will experiment with real Swift code in a playground.

In this chapter, we will cover the following topics:

- Installing Xcode
- Exploring playground
- Different options available in Xcode
- Markup items

## Installing Xcode

First, Xcode runs on macOS only. This means you have to find a macOS-compatible computer that is running macOS 10.13 or later.

It is possible to have macOS running on a virtual machine, but having a hardware one is better.

We will install Xcode version 9.3. This is the latest version available in the App Store at the moment, but it may change in the near future, so no worries if you install a slightly newer version. The IDE looks the same way.

Start your computer and open the App Store application. This application is used to download extra software on to your macOS. You can find its icon on the dock, as shown here:

Once you've clicked the icon, you should see the App Store application displayed. At the top-right corner, there is a search field. Select it and start typing Xcode. You will see many suggestions as shown in the following screenshot:

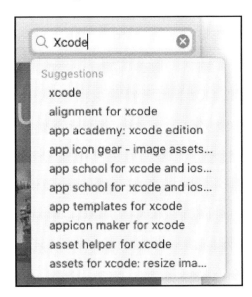

Select the first item, which is what we are looking for. The next screen that will be displayed is the search result screen, something similar to this:

The only difference will be that the button will say **INSTALL** instead of **UPDATE**. Xcode is free software, provided by Apple, so you will be able to install it at no cost. Just press the **INSTALL** button and the download process will be triggered. The initial installation may take hours, based on your internet connection and computer speed. Don't worry—leave the computer doing its own job and you can keep reading this chapter. Once the process has finished successfully, you will see that the App Store displays another button, **Open** as shown in the following screenshot:

You have to click **Open** to start the Xcode. Another option is to find it in **Applications Installed** and to click on the blue icon (you have seen the icon already, while installing). The next section explores the Xcode application.

# Exploring Xcode

The Xcode application is installed and it is running. You will see the following start screen:

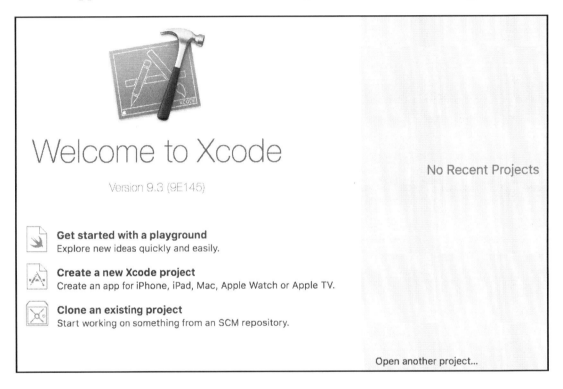

On the right, you will see **No Recent Projects**, but this just shows a list of the last few projects you have worked on. On the left, you will see the version of Xcode 9.3 and a few shortcuts. We will start with the first one to get familiar with the playground. Go and click **Get started with a playground**. A new window is displayed, as shown in the following screenshot. Don't panic; this is the window in which you have to select the template for your playground project. For now, we will stick to iOS:

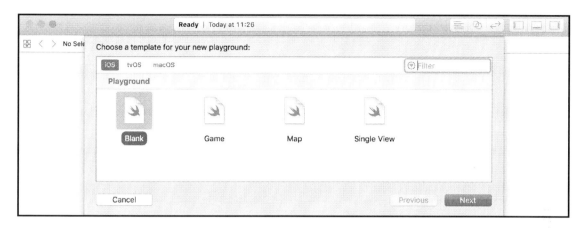

When you click **Next**, you have to enter the name of the playground. Let's start with `Swift 4 by examples`. We can change the platform if we want to explore the different features of other platforms. Xcode has a really powerful simulator which can simulate different OS (tvOS, iOS). The development for these platforms is a breeze once we know Swift.

You have to pick a folder to store the playground project. A good place is the `Documents` folder, (click on it; it should be located on the left) and then you can create a subfolder, `Swift 4`, using the button at the bottom left, **New Folder**. Another option is to pick a place on your own. Once you are ready, click on the **Create** button, which is located at the bottom-right of this window. Xcode initiates a process and generates a simple playground for us:

```
1  //: Playground - noun: a place where people can play
2
3  import UIKit
4
5  var str = "Hello, playground"              "Hello, playgroun...
6
```

The Xcode windows looks a bit empty, but don't panic. It's because you should focus on the development process, but this chapter is to get familiar with Xcode; that's why we will start exploring the IDE. After the exploration part, we will get back to the playgrounds and why they are cool.

# What do we see on the screen?

In this section, we will present all the important parts of the Xcode application, such as panels, toolbars, buttons, and their use. Once you are ready, you will know where you can find specific information about your project or how to find and edit a specific part of a mobile project.

## Toolbar

This is the topmost part of the screen. We have the status line, which says **Ready | Today at 7:28 PM**, as shown in the following screenshot. This is the place where Xcode communicates with us. The app prints all errors here and we can dive into the details by clicking on the errors. There are no errors at the moment, but they may appear at times.

Successful messages such as the one on the previous screen and the following screen can't be explored:

We have the basic controls located on the right. There are two groups of buttons. The first group consists of the following options:

- **Show the standard editor** : This option presents a single window to edit the project (usually, a view of our source code).

- **Show the assistant editor** : This option splits the screen in two. There is a small down arrow at the bottom of this option. Once you activate this mode, the second click will present a menu with different options. You can explore all possible options. We won't use this mode of the Xcode now. It will be explained in detail later, when we are about to use it (this will happen when we start developing the UI using storyboards).

- **Show the version editor** : This one is used when the project supports versions and Git. (We will get briefly to this option once we discuss Git and version control integration.)

The second group also has the following three buttons which activate advanced panels of the Xcode. These are toggle buttons, which activate (show) or deactivate (hide) different parts:

- **Hide or show the Navigator button** 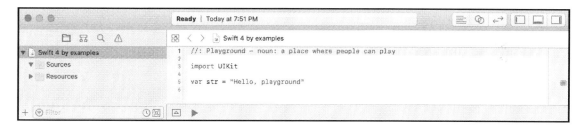 : This button activates the **Navigator** panel, which is located to the left. Once activated, the editor (main part) is squeezed. If it's deactivated, then the editor is expanded to take the whole window estate as shown in the following screenshot:

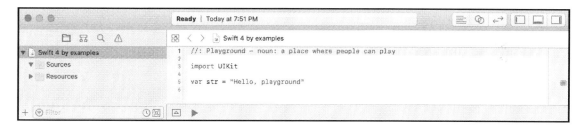

For more information, check the sub-section which explains the **Navigator** panel.

- **Hide or show the Debug Area button** 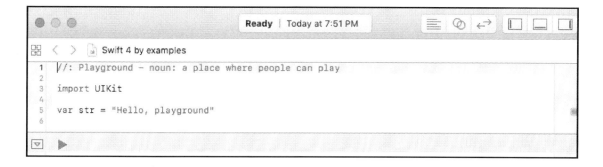 : This activates the **Debug** panel, which is located at the bottom:

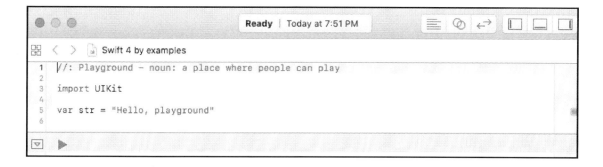

For more information, check the sub-section which explains the **Debug** panel.

- **Hide or show the Utilities button**  : This activates the **Utilities** panel, which is located on the right as shown in the following screenshot:

For more information, check the subsection which explains the **Utilities** panel.

Each one of these three panels gives the user extra control of the project and an easy way to change its configuration. We can add and explore all files and assets from the **Navigation** panel. We see the output from the app in the **Debug** panel. There are too many buttons to be clicked, which could lead to confusion. Don't try to remember everything now, just start exploring the IDE and you will get used to it. Then you will learn the shortcut keys, and step-by-step you will become an Xcode master.

The panels are contextual, which means they look different based on the active (selected) file.

We can see the active file at the very top of the editor. In our case, `Swift 4 by examples`, as shown in the following screenshot:

The playground can contain many files and assets, but the main file is displayed, once the playground is opened.

The Related Items button provides a menu to explore all files, which have been opened as shown in the following screenshot:

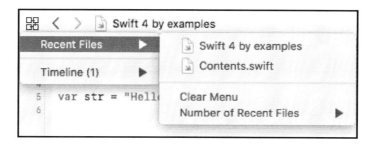

 `Contents.swift` is the main file of every playground; it contains the code which is executed when the playground is run.

The back arrow button helps us to go to the previous file that was explored in the editor. In our case, when we have a playground with a single file, it's not very usable; but when we start to build real mobile apps, then it will become handy.

The forward arrow button does the opposite of the back arrow button. You can use it to go to the next file.

The filename, `Swift 4 by examples`, is a visual tree that shows the playground project structure. It's pretty close to what you will see in the **Navigator** panel. You can use it to switch between different source files in the editor area as shown in the following screenshot:

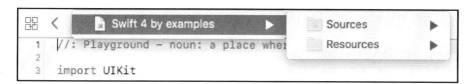

The rest of the editor area is used to render the selected file at the top. In our case, we see the code of the playground project. To be more precise, the `Contents.swift` file. At the

very bottom, we see the **Debug** panel action bar. It looks like this: There are two buttons: the first one is to open the console, which triggers the **Debug** panel button in the top-right part of the Xcode window (the middle button). The second is the Play button which evaluates the whole playground. We can use it to run the code that we have written. If we press it, the status bar (part of the toolbar) will start and will say **Ready | Today at 12:00 PM** (where the time will be your current time of execution).

# Menu

Xcode has a menu bar, which is common to all the macOS software as shown in the following screenshot:

We won't discuss all options from the preceding screenshot, but will try to briefly point out the most important ones:

- **Xcode**: You can open the preference window from this menu option **Xcode | Preferences...** or by using (*cmd* + ,). The preference window can be used to configure the Xcode so it suits you. It's really important to customize the IDE so it's a friendlier place to spend the time with. For more information, check the Xcode preferences window section. You can open different developer tools that are part of the Xcode, such as **Instruments** or **File Merge**.
- **File**: The following actions can be started:
    - **New**: This opens a new tab (Xcode supports many tabs), a new project (Xcode can have several projects opened at one time), a new window (one project can be edited in two different windows), and so on
    - **Open**: This opens projects and triggers the **Quickly Open Windows** tool, which helps you to jump without hassle through the source code of the project when it is huge
    - **Save**: This saves files and projects
    - **Close**: This closes the files

- **Edit**: A typical edit menu, containing **Undo** (*cmd + Z*) and **Redo** (*cmd + Shift + Z*), is here, as well as copying and pasting items, and different types of filtering and sorting.
- **View**: Access to the different panels and their subtabs. Open the Xcode in full-screen mode (*cmd + Ctrl + F*).
- **Find**: Different options to find and/or replace text in a project.
- **Navigate**: Use this to open different parts of the Xcode or to move around.
- **Editor**: Various options to indent the text. Also, to insert different symbols.
- **Product**: Triggers builds or tests. Everything related to building (compiling) a project can be found here.
- **Debug**: Different options to initiate a debug session. Please note that this is not applicable to playground.
- **Source Control**: Manage source files using Git. We will get familiar with this, once we start working on mobile apps.
- **Window**: Easy way to organize the Xcode windows, once there are several of them.
- **Help**: To find help about the Xcode or to access the language documentation.

 The best place to get familiar with Xcode is to read what Apple has prepared. Navigate to **Help | Xcode** to get detailed explanations about each part of the Xcode.

Now let's get familiar with the basic options in the three main panels, starting with the **Navigator** panel.

# The Navigator panel (located to the left)

The **Navigator** panel displays the project structure on the left. It has root item(s). Usually, this is the project and the project looks like a tree. We can use the arrows to expand each level of this visual tree. Using right-click, we bring up a menu, where some handy shortcuts are displayed as shown in the following screenshot:

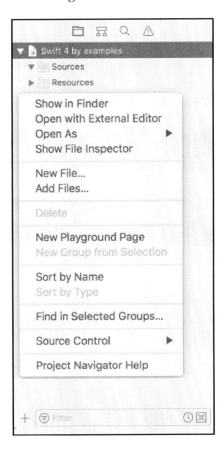

The **Navigator** panel contains a bottom menu which has the following options:

- **+ button**: To add new files to the project.
- **Filter text field**: A textbox which can be used to filter the content of the preceding list. For example, if we want to see all images which are the .png files, then we can simply enter PNG in the filter. In our case, with the currently opened playground, this will display the text **No Filter Results**.
- **Show only recent files**: The clock icon, if it's activated, will show the recent files only.
- **Show only files with source control status**: The square icon, if active will display the files under **Source Control** (included in the Git repository).

The **Navigator** panel has four tabs when we are exploring the playground project. It has a few more when the project is a mobile one.

The first tab is the project navigator, as we already know. The next is the symbol navigator, the place where we can explore the source code structure. (Don't panic—we will learn how to create all these structures and will be able to use this panel.) The third is the find navigator, the place that is used when we want to locate something in a project, not only in the source files. This tab contains different options to tweak the search. Don't be afraid; explore them to narrow down what you are looking for.

The last tab is the issue navigator. In this tab, we have a list of all build-time and runtime issues caused by our project.

At the bottom, there is a filter on each tab, which is similar to the one we had discussed earlier. You can use it to filter the results presented in the tab.

# The Debug panel (located at the bottom)

The Debug panel is located at the bottom of the Xcode. While developing a playground project, we won't be able to actually see its power. We will be presented with the console where the app prints information. We will use it to print debug information to validate our code.

When working on a mobile application we will discuss how to debug the app. This will be tightly related to the debug options located in the Debug panel. We will get to this part once we have created a regular app, and we want to improve it.

# The Utilities panel (located to the right)

The Utilities panel gives us extra options to configure each active element. At the bottom part, we have sections with various templates which we can use in our development process.

At the top, there are two tabs. The first one is called **File inspector.** It's denoted with an icon like a new blank page. This tab shows information about the selected file. You can find information where the file is located on the hard drive and a few other options, as shown here:

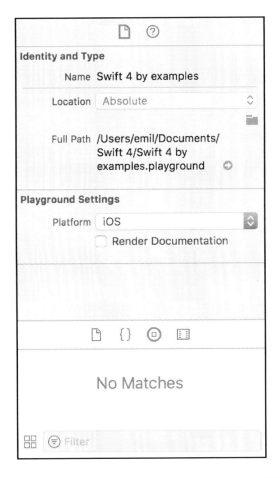

We see the file location of the playground project. Also, it's using iOS as a platform and we can change that by picking another platform from the list. We can enable text markup in the playground or disable it. The markup will be discussed later in this chapter.

The second tab is called **Quick Help Inspector**. It provides extra contextual information based on the last, focused item in the editor. It's really handy when using a public interface (API) from Apple or any other third-party well-written (documented) library. We will learn more about external libraries and how to use them later in this book.

The number of tabs is more than two, when the project is a regular mobile app. Don't feel that we are skipping them; we will discuss them when they appear.

At the bottom of the Utilities panel, there is another section, which contains several tabs. This part contains different templates:

- The first is the **File Template Library**, which can be used to add different files to a project
- The next is the **Code Snippet Library**, which contains different code snippets
- After that is the **Object Library**, a collection of objects which can be added to a storyboard
- Finally, there is the **Media Library**, a list of all media items, which are part of your project or workspace

These panels are there to save you time when looking for something in your project. There is a neat filter function at the very bottom. Here is a screenshot that shows you how to get access to a list of all Swift code templates:

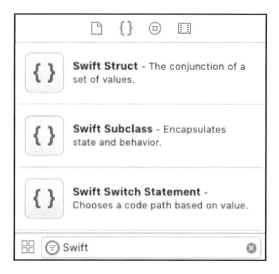

There is a small icon to the left of the filter text field. It switches between a list and grid view of the template tabs:

Next, we discuss the preferences of the IDE, so we can match our personal preferences.

## Xcode preferences window

In this section, we present the preferences window briefly. If we open it, we can see several tabs, each containing different options about the Xcode:

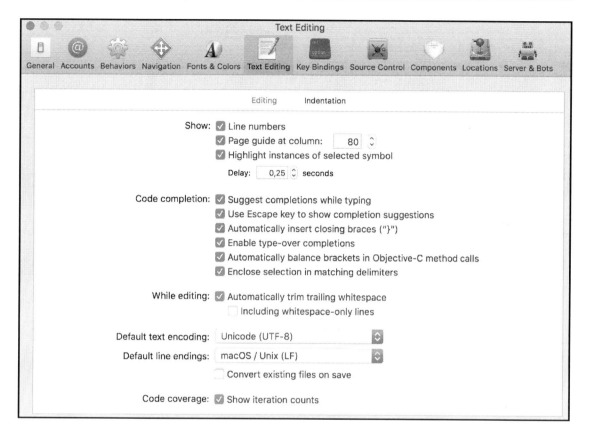

Let's describe each tab, its role, and what you can find in it.

- **General**: Contains settings about the general build behavior of the Xcode.
- **Accounts**: The tab where the user can link different Apple accounts and source code repositories. The settings can store the username and password, so the Xcode can do some actions on the user's behalf.
- **Behavior**: Here, each step/action done by Xcode can display a notification or even play a specific sound. It's possible to trigger a script or speak the phase name.

- **Navigation**: Configures where the new code should be opened, once the user clicks on a source file using the modifier keys such as *cmd, Option, Shift*.
- **Fonts & Colors**: The Xcode can look different; it's up to you:

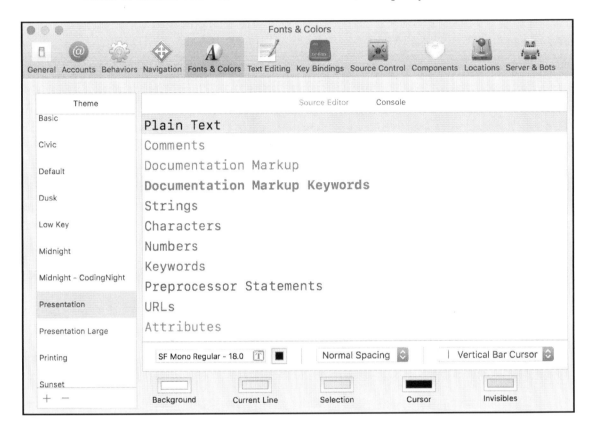

- **Text Editing**: A place where you can customize the behavior of the editor.
- **Key Bindings**: If you are a fan of keyboard shortcuts, then this is the place to customize Xcode. You could become a master if you add some extra shortcuts or make some predefined ones to fit your needs.
- **Source Control**: Configure the general behavior of the source control integration.
- **Components**: This is the place where you can download an old version of the simulator.

In general, you will be able to download simulators which are supporting specific versions. For example, the oldest one for Xcode 9.3 is iOS 8.1.

- **Locations**: Configure which folders should be used by Xcode for temporary files. You can change the version of the **Command Line Tools**, which can be used from the Terminal window.
- **Server & Bots**: This is a special tab where you can configure the Xcode to continually build and test your apps.

We aren't new to Xcode anymore, so now is the time to dive into details, such as what's a playground and how we can use playgrounds to do experiments with Swift.

# Playground

Before diving into a mobile project, we will start with a special type of project that will help us master the Swift language. These projects are a cool place to experiment, without the extra hassle of setting up a real mobile project. We can experiment with real mobile functions, without even working on a full mobile project. Playground projects are a really nice place to prototype algorithms or UI, and simply to have small building blocks, ready and fully tested, before plugging them into a mobile app.

# What is a playground?

Straight from the file generated by Xcode:

> *"Playground – noun: a place where people can play."*

Playground is a simple project, which can be used to practice, experiment, prototype and play with code and the underlying OS. It's easy to write some code to sketch an idea or to clarify a concept. The best thing is that you can mix text (markup) with code. Also, it's possible to use the native functions that are specific for the platform (for example iOS). This makes playground projects very expressive and realistic.

Let's create a playground and dive deeper into it:

1. Open Xcode
2. Select **File** | **New** | **Playground** or simply press "*Option + cmd + Shift + N*"
3. Pick a nice name—for example `Swift 4 by examples`
4. Set the platform to **iOS**
5. Click **Next**
6. Select a place to save the file
7. Press **Create**

As a result of these steps, you will have a new playground, which will only have a few rows.

The playground can contain more than one page.

In our example, we are using just a single-page playground, but if you want to express something complex, you can add another page using the + button in the Navigator panel (at the very bottom).

# Let's add some code

Let's get our hands dirty with some code. We can try using the template panel to implement a switch statement and a `for` loop. How do we do this?

1. Let's open the Utilities panel. To do so, use the topmost right icon on the toolbar or simply press *Option + cmd + 1*.
2. Then select the second tab in the bottom part {} to open the code snippets library.
3. Next, type the following in the filter field—`Swift switch`.
4. You should see just a single item.
5. Drag that item to the editor:

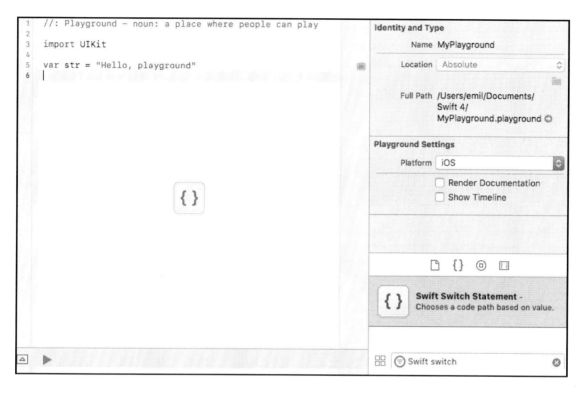

6. Once you drop it, you will see the switch structure with a few placeholders to fill in.

7. Try to fill the gaps, so the switch looks something like this:

```
switch str {
    case "swift":
        print("Hello, Swift 4!")
    default:
        print("Who are you?")
}
```

8. Then, we can open the console at the bottom to see the output of our program.

   Use the [▽] button to open the Debug console where all print messages are displayed or press *cmd + Shift + Y*.

9. You should see: **Who are you?**

Now, let's try to create a `for...in` loop, which prints all numbers from one up to five inclusive. Let's use the same procedure as before, but at step 3 we should use `Swift for` for filtering. Then, at *step 7* we should try to reach the following:

```
for i in 1...5 {
    print("\(i)")
}
```

It's normal while you are writing code to see some warnings or even errors. Playgrounds are built automatically on every change in the code, thus, the compiler is showing errors when the code is not valid. When you are ready, all errors should be gone and in the output of the program, you will see all numbers from one to five.

To switch to manual mode, press the **Play** button at the bottom menu and hold for a bit. A menu with two options should pop up—**Automatically Run** and **Manually Run**. The first one is selected, but you can switch to manual mode.

If you are in **Manually Run,** once you change the code of the playground, you will have to **Run** the playground to reflect the changes. A simple save action is not enough, compared to the **Automatically Run** mode.

When you start a manual build (or an automatic one was executed), the toolbar at the top changes briefly. The progress indicator appears while the execution takes place.

If there is an output of the playground, it is printed on the console. But this is not the only way to see the evaluation of the code. There is a right panel in the editor, which is really handy when exploring the playgrounds. Unfortunately, it's not expanded by default, but it shows the evaluation of each statement. You can resize it with your mouse to make it visible. Just grab the leftmost edge of the gray panel to the right of the editor—it's easily distinguishable:

```
Swift 4 by examples

1   //: Playground - noun: a place where people can play
2
3   import UIKit
4
5   /*: your code goes here */
6
7   var str = "Hello, playground"
8
9   switch str {
10  case "swift":
11      print("Hello, Swift 4!")
12  default:
13      print("Who are you?")
14  }
15
16  for i in 1...5 {
17      print("\(i)")
18  }
```

```
Who are you?
1
2
3
4
5
```

Here is the expanded version of the panel, which shows the value of each line. It looks nice, when you have just a single statement on each row:

```
    Swift 4 by examples
1   //: Playground – noun: a place where people can play
2
3   import UIKit
4
5   /*: your code goes here */
6
7   var str = "Hello, playground"                    "Hello, playground"   ▣
8
9   switch str {
10  case "swift":
11      print("Hello, Swift 4!")
12  default:
13      print("Who are you?")                        "Who are you?\n"      ▣
14  }
15
16  for i in 1...5 {
17      print("\(i)")                                (5 times)             ▣
18  }
```

```
Who are you?
1
2
3
4
5
```

This is not the case when there are two or more statements separated with ; .

 Keep the code clean and simple by adding just a single statement on each line. This will help you to write understandable and easily maintainable code.

Now let's explain the default screen. There are two icons which you see on the line which is hovered. The first one is **Quick Look**, which shows the evaluation in a pop-up window. The other button is **Show results**. When it's activated, the results are displayed inline. (To activate this, you can use **Editor | Show Result for Current Line**):

```
Swift 4 by examples
1   //: Playground – noun: a place where people can play
2
3   import UIKit
4
5   /*: your code goes here */
6
7   var str = "Hello, playground"
8
9   switch str {
10  case "swift":
11      print("Hello, Swift 4!")
12  default:
13      print("Who are you?")

            Who are you?

14  }
15
16  for i in 1...5 {
17      print("\(i)")

            5

18  }
```

Different values are presented in a different fashion such as a chart, a list of values, or simply the last value stored in that variable.

Here is an example, which shows how the value stored in the sum variable is growing over time. With the mouse, you can explore the exact value at every single moment:

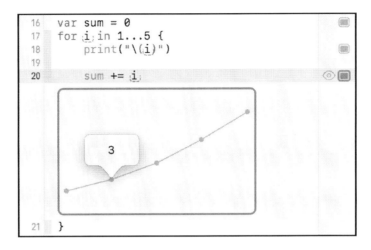

You can explore the result with the mouse. It's pretty easy to resize the answer area too; just move the mouse close to the edges, until the pointer changes to a double-headed arrow. If you want to change the way a result is presented, then use the following option, but it should be selected first: **Editor** | **Result Display Mode**; then three options will be presented:

- **Latest Value**: Displays the last value of the statement
- **Value History**: Displays a list of all values
- **Graph**: Plots the values

 We can see the whole sequence of the invocation in the console (*cmd* + *Shift* + *Y*).

Playgrounds can contain a lot of code. But there is a neat way to add it to a project by using auxiliary files.

# How to add auxiliary code to a playground

Each playground may need a bunch of classes which are helping to illustrate the problem or a solution. There is a handy way to add a chunk of code, which is compiled once it is added or changed. This means that those parts won't be compiled each time the playground is executed. The files containing code are called auxiliary files. To add such a file, we should do the following:

1. Open the Navigator panel (*cmd* + *1*).
2. Select the **Sources** folder.
3. Press the **+** button at the bottom of the Navigator panel.
4. Select **New File.**
5. Give the new file a nice name related to its role.
6. Add the code which you want to reuse in the playground. Don't forget to add the `public` scope modifier to make it *visible* in your playground
7. Try to use it in the main playground:

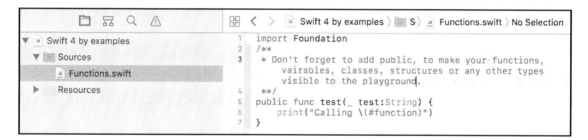

Playgrounds can contain different resources such as images, statistic data, sound, and so on. These are placed in the `Resources` folder. Here is a step-by-step guide on how to add a resource (image/asset) to a playground.

# How to add resource to a playground

Follow these steps to add an image to your playground. Try to use a `.png` or `.jpg`—images look great once you load them in a playground:

1. Open the Navigator panel (cmd + *1*)
2. Select the `Resources` folder
3. Press the **+** button at the bottom of the Navigator panel

4. Select **Add Files to 'Resources'...**
5. The file is automatically copied to the `Resources` folder
6. Try to use it in the main playground

For example, to use an image in the iOS playground you can use the following code:

```
let img = UIImage(named: "open_xcode.png")
```

Where the name of the file is `open_xcode.png`. Don't worry about the code and what `UIImage` means. We will understand this a bit later on in the book. Take a look at the following screenshot:

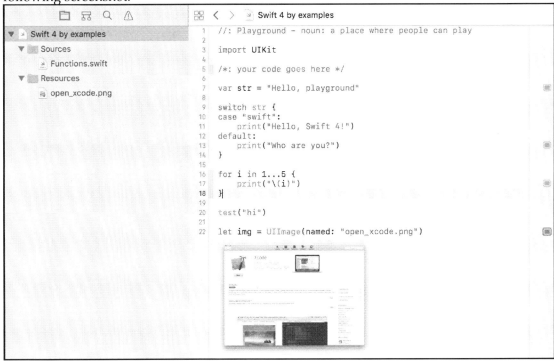

Adding an image to your playground

# Converting a playground to a workspace

If you want to add a custom framework (external library of code) to your playground, you have to convert the playground to a workspace. This can be done using **File** | **Save As Workspace...**.

Just pick a new name and save the file. Xcode will switch to advanced mode and you will see a lot of options available. We will discuss how to add third-party libraries to a workspace later in the book. But it's good to know that you can use playgrounds to test your framework without any problem.

So far, we know the basics of the playground. Now let's introduce the markup language and an easy way to make your playgrounds outstanding.

# Markup in playgrounds

The playground supports an easy way to write documentation for your code. It's like comments, which we are familiar with, but the Xcode renders them nicely. Let's do it step-by-step:

1. Open a playground project
2. Open the Utilities project
3. Select the **File Inspector**
4. Mark the option **Render Documentation**
5. You should see that `//:` `Playground - noun: a place where people can play` is converted to a good-looking text

# Different items in the markup language

First, let's clear up what a markup language is; it is an easy way to write styled text, which will be rendered using a set of rules. The final result is nicely formatted text.
Here is a code that creates markup (in a playground):

```
/*:
# Header Big
## Header Normal
### Header Small
List
* option 1
* option 2
* option 3
    - option 3.1
This is _italic_ text.
This is __bold__ text.
This is ___bold & italic___ text.
This is **bold** text.
A code ```let x = 5``` has different style.
```

```
An example follows:
        var a = 13
        var b = a + 7
- Note:
"You can learn Swift 4."
\
\
Playgrounds are really nice place to learn Swift 4.
*/
```

To create nice documentation, we should learn how to use markup. The benefit is that we can use most of the formatting while writing documentation for each function, which will be used in the Utilities panel (the **Help** tab) in Xcode.

Here is what the previous markup looks like once we enable the **Render Document** mode (from the Utilities panel):

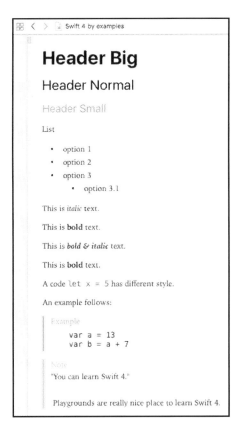

To start new markup section in a playground, you should write the following instead of a typical comment block:

```
//: your new rich documentation
```

You can also write a comment block like this:

```
/*: your code goes here */
```

This will be converted to a markup, if you are using one of the special structures (see the following). To enable the **Render Document**, we can do it using **Editor** | **Show Rendered Markup**. An alternative option is to mark the checkbox **Render Document** in the Utilities panel on the right.

 If **Render Documentation** is on, then you won't be able to edit the markup-comments, because they are converted immediately. You have to switch off the rendering mode. This can be done using **Editor** | **Show Raw Markup**.

## Basic markup items

First of all, when writing markup, we need to add titles for different sections. To do that, we have to add the # symbol in front of the text and it automatically becomes a header text with a bigger bold font. For example:

```
//: # Header Big
```

If we keep adding more # in front then we demote the text:

# Header Big
## Header Normal
### Header Small

If we want to use lists in the text, then we should structure it as follows:

```
//: List
//: * option 1
//: * option 2
//: * option 3
//:    - option 3.1
```

With adding an extra offset, we can push the bullets to the right, simulating subsections. To create enumerated lists, you should start each option with `1.` like this:

```
//: Enumerated list
//: 1. option 1
//: 1. option 2
//: 1. option 3
```

Here is the result of both lists when they are rendered:

List

- option 1
- option 2
- option 3
    - option 3.1

Enumerated list

1. option 1
2. option 2
3. option 3

When describing some functions or classes, we want to stress some properties. To do that, we can change the font style easily. Here is how we can write in bold, italics, or mixed:

```
//: This is _italic_ text.
//: This is __bold__ text.
//: This is ___bold & italic___ text.
//: This is **bold** text.
```

Here is how this text is rendered:

> This is *italic* text.
>
> This is **bold** text.
>
> This is ***bold & italic*** text.
>
> This is **bold** text.

Sometimes, we want to quote a variable or a short code snippet. It's really nice if we can distinguish it easily from the rest of the text. This can be achieved by surrounding the text in ` —the ascent symbol.
Here is an example:

```
//: The code `let x = 5` has different style.
```

If you want to add an example block, then simply add an empty line, to separate the block and add in an extra offset:

```
//empty line
//: var a = 13
//: var b = a + 7
```

The preceding code creates this:

> The code `let x = 5` has different style.
>
> An example follows:
>
> Example
>
> ```
> var a = 13
> var b = a + 7
> ```

Sometimes, images are really important; here is the easiest way to show an image:

```
//: ![Image from resources](open_xcode.png)
```

If you need to add some links here, this is how you can do it:

```
//: [Text](URL)
//: [Swift](https://swift.org)
```

Finally, if you want to add a note to explain something important in a playground, you can use the following code:

```
//: - Note:
//: "You can learn Swift 4."
//: \
//: \
//: Playgrounds are a really nice place to learn Swift 4.
```

The rendered note looks slick and can be used to outline something really important:

Note

"You can learn Swift 4."

Playgrounds are a really nice place to learn Swift 4.

We have presented some popular markup formatted text, which will add a final touch to your documentation. Some of the styling could be used to improve your documentation, which is rendered in the Utilities panel.

# Summary

In this chapter, we learned how to install the Xcode app and how to use it in general. We are familiar with the basic components of the IDE and we have created our first playground. It was pretty basic, but we know how to write Swift code, which is automatically evaluated. We can read the errors and we can try to resolve them.

The next chapter will teach us how to create our first mobile app. It will explain the structure of a mobile project and how to start adding simple features to it. Let's dive deep into iOS and produce something which can be executed on mobile devices.

# Creating a Minimal Mobile App 3

In this chapter, we are going to develop our first mobile app using Xcode and our basic Swift knowledge. We will get familiar with the basic organization of an iOS project. We will run it in a simulator, which will be our first friend through the development process. A Git version control system will be introduced, because it's part of Xcode. With it, through the development process, we can track our changes to the source code. Then, at some point, we can easily switch back to a specific version. We will learn how to keep our code under control and to jump to a specific version, developed earlier by us.

In this chapter, we will cover the following topics:

- Developing our first mobile app using Xcode
- Git

# Your first iOS application

Let's start with creating your first iOS mobile project using Xcode. Here are the steps that will guide you through the process.

1. Go ahead and start Xcode. If you start Xcode for the first time or there is no active project opened, then you will see the following screen (please check Chapter 2, *Getting Familiar with Xcode and Playgrounds*, if you don't have Xcode already installed on your Mac):

2. Click on **Create a new Xcode project**. If you have an opened project, then simply use the menu at the top to create a new project by navigating to **File** | **New** | **Project** (*shift + cmd + N*):

3. Select the **iOS** tab at the top.

This book is focused on iOS development, but, in general, there is no huge difference between all other platforms—macOS, watchOS, or tvOS. They have different capabilities, but they can run apps developed in Swift.

4. Then select **Single View Application**.

This is a special type of application, which consists of a single-view controller which presents a single view.

Xcode will generate an **empty** starting project, based on the selected template, which has just a single view. The project is not empty, it contains the very basic building blocks. Don't worry; we will learn how to add extra views and improve the project's structure.

Here are all the other types of projects that are available in the current Xcode version:

- Application projects: These are mobile applications which present data to the user.
    - **Game**: You should pick this project template if you want to develop a game for iOS.
    - **Augmented reality app**: A project template that boots the augmented reality scene setup. We will be working on a limited number of iOS devices—the ones which support AR.
    - **Document based app**: A special template that easily enables document manipulation on the device and in the cloud.
    - **Master-detail application**: A special project template, which is a good start if you want to display data in a table/list. The project could be universal (for iPad and iPhone), or for iPhone only, or for iPad only.
    - **Page-based application**: A special template, which displays a set of views (pages). There is a nice way to navigate between them.
    - **Tabbed application**: An application template, which has a tab bar control (a menu of several items at the bottom) that can be used to switch between different sections in the app. This is quite a popular template because many apps which present data in sections use this neat approach.
    - **Sticker pack application**: This template project is an extension of the iMessage app, which is part of the iOS, which will define new Stickers that can be used in the app. It's something new starting from iOS 10.
    - **iMessage application**: A template project which helps you develop an iMessage app integration. This special type of project is used when you want to provide a seamless integration of your app and iMessage app.
- Framework and library project:
    - **Cocoa Touch framework**: A template which helps you to create a custom framework (a set of classes and resources, larger than a library) that can be shared across several iOS projects. There is a chapter later in which we will learn how to integrate open source frameworks within our iOS project(s).

- **Cocoa Touch static library**: A project template which should be used when you want to define a separate set of classes, resources and assets, which can be distributed separately and reused in different iOS projects. Compared to the previous framework project, the static library is much more specific. In general, several libraries can form a framework, but sometimes it's just a single one. The distribution of static libraries is harder, compared to the distribution of frameworks.

- **Metal library**: A template that should be used in case you want to deliver a Metal-based framework (for games or Metal-enabled apps).

5. Click on **Next** and the following screen will appear.

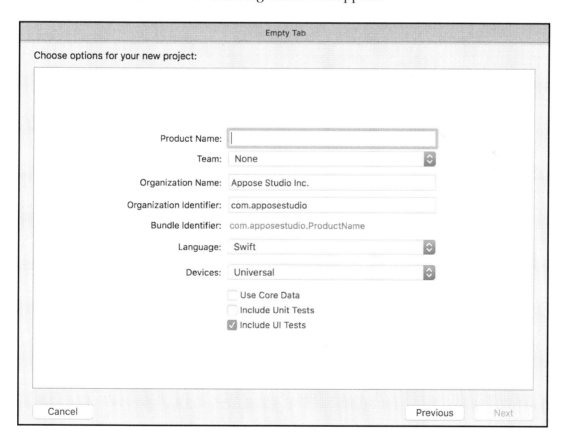

6. On this screen, we should fill in some details, which we can alter later from the project's settings:

    - **Product Name**: This is the name of the app. We can use `My First iOS app`.

    - **Team**: Leave that as **None** for now. Here, you can pick on behalf of which team you are going to develop this app. You may be part of several teams or accounts in the App Store.

    - **Organization Name**: This is the name of the company that is the owner of the app. You can enter arbitrary text here.

    - **Organization Identifier**: The bundle identifier prefix of your organization. Usually, people use the domain of the organization in reverse order. For example, `apposestudio.com` is converted to `com.apposestudio`.

    - **Bundle Identifier**: This is a read-only field, but it's composed by appending the organization identifier and the product name (after a small transformation). For example, if you use `com.mycompany` and `My First iOS app`, the value there will be `com.mycompany.My-First-iOS-app`.

    - **Language**: Keep it as it is; Swift is what we are learning. You may change it with Objective-C.

    - **Devices**: Leave it as **Universal**. This means that the app will run on both device families, iPhone and iPad. You can decide to develop it just for phones or for tablets only, then pick the corresponding value.

    - **Use core data**: You can check this if you are planning to use core data for storing data locally on the device. This won't be discussed in the book, but you can find about it at `https://developer.apple.com/library/content/documentation/DataManagement/Devpedia-CoreData/coreDataOverview.html`.

    - **Include Unit Test:** Xcode will generate a simple test, which could be used to test some parts of your app. This is great in case you want to test your code.

    - **Include UI Tests**: Leave it selected. Xcode will generate separate projects with UI tests, which should be developed in case you want to test the UI of your app.

7. Click on **Next**.

8. Select a folder where the new project will be saved on the disk. For example, in the `Documents` folder, create a new folder called `Swift projects`. Keep the **Source Control** option marked to create a local Git repository, as shown here:

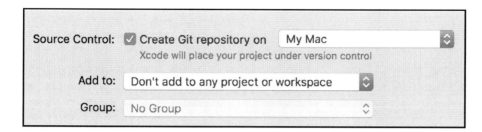

 You will learn about it later in the chapter.

8.  Click on **Finish**.

Xcode will start generating a bunch of files and will open the project for you:

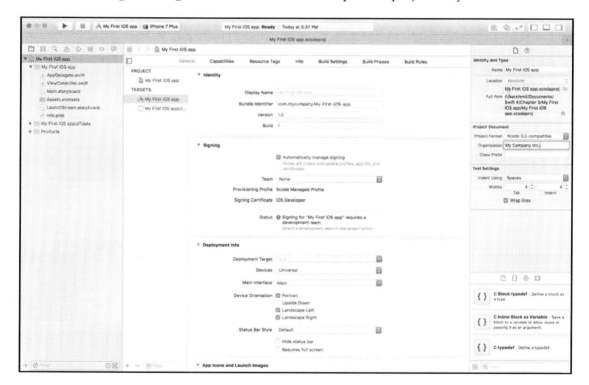

Project

You will see the project settings screen. There are two targets: **My First iOS app** and **My First iOS appUITests**. This is in case you have used the proposed name, but these could be named differently based on the name that you picked for your product earlier.

On this screen, you can change the bundle identifier, in the **Identity** section at the top. In the **Display Name** field, you can specify the name of the app, which will be visible below the icon of the app on the device. The **Version** field is used to set a specific version of your application. Usually, the versioning starts from 1.0.0, but you can use a different approach. The build number is there to distinguish different builds from the same version. It should be increased if you upload a different version in the App Store.

In the sign-in section, you have to pick a team. You can pick **Add an Account...** and if you have an Apple ID, you can use it. If you haven't, then simply use the **Create Apple ID** button and follow the instructions (everything is done in Xcode):

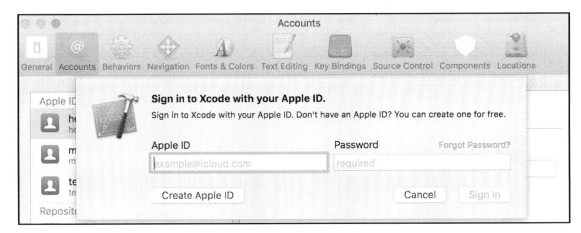

 With your personal account, you can run the app on an iOS device.

To run the app on an iOS device, you have to connect it with a USB cable to your computer. The device will ask you whether you trust this computer (pick **Trust**) and the device will appear in the list, next to the target, at the top of Xcode:

To pick the device you have to click on **iPhone 7 Plus** and you will see the following menu, where you can see your device listed:

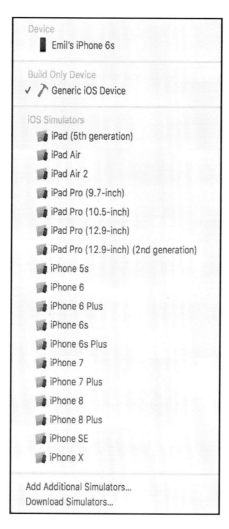

The next section is **Deployment Info**. It is used to specify the device family (keep it as it is).

The main interface points to the `Main.storyboard`, which we will discuss a bit later in the chapter. The role of this field is to show the main storyboard. A `storyboard` is a special type of file that is used to describe the UI of an application or framework. One application can have multiple storyboards. It's possible to have applications without storyboards, but by using them, it's much easier to describe and depict complex UI dependencies.

A device orientation list of checked options defines the supported orientations by the app. If you want to support only **Portrait** mode, then you have to deselect the other options. In the current case, we should deselect **Landscape Left** and **Landscape Right**.

The status bar style can be configured next. The default can be replaced with **light**, which means that the text color will become white. There are two sub-options: to hide the status bar completely once the app is started, and to request full-screen mode wherein the app will be using the whole screen estate.

 Most of these settings can be configured programmatically using code, but it's much easier if we do it through the General panel.

The other sections are for configuring icons and embedding external code in the app. These will be explained later in the book, so don't bother with them right now.

The rest of the tabs on this screen are:

- **Capabilities**: From here, we can add extra capabilities to our app. For example, support of maps, background execution, data protection, key-chain sharing, integration with wireless accessories, and interaction with HealthKit or HomeKit. If you are using a paid account, then you have access to some more, such as Siri integration, push notification, iCloud, GameCenter, Wallet, Apple Pay, In-App Purchase, Personal VPN, and Network Extensions.

Not all capabilities are available, if you are using a free personal account. You have to register for a paid account in the App Store, which costs $99 per year, but this will be needed once you want to use something that is not part of the free tier. For example, if you want to publish your app in the App Store, then you have to switch to a paid account.

- **Resource Tags**: This is place where you can categorize different resources, so they are fetch on the go. It means that not all resources will be downloaded with your app at the very first moment. Some categories will be fetched later, so the user can download the app easily. This technique is advanced and it's applicable for huge apps, which benefit when the user is downloading just part of the resources. If you need further details you can read them here – `https://developer.apple.com/library/content/documentation/FileManagement/Conceptual/On_Demand_Resources_Guide/index.html`.

- **Info**: This tab presents application information. The same information can be found if you open the `Info.plist` file (*cmd + shift + O* and then type `Info.plist`).

- **Build Settings**: This tab contains advanced options of the compiler and your application. To see all the settings, you have to select **All** (it's next to **Basic** and **Customized**):

Use the search box on the right to find what you need. There are too many options to be tweaked, so don't waste time; simply filter.

- **Build Phases**: On this screen, all phases performed while building the project are listed. You can add extra ones or remove one of these–please, don't remove any!

A really important part is **Compile Sources**. You can explore the list of files, which should be compiled:

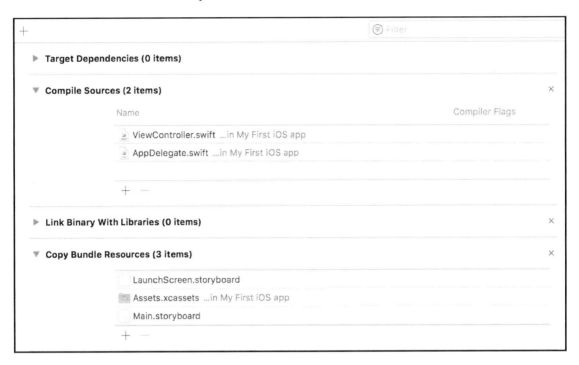

The other key phase is **Copy Bundle Resources**. Xcode is copying the resources which describe the UI of our app.

- **Build Rules**: This last tab contains all default rules which are executed by Xcode.

You can add custom rules which can transform your source code. For the default tasks, Xcode already has a set of default rules.

We learned a bit more about the project settings and how to change those. This is the time to start our app in the simulator. Please pick the type of simulator which should be used; it's located next to the target (at the very top of the Xcode). It should say **iPhone 7 Plus,** for example. Then, click on the big **Play** button to run the project. You should see a **Build Succeeded** message fading in and out at the bottom of your screen.

The simulator will be started automatically. You should see something similar to this:

Yeah, that's right: the app running on the screen is blank. Next, we will understand more about the project organization and, in the next chapter, we will start adding new things to it.

The simulator is a separate application, which simulates an iOS device. It could simulate on an iPad. You have a separate menu to control it. You can do a lot of actions, which the real device can do.

For example you can do the following:

- Take screenshots
- Rotate the simulator to the left (*cmd* + left arrow)
- Rotate the simulator to the right (*cmd* + right arrow)
- Shake gestures (*ctrl* + *cmd* + *Z*)
- Go to the home screen (*cmd* + *shift* + *H*)
- Activate Siri (*alt* + *shift* + *cmd* + *H*)
- Reboot the device
- Simulate TouchID
- Simulate memory warning

- Simulate call
- Toggle hardware keyboard
- Simulate force touch
- Simulate external display
- Send fake locations
- Open System log
- Trigger iCould sync

These are the most popular ones and they can be found in the menu. Feel free to explore them and don't forget that this is similar to a regular phone. So, you have settings and you can configure your device.

> You can copy images from the filesystem by simply dragging and dropping those on top of the simulator. The images will appear in the photos app.
> Not all apps, which are part of real iOS devices, such as App Store, Camera, Notes, and others, are part of the simulator.

Now is the time to explore the project structure. Let's take a look at the Navigator panel on the left. (You can open it using **View** | **Navigators** | **Show Project Navigator** or *cmd + 1* (see more in `Chapter 2`, *Getting Familiar with Xcode and Playgrounds*):

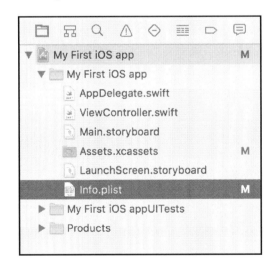

# Project structure

At the top, we see the project's icon **My First iOS app** and its internal structure.

The first is the **My First iOS app** group (folder in this case).

 It's up to you to create a corresponding folder on the filesystem. The project structure may match the file structure, but it could be different.

The yellow folders are called groups and we see three groups in the Navigator.

 Dragging files to different groups doesn't affect the real file on the filesystem.

Let's describe each file in the main group, named after our project:

- `AppDelegate.swift`
- `ViewController.swift`
- `Main.storyboard`
- `Assets.xcassets`
- `LaunchScreen.storyboard`
- `Info.plist`

We will start with `AppDelegate.swift`, which manages the interactions between the app and the underlying OS.

# AppDelegate

The delegate pattern is used to delegate some responsibilities to another class. It's broadly used in Cocoa and Cocoa Touch. In our case, `UIApplication` (our application main class) delegates the control of the interaction between the app and the iOS. We will discuss structure, classes and inheritance in the next chapters—which will help you understand more about delegate software design pattern.

The `AppDelegate` class contains some key methods, which are cool extension points.

 Xcode has added some comments to each function, to help you understand what it does and when it is called.

```
func application(_ application: UIApplication,
didFinishLaunchingWithOptions launchOptions:
[UIApplicationLaunchOptionsKey: Any]?) -> Bool {
        // Override point for customization after application launch.
        return true
}
```

There is a function which is called once the app goes into background mode (the user switches to another app) and when it goes to foreground mode (the app was activated).

The delegate is in a good place to respond to incoming notifications (such as push notifications, memory warnings, and download notifications). In short, these are external events, sent from the iOS, which the app could handle. Here is the place to respond to all events that target the app, not any visual part of it.

The state of the app can be preserved and restored in here. It's important to take care of the user data and the app's internal state, so that next time the user comes back, they can continue their interaction with the app.

Here is a list of some other important actions which should take place here:

1. Register for remote notifications.
2. Check the launch parameters to understand why your application was started (from a deep link, from a push notification, and so on).
3. Open a specific URL sent to your app.
4. Handle notifications remote and local.
5. To initiate background download (when the iOS gives you a green light).
6. Remote protected data when the device is locked.
7. Re-establish access to the protected data, when the device is unlocked.

We will use some of these in the book, but not all of them. You can find further details about each one of them in the official iOS documentation.

# Application states

There are five different states in which an iOS application can exist. Here is a diagram of the states and the relation between them:

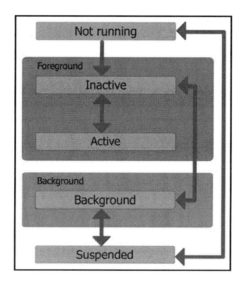

- **Not running**: The app is not running.
- **Inactive**: The app is in the foreground, but doesn't receive any events; probably, the app is changing states.
- **Active**: The app is running and this is the normal mode, when the user is interacting with it.
- **Background**: The app is running, but it's not presented on the screen. In this state, you should do short tasks and return the control back to the OS.
- **Suspended**: The app is in the device's memory, but not doing anything. The OS may remove these apps, to free up some resources for new apps.

These are the methods which are called when the application transitions from one state to another:

```
//when the app is launched
application(_:willFinishLaunchingWithOptions:)
application(_:didFinishLaunchingWithOptions:)
```

When it transitions to:

```
//the foreground
applicationDidBecomeActive(_:)
//the background
applicationDidEnterBackground(_:)
//inactive state, after it leaves the foreground
applicationWillResignActive(_:)
//when it's leaving the background state
applicationWillEnterForeground(_:)
```

This one is called only, when the app is running:

```
applicationWillTerminate(_:)
```

We have learned a lot about `AppDelegate`. Now we should explore the other key file–`ViewController.swift`.

# ViewController

The `ViewController` is responsible for managing the visual part of the app. The logic of the app is spread across many different classes derived from `UIViewController`. It's responsible for saving the data in the model and for reacting to users' interactions, by managing the views.

The class that is generated is pretty basic, but it could be expanded to handle different events. Some of the notable ones are as follows:

- Updating the views, when the underlying model has been changed
- Responding to user actions with the app's UI
- Resizing, animating, and modifying the UI

Each app has at least one `ViewController`. Every one is tightly coupled with the current view hierarchy. The template project which we are using now is blank, thus the current `ViewController` contains almost no code. Later in the book, we will get familiar with other types of `ViewController` that provide a lot of functionality out of the box. Some of them are part of the other project templates, which we can pick from when creating a new project.

Next in the list is `Main.storyboard`. This is the file that defines the visual part of the app. It's like a huge blank page, where we can place all different app screens and we can define the connections between them. It's great that we can visualize different user flows and check whether they are implemented:

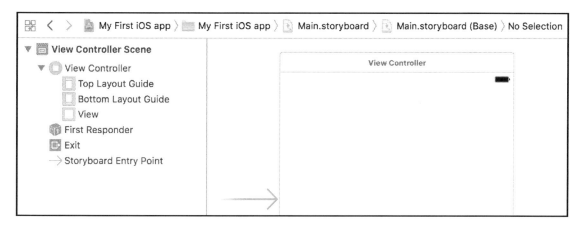

As you can see, the editor panel has become a visual editor, not a text editor, as before. We see that we have a single empty view controller. It has a single view, first responder, and it's marked as an entry point–the arrow denotes this.

We won't spend much time editing the current storyboard, but this is the place where you should start from when you want to add a button or any other UI component.

Next is the blue group – `Assets.xcassets`. This is a special type of resource catalog of all images which are part of the application. At the moment, we have a single one, namely an empty icon.

> Pick the icon of your app carefully. It should be well designed as a single square image which is 1,024 x 1,024 pixels. Then you will have to scale it down to many different resolutions, to support all the different iPhone models.
> There are pretty handy apps or scripts which can be used to generate all the needed assets from the initial one.

Finally, we should check the `LaunchScreen.storyboard`. This is a special storyboard, which is used to define a dynamic version of the loading images. The loading image is shown briefly once the app is started from a cold start (the app has not been started yet) while it's loading the `Main.storyboard`. Here, you can decide what should be displayed in front of the user. Think carefully; this is the first impression which your app makes.

> The best practice is to clone the UI which will appear first (the one part of the `Main.storyboard`.)

For example, if the main view loads some data from the internet, then the launch screen can be similar but without any data.

We won't discuss the `Info.plist` because we got familiar with this file earlier in this chapter.

Next, we will discuss how to use the Git source control system locally, to create snapshots of your app source code. Even though the project is almost blank at the moment, it's good to know how to keep the code safe and how to revert to certain versions.

# Git

Let's try to explain what Git is briefly. This is a distributed version control system. All version control systems are storage of the code, which help you to keep track of all changes of your code. You may think of it as a nice way to do copies of the code and move them around in such a way, so you can go back and forth between different versions. In fact, there are many version control systems, but Git is really popular. Different services such as **GitHub**, **Bitbucket**, and **GitLab** have contributed to make it popular.

Xcode comes with Git integrated. It automatically creates a local repository for your project. Do you remember that there was a **Source Control** option when creating the project? We already have a local Git repository ready for us.

> Distributed version control systems (such as Git) work as a client and a server. This means that they may function without a special centralized place (server) to be fully functional. Another benefit is that every instance may become a server at some point.

It's easy to use the local Git repository. We will learn how to *commit* our code. But, first, let's verify that everything is working fine. You may have noticed that there are some strange symbols next to your files, such as the letter **M**. This denotes that this file has been modified.

> The source control is a safety measure, while you are developing your project. You have to learn that it's good to *commit* (save) your code at some period when coding, because at some point in the future you may decide to go back to a certain *commit* (certain version).

To do your first commit, you have to open the Commit window. Use the menu **Source Control** | **Commit...** (*alt* + *cmd* + *C*):

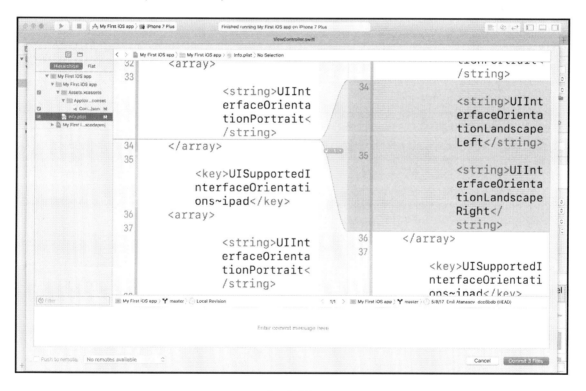

Commit window

This view shows the differences in the files. Once a file is selected in the Navigator panel, it is displayed on the right, in the editor. It's not a typical editor. Here you see the old version on the left and the new version on the right. Xcode shows each difference, and you can decide whether you like this change or you want to revert it to the original state. Just click on the button which has a number:

You have two options. The first one is **Don't Commit**, which will leave that change out of the commit. So, you will have it locally, but it won't become part of the Git (and the tracked history). The other option is **Discard Change**, which will discard the code and leave it as it was in the previous commit.

 If you discarded a change, then it will be lost and you have to do it manually. In Xcode, you can reverse it using the Undo action (*cmd + Z*).

Once you have verified all changes, then you write a nice summary of all your changes in the commit message at the bottom. For example, one of the changes which we had made is to deselect the **Landscape Left** orientation and **Landscape Right** orientation. We can summarize this as *Support only Portrait orientation* in the commit message.

 Don't list the files in the commit message which has been affected. These are easily visible, once someone explores the commit.

Click on the **Commit 3 Files** button. This means that you agree with the changes and they will be stored in the Git repository. All letters in the Navigator panel will be gone. It means that everything is saved and you can switch to this exact version of your project.

To prove it, we will perform an experiment. First, we are going to remove a file and then we will recover it using Git. It sounds like magic, but it's something which Git is used for.

> This example shows how to recover if you remove any file which is under Git control.

Here is what you should do to remove a file. Please be careful when you remove files. If they are not part of the Git repository, then there won't be an easy way to recover them:

1. Open the Navigator.
2. Select `AppDelegate.swift`.
3. Right-click on top of the file.
4. Pick **Delete**:

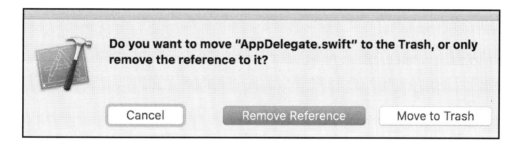

5. Click on **Move to Trash**.

   At this point, the missing file is in the trash. To make this completely transparent, go and empty your macOS **Trash**.

6. You should see that the file is not part of the project. If you try to run the project from the **Play** button it will fail.
7. To recover it, you can use the following command: **Source Control | Discard All Changes...**.
8. Click on **Discard All Changes**.
9. The missing file is here!

> All changes are discarded. Be careful not to lose any important change.

If you need better control, then open the Commit screen (we have done that earlier in the chapter) and you will be able to recover just a single file–use right-click .

The deleted files have **D** next to them.

Git is pretty powerful and there are many features which we won't be able to cover in the book. If you are curios, then you can read much about Git at `https://git-scm.com/book`.

But one important feature is the ability to branch the Git repository. A branch is a point in time where the project code is cloned. All the changes in this branch will co-exist with the other branches. The repository has one main branch called *master*. It's nice to follow a specific policy when developing a software product. One very popular practice is to use the following Git flow/branches. The main development happens in the *develop* branch. Each release is merged back to the *master* branch and those are tagged.

Every new feature is developed in a separate branch which starts from *develop*. This way the developers don't block each other. Once the development is finished, the branch is then merged back to the *develop* branch. If the *develop* branch has progressed since the creation of the feature branch, then all conflicts should be resolved (merged).

We won't discuss all possible scenarios, but you can use Git to merge only the features which you want to include in the next release. Every other feature should catch up the *develop* version of the app.

Git will help you to manage the source code of your app, but it's good to spend enough time exploring it. We've scratched the surface of the version control universe, which can teach you how to manage the project source code.

# Summary

In this chapter, we learned to create a simple mobile app using Xcode. We can set up a Git repository in which we can commit our code. We can switch to a previous version and even to create a new branch, where we can develop different functionalities of our app.

# 4
# Structures, Classes, and Inheritance

In this chapter, we will get familiar with structures and classes. At the end, you should feel comfortable defining your own class or inheriting from any class that is part of iOS and could be inherited.

Now let's dive into structures and classes in Swift. Then, we will continue with two different techniques used to add extra functionality to a class—inheritance and extensions. The chapter discusses the MVC design pattern and why it is good to use it.

In this chapter, we will cover the following topics:

- Structures
- Classes
- Inheritance
- Model-View-Controller (MVC)

## Structures and classes

In Swift, structures and classes are used to define custom data types. They have similar features but are distinct. (We already know that `Bool`, `Double`, `Float`, `Int`, and `String` are basic data types.) Structure and classes define a set of different fields (stored properties) and functions (methods) that are applicable to the object and all related types. The good side of these custom types is that we can combine them when we are implementing our software ideas.

Basic data types are implemented as structures.

Here is how we define a structure:

```
struct Car {
  var name:String = "missing name"
  var speed = 0
  var maxSpeed = 200
}
```

Here is how we define a class:

```
class Ship {
  var speed = 0
  var isFlying = false

  var description:String {
    get {
      return "The ship speed is \(self.speed) and it
              can\(self.isFlying ? "" : "not") fly."
    }
  }
}
```

The first difference is that we are using different keywords, `struct` and `class`. But the final result is that we have two custom types. One is called `Car` and it's a value type. The other one is called `Ship` and it's a reference type.

All instances of both types are called objects. These objects can have functions that belong to them. Let's define some:

```
struct Car {
 var name:String = "missing name"
 var speed = 0
 var maxSpeed = 200

 //method
 func getDescription() -> String {
     return "\(self.name) has maximal speed of \(self.maxSpeed)"
 }
 //property - getter (again method), but it's
 //invoked slightly different
 var description:String {
     get {
```

```
        return self.getDescription()
    }
  }
}
```

The preceding code shows how to define evaluated property, which is different than the three stored properties. The code adds a method which can be called when there is an instance of the Car type.

We can create instances from each of these two types like this:

```
var ferrari = Car(name:"Ferrari F40", speed: 280, maxSpeed:320)
print(ferrari.getDescription())
print(ferrari.description)
//the lines above print:
//Ferrari F40 has maximal speed of 320
//Ferrari F40 has maximal speed of 320

let ship = Ship()
ship.speed = 10
ship.isFlying = false
//The ship speed is 10 and it cannot fly.
```

As you've already seen in the preceding snippet, both instances were created using their respective names followed by (). This is an implicit call to the appropriate init method that handles the object creation and initialization of all fields (stored properties), which are part of this object.

When we have a structure with all fields initialized with default values, then we get two init listeners for free—one without any arguments (the default one) and one which has all fields as arguments. If we call Car() (the default one), then all fields will be initialized with the default values. The other constructor—Car(name:"Ferrari F40", speed: 280, maxSpeed:320)—sets the passed value to the corresponding properties. If we have a class, then we either have explicit default values to all fields, or we need a constructor which will initialize all fields.

Swift forces you to initialize all fields (properties) before instantiating a new object. This is really important since every field should have a value. Otherwise, the new instance could contain undefined information and thus it can't be used safely in a program.

`self` is a keyword, which is used to refer to the very same instance/object. It's used when you want to access specific properties or methods of the same class. It could be used to resolve ambiguity between an instance property and a function parameter with the same name (check the following example).

Here is how we can create a custom `init` method in a class or a structure:

```
class Ship {
 //... the same fields

 //designated initializer
 init(speed:Int, isFlying:Bool) {
 self.speed = speed
 self.isFlying = isFlying
 }

 //convenience
 convenience init(speed:Int) {
     self.init(speed: speed, isFlying: false);
 }


}
```

The code sample in which we create a `Ship` instance should be updated, so that we are using the new initializer with speed:

```
let ship = Ship(speed: 10)
print(ship.description)
//The ship speed is 10 and it cannot fly.
```

We have to remember that all fields should be initialized; otherwise, the compiler will complain. When we are using classes, we should distinguish between two types of initializers. The first type, designated `init` methods, which handle the full object initialization, and the other type, **convenience** initializers, which they should call either another convenience or designated initializer. Such a sequence always ends with designated initializer call.

Every class should have at least one designated constructor. The default constructor is a designated one if all fields have default values.

Designated initializers don't delegate the initialization of the object (except in cases of inheritance, when they delegate that to the super initializer).

When we are defining a structure we can follow the same rules, but we shouldn't add a **convenience** word in front of a constructor. The rules are the same—all fields should be initialized.

So far, we have learned how to define structures and classes. These data types can have methods and properties which store values. Not all properties should be fields; they could be evaluated properties. Such types of properties are accessed (called) like regular properties, but instead of that, a function is triggered. The preceding code defines the description property, which returns a String object, describing the instance of the type. Let's define the generic property, which consists of a getter and a setter:

```
class Ship {
    ...
    private var _id:String = "no-id"
    var serialNumber: String {
        get {
            return self._id
        }
        set {
            _id = newValue
        }
    }
    //...
}
```

The preceding code helps us to do the following actions using every ship instance:

```
//ship is an instance of Ship from above
ship.serialNumber = "my-first-ship"
print(ship.serialNumber)
//my-first-ship
```

We can see the different usages of the property notation:

- The setter is called when the instance is the left part of an assignment such as the following:

```
ship.serialNumber = "my-first-ship"
```

- The getter is called when the instance property is used in any other code statement different from association with a new value. In all cases when the = operator is missing, the getter is invoked.

Properties, classes, structures, enums, and tuples have a scope of visibility or access level. The following scopes are available:

- `private`
- `fileprivate`
- `internal`
- `public`
- `open`

A module is a logical unit of code. For example, an app is a module. A framework, which can be used in one or more apps, is another module. Every scope has different visibility in the module(s) in which it takes part. The less restrictive is the `open` access mode and most restricted is `private`. In the preceding code, we are hiding the internal organization of the `Ship` class, thus we need to use private. It means that we can't access the `_id` property, because it's marked as private from outside of the class. It still can be used in our internal function like the setter, getters, and any other internal methods.

> It's possible to restrict the setter access level when we explicitly define it. The new access level should be restricted compared to the getter.
>
> `private (set) public var myProperty: String?`

The `fileprivate` scope limits the usage to the same source file, which is a slightly broader than the pure private access mode. The `internal` scope is the default mode. It means that the visibility is restricted to everything inside the current active module (framework or application).

The `public` means that other modules will be able to see the file, but they won't be able to inherit it. To enable inheritance from other modules, then you need the less restricted access level open. This is intended to be used when designing frameworks since once the public interface is fixed, every next change in the public interface defined by the framework should be backward compatible.

If a property has only a getter (no setter included), then we are talking about a read-only property. Here is how we can implement a `version` property:

```
class Ship {
 //...
 var version: String {
     return "1.0.0"
 }
 //...
}
```

It can be used as a regular property:

```
print("Ship version: \(ship.version)")
```

But it should never be a left part of an assignment. The following code won't compile:

```
ship.version = "4.0.0"
```

The Swift compiler complains with the following error:

```
cannot assign to property: 'version' is a get-only property.
```

There is one special type of property—these are the lazy properties. They are different than regular ones because they are not initialized before their use. Let's define a custom class, `Permit`, to illustrate the lazy properties properly:

```
class Permit {
    var validUntil = 2017

    init(validUntil: Int) {
        self.validUntil = validUntil
        print("Permit object is constructed")
    }

    deinit {
        print("This instance is destroyed.")
    }
}
```

Then we have to add a lazy property to our `Ship` class:

```
class Ship {
    //...
    lazy var permit:Permit = Permit(validUntil: 2100) ...
}
```

As you can see, the `lazy` property already has a value, which will be evaluated immediately before its use.

Here is how we can use the `permit` property:

```
print("Ship's permit is valid until \(ship.permit.validUntil)")
//Permit object is constructed
//Ship's permit is valid until 2100
```

As you can see in the console, there is one extra row printed, which is part of the permit `init` method. If we never use this particular property, then it will never be constructed, thus the console will stay empty.

We have learned the basics of structure and classes, and how to define properties and methods (known as object functions). We will discuss the static (also called class methods a bit later); but, first, let's get familiar with a pretty handy way to add additional functionality to already defined classes or structures.

# Extensions

The extensions are used to add new functionality to different data types, such as structures, classes, enumerations or protocols. We will focus on classes and structures, but in future will see some handy applications of the extensions.

Let's see what we can do in an extension and how it's defined.

 You can't add stored properties to a class and a structure in an extension.

Let's see an example that adds constructors to our data types. This includes structures and classes:

```
//class extension
extension Ship {
    convenience init(type:String) {
        if(type == "super-sonic") {
            self.init(speed:2000, isFlying: true);
        } else {
            self.init(speed: 10, isFlying: false);
        }
    }
}
```

```
//struct extension
extension Car {
    //no need to add convenience in front
    init(name:String) {
        self.name = name
    }

     init(name:String, maxSpeed: Int) {
        self.name = name
        self.maxSpeed = maxSpeed
     }
}

var cars = [Car(), Car(name:"Ferrari"), Car(name: "Tesla", maxSpeed: 320),
Car(name:"Porshe", speed:50, maxSpeed: 260)]

var ships = [Ship(speed:20), Ship(type:"super-sonic")]
```

We can use the extensions to add one of the following items:

- Any type of computed properties (class and instance ones)
- Any type of functions (class and instance)
- Define subscripts
- Provide new initializers
- Define nested types
- Use nested types
- Mutating functions (for structures)
- Conform to a protocol

You will see some of these used in the book. Be aware that without the extension, the type doesn't include those new functionalities. Once the extension is evaluated, then all the new functions can be accessed.

 When defining additional (convenience) constructors, it's good to add those to an extension.

For example, if you have default values to all properties of a structure, then you get two init methods for free. If you define new init method in the structure body, then you will lose the ones which are provided for free by Swift. If you want to keep those, define the extra constructors in an extension.

Extensions can't add property observers to existing properties.

Here is a short example that improves the `Car` structure:

```
//add color
extension Car {
    enum Color {
        case red, blue, silver, green, pink, undefined
    }

    func getTypicalColor() -> Color {
        if self.name == "Ferrari" {
            return .red
        }

        if self.name == "Tesla" {
            return .silver
        }

        if self.name == "Tesla Blue" {
            return .blue
        }

        return .undefined
    }
}

print(Car(name: "Tesla Blue").getTypicalColor() == Car.Color.blue ? "The
car is blue." : "What color is this?")
```

When we are discussing classes, we should be aware that each instance of a class type takes some memory and it's stored in the heap memory when it's allocated initially. The process of allocation happens automatically once you call the `init` function. The class instances can be shared, which means that several variables can use the same place in the memory. We will dive into the memory management in the next chapters. But, before that, we should know that to free up the memory which was taken by our instance, we have the handy function which is called immediately before the instance is de-allocated from memory—the `deinit` method.

# The deinit method

Usually, you won't implement this method, but if your class is using some OS resources such as files, sockets, connections, extra memory—it's good to clean up once the instance responsible for this is going to be de-allocated. Each class may have a `deinit` function, which is written slightly differently:

```
deinit {
    //clean up the resources which the class is using, so they can be
        re-used later
}
```

It's similar to the `init` methods, but it doesn't have `()` after it. This method is called automatically.

> You can't explicitly call the `deinit` method. It's called automatically immediately before the de-allocation of the instance.
>
> If the class inherits another class then the de-initializer is called automatically after the de-initializer of the subclass. The supper class de-initializers are always invoked, even in cases when the subclass doesn't define the `deinit` itself.

Each instance has its own properties. When a new instance is allocated then a new set of properties is created for it. If we want to have something common between all instances of a particular type (such as data or action), then we should use type properties or type functions.

# Type properties and functions

**Type properties** are used when we need to have access to data from any instance of that type (we could think from many different places). Compared to instance properties, their properties are accessible through that particular instance. It means that a single copy will exist and it will be attached to a specific type. The phrase *type* properties suggest that those properties will be special properties, which could be accessed through the type itself, as shown in the following code:

```
class Ship {
  ...
  static let madeIn = "UK"
  ...
}
```

```
//we use the type property in the print function
print("Made in \(Ship.madeIn)") //Made in UK
```

To mark a property as a type property, simply add `static` in front of it. From now on, when the text refers to a static property it means a type property.

There is an alternative way to add a static (type) property to a type, using `extension`. Here is how the preceding code looks when using what we already know:

```
extension Ship {
    static let madeIn = "UK"
}

print("Made in \(Ship.madeIn)")  //Made in UK
```

The typical usage of a static (type) property is to share values across all instances. There is no limit to what type of properties will be used as static. They could be constants, variables (stored properties), and computed ones.

Every type is a special object, which is responsible for creating instances of that particular type.

All stored type properties should have a default value because the type is a special type of object, which doesn't have its own initializer. (Every instance uses an `init` method like we had discussed earlier. Unfortunately, the type itself doesn't use any `init` method.)

Here is some code, which illustrates this:

```
extension Car {
    //computed read-only property
    static var bestCarBrand:String {
        get { return "Tesla" }
    }
    //type stored property
    static var totalNumberOfCars = 0
}
```

The type could be used to store shared data using static stored properties, but be careful who else has access to this field and how it's managed.

If you want to check the type on an instance, the following function comes in handy: `type(of: yourVariable)`.

Here is an example that shows how to use it:

```
let ship = Ship(speed: 10)
//get access to a type metadata
var typeOfShipConstant = type(of: ship)
var typeShip = Ship.self
print("My type is \(typeOfShipConstant)")
print("My type is \(typeShip)")
print("The type of Ship.self is \(type(of: typeShip))")

//My type is Ship
//My type is Ship
//The type of Ship.self is Ship.Type
```

Static (type) functions are similar to static properties. They can be called using their full name—`Type.functionName(parameters)`. There is no need for an instance and these methods could be called from any code, where the type is accessible, (for example, everywhere in the current module, if the type is not private). For more information, check the previous access modifiers in this chapter.

In the next section, we will discuss how to add some custom classes and structures to a playground.

# Adding custom data types to a playground

We know how to create our own data types to model the real world. Let's try to add some classes to a playground so we can present the weather for a particular location to the user.

To add a new file to the playground, you have to open the Navigation pane on the left. Then you can expand the `Source` folder, then, right-click on it and pick **New File**. Then simply give it a name and you are ready to edit the new `.swift` file.

First of all, we will need to model the weather. So, let's start with a structure called `Weather`. It will contain a list of simple objects, which describe the temperature for a particular hour. These objects can be stored in a list and each index can match specific hours of the day. We need a type which will contain this information—we will call it `ForcastData`.

 Good practice is to keep each data type in a separate file.

There are many benefits to this approach; here are a few:

- Encapsulation—each class should access only its own properties
- Faster builds—incremental builds are part of the Swift compiler; only changed files will be recompiled
- Better organization—correct definition of responsibilities, who does what
- Easy support of a huge code database
- Easy collaboration when working on huge projects

Here is the code. Each file should contain only a single structure and its extensions.

We are starting with `Weather.swift`:

```swift
// use import to link other modules/frameworks to the code
import Foundation

/***
 * Structure which describes the Weather.
 * It contains an array of ForcastData for each hour.
 * The location property contains the location where the forcast is
applicable.
 * The date filed contains the day of the forcast.
 **/
public struct Weather {
    public var hours: [ForecastData]
    //public getter, internal setter
    internal (set) public var location: String
    //public getter, internal setter
    internal (set) public var date: Date

    // public initializator, because it should be visible
    public init(hours:[ForecastData], location:String, date:Date) {
        self.hours = hours
        self.location = location
        self.date = date
    }
}

public extension Weather {
    init() {
        self.hours = []
        self.location = "Nowhere"
        self.date = Date()
    }
}
```

Then we move to `ForecastData.swift`:

```swift
import Foundation

/**
 * Structure which describes the weather in specific point in time
 * It contians the most important details.
 **/
public struct ForecastData {
    public var hour: Int
    public var temp: Double
    public var minTemp: Double
    public var maxTemp: Double
    public var pressure: Double
    public var humidity: Double

    public var clouds: Double
    public var wind: WindData

    public var description: String
    public var icon: String?
}

public extension ForecastData {
    init() {
        self.hour = 0
        self.temp = 0
        self.minTemp = 0.0
        self.maxTemp = 0.0
        self.pressure = 0.0
        self.humidity = 0.0
        self.clouds = 0.0

        self.wind = WindData(speed: 0, degrees: 0, direction: "none")
        self.description = "Empty object"
        self.icon = nil
    }
}
```

If you add new `init` methods in an extension (not in the main definition), you will keep the autogenerated ones. If you define at least one `init` in the main definition, then you won't have any autogenerated initializer.

Finally, we finish with the shortest file—`WindData.swift`:

```swift
import Foundation
/**
 * Structure which contains extra data, describing the wind.
 **/
public struct WindData {
    public var speed: Double
    public var degrees: Double
    public var direction: String
}
```

Here is what your playground should look like:

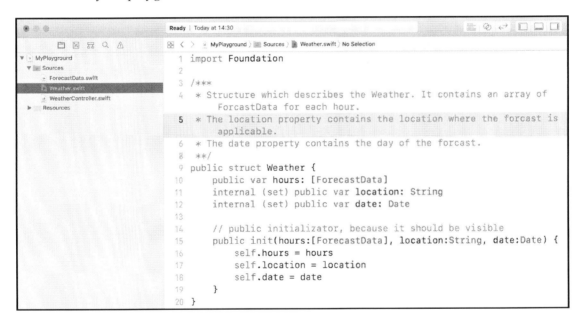

Then you can experiment with the following code to verify that the new data types are working as expected:

```swift
// Weather structures in action
var emptyForecast = ForecastData()
var weather = Weather()
weather = Weather(hours:[emptyForecast], location:"London", date:Date())
print(weather.location)
```

One thing which we should note is that the structures should be marked as `public` to be accessible (visible) in the main playground and its properties too. Because we want to allow only read access, the setter is marked with the `internal` access level. This is needed because all supporting playground classes are in a separate module. We have discussed this in `Chapter 2`, *Getting familiar with Xcode and Playgrounds*.

In the next section, we will discuss a handy mechanism, which helps when developing complex class models.

# Inheritance

**Inheritance** is a mechanism that helps developers through the process of implementing complex hierarchical data structures. All inherited features become part of the new class. To put it simply, a class can inherit properties and methods from another class. The class which is inherited is called a **parent** class or **super** class. The new class which inherits another class is called a **child** class.

 The inheritance is applicable to classes only.

Each class which inherits from another class can provide a specific implementation of the inherited features. All other functions, properties, subscripts, and so on, can be accessed from the child class.

# Base class

Every class which doesn't have a super class is called a base class. In contrast with other programming languages, there is no universal class which all classes inherit from. So, every base class can be used as a super class (except if we explicitly forbid a class to be inherited).

Let's try to create a subclass of our class `Ship`:

```
// SpaceShip inherits Ship
class SpaceShip: Ship {
    var numberOfLazerGuns:Int
    init() {
        //initialize local properties
        self.numberOfLazerGuns = 4
        //initialize the inherited ones
```

```
            //calling a designated initalizer
            super.init(speed: 50000, isFlying: true)
        }
    }

    extension SpaceShip {
        convenience init(lazerGuns:Int) {
            //call designated constructor
            self.init()
            self.numberOfLazerGuns = lazerGuns
        }

        convenience init(speed:Int, lazerGuns:Int) {
            //call designated constructor
            self.init()
            self.speed = speed
            self.numberOfLazerGuns = lazerGuns
        }
    }
```

When inheriting from a class, we simply list the name of the super class after the name of our class. This action is called subclassing, as in the following code:

```
class SpaceShip : Ship
```

`SpaceShip` is a subclass of the base class `Ship`. `Ship` is a base class because it is not a subclass of any class.

Subclasses can be subclassed.

We can access all the methods and properties of the parent class, which are inherited. Here is how to do it:

```
var spaceShip = SpaceShip(lazerGuns: 5)
print("SpaceShip speed is \(spaceShip.speed)")
```

When subclassing, our class inherits all methods and properties from the parent class, but with *overriding* we can modify and further refine each function. If you want to provide a new behavior for the same function, then you have to explicitly declare that by adding the keyword `override` before the function.

Let's see an example. Look at the following code:

```
print(spaceShip.description)
```

It results in the following output:

```
The ship speed is 50000 and it can fly.
```

We can override the description property as follows:

```
class SpaceShip: Ship {
 //...
    override var description:String {
        get {
            return "The space ship (🚀) speed is \(self.speed) km/s."
        }
    }
}
```

After this tiny change, the code produces the following output:

```
The space ship (🚀) speed is 50000 km/s.
```

 You can't use extensions to override existing functionality.

If you do want to keep or reuse the provided functionality from the super class, you can use the super keyword to refer to the parent class. You can call any functions and use their result. For example, if we want to keep the result from the description property, we can do the following:

```
class SpaceShip: Ship {
    //...
    override var description:String {
        get {
            return super.description
        }
    }
}
```

When overriding a property and if the property contains only a getter, then we can provide a setter and a getter in the subclass. If it has a setter and a getter, then we should provide an implementation for both when overriding it. If we do want to keep the super implementation we can delegate it, as in the last example, and just pass the parent value.

Overriding a method is similar to overriding a property. Simply add the override before the method definition (name, parameters and result type).

If we assume that the Ship class contains the following function:

```
class Ship {
    //...
    func calculateDistance(time:Int) -> Int {
        return self.speed * time
    }
}
```

We can override this function like this:

```
class SpaceShip: Ship {
//...
    override func calculateDistance(time: Int) -> Int {
        return super.calculateDistance(time: time) * 2
    }
}
```

Sometimes, when designing complex relations between many classes or when designing software frameworks (a set of handy classes—such as iOS frameworks), you may like to prevent some methods from being overridden. This is possible and, to do so, you have to add the final keyword in front.

If we want to prevent a whole class from being subclassed, we can mark it with final—so it will become the following:

```
final class <Name of the class> ...
```

Now is the time to discuss special type properties. They are part of the class definition similar to the static/type properties, but they are slightly different.

# Class properties

These are special types of properties which are similar to type properties. They can be overridden in the classes which inherit the class property from another class, in contrast to static (type) properties which can't and they are not inherited.

We already know about inheritance and how to define custom types. Now we should get familiar with the most popular way of organizing your code in an iOS app.

# Model-View-Controller (MVC)

MVC is a design pattern, which helps you to organize your code. It separates the classes by roles, which maximize the reuse and independence of the code (loose coupling):

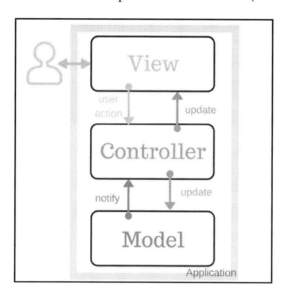

The **Model** stores the data of the app. There you can keep the state of the app, the data entered by the user, and so on. Only the controller interacts with the model. When the **Model** is updated, this change is reported to the controller. On the other hand, the **Controller** sends updates to the **Model**.

The **View** is responsible for presenting data to the user. The user interacts directly with the **View**. Every user event is reported to the **Controller**. The **Controller** decides whether it should be propagated to the model or it should just modify the view.

The **Controller** is the mediator, which is responsible for coordinating the views and the models. By having this extra layer, we can design our iOS apps in such a way that the views can be reused easily and the models can be reused as well.

Here is an abstract scenario in which we can have data which can be displayed in different types of charts. The **Controller** can decide what part of the data (the **Model**) should be passed to every single presentation (the **View**). When the user decides, a different presentation of the data could be rendered.

Before diving into the source code, you should know something about protocols. This is the blueprint of a class/structure. It's the contract that a type can decide to fulfill; we will discuss protocols in detail in the next chapter.

Here is a simple code which sketches the MVC concept with our own `Weather` class.

```
//MVC example
var dc = DateComponents()
dc.year = 2017
dc.month = 7
dc.day = 7
//create a date
let coolDate = Calendar.current.date(from: dc)!

var newYourWeather = Weather(hours: [emptyForecast], location: "New York",
date: coolDate)
var sanFranciscoWeather = Weather(hours: [emptyForecast], location: "San
Francisco", date: coolDate )

var model = WeatherModel(weather: newYourWeather)
var controller = WeatherController()
//the controller needs a model
controller.model = model
model.modelObserver = controller

var view = WeatherView(location: controller.location, date:
controller.date, listener: controller)

//the controller needs a view
controller.view = view

//initial view rendering
view.draw()

//simulate model update and the view is updated if needed
model.setNewWeater(weather: sanFranciscoWeather)

//simulate user action and the model will be updated if needed
view.simulateUserAction()
```

We have the following three files in our playground.

The first is `WeatherModel.swift` which stores our Model:

```swift
public protocol WeatherModelObserver {
    func modelHasChanged(model:WeatherModel)
}

public class WeatherModel {
    private var weather:Weather
    public var modelObserver:WeatherModelObserver?

    public init(weather:Weather) {
        self.weather = weather
    }

    public func setNewWeater(weather:Weather) {
        print("[Model] The model has been changed.")
        self.weather = weather
        if modelObserver != nil {
            modelObserver?.modelHasChanged(model: self)
        }
    }

    public func getWeather() -> Weather {
        return self.weather
    }

    func update() {
        print("[Model] Update the model")
    }
}
```

Then we have `WeatherView.swift`:

```swift
public protocol WeatherViewListner {
    func showWeather(forDate:Date)
}

public class WeatherView {
    private var toNotify:WeatherViewListner?
    private var location:String
    private var date:Date
    private var dateFormatter:DateFormatter

    public init(location:String, date:Date, listener:WeatherViewListner?) {
        self.location = location
        self.date = date
```

```
            self.toNotify = listener

            self.dateFormatter = DateFormatter()
            dateFormatter.dateStyle = .medium
            dateFormatter.timeStyle = .none
            // DateFormatter.dateFormat(fromTemplate: "yyyy-MM-dd",
                options: 0, locale: Locale(identifier: "en_US"))
    }

    public func simulateUserAction() {
        print("[View] Detect user interactions and react.")
        // update the visual part
        // and notify the controller
        if toNotify != nil {
            toNotify?.showWeather(forDate: Date())
        }
    }

    public func draw() {
        let d = self.dateFormatter.string(from: self.date)
        print("[View] \(d) - \(self.location) =>")
    }

    public func refresh(location:String) {
        print("[View] The view is updated and will be redrawn")
        draw()
    }
}
```

And finally, we have `WeatherController.swift`, which defines the connection between our Model and View:

```
public class WeatherController {
    public var view:WeatherView?
    public var model:WeatherModel?

    public init() { }

    public var location:String {
        get {
            return model?.getWeather().location ?? "Unknown"
        }
    }

    public var date:Date {
        get {
            return model?.getWeather().date ?? Date()
```

```
            }
        }
    }

    extension WeatherController: WeatherViewListner {
        public func showWeather(forDate:Date) {
            print("[Controller] Handle all user interactions.")
            print("[Controller] If necessary the model is updated.")
            model?.update()
        }
    }

    extension WeatherController: WeatherModelObserver {
        public func modelHasChanged(model:WeatherModel) {
            print("[Controller] The model has been updated.")
            print("[Controller] Check if the view should be updated.")
            view?.refresh(location: "New York")
        }
    }
```

We see that the Model can exist on its own. The same thing is applicable to the View. The Controller is the glue which sticks both and controls them.

# Summary

In this chapter, we discussed how to define custom data types—structures and classes. Then, we defined some custom types in our playground to see this in practice. You should be able to define your own data types. We've learned what is subclassing and inheritance. You now know how to override methods and properties. We explored the very popular design pattern, MVC. If you organize the app following the MVC pattern, then some parts of our apps can be reused in other apps without further improvements. They will be designed for future reuse.

In the next chapter, we will add interactivity to our first application. We will try to apply the MVC in practice in our mobile app. Let's get started with storyboards and views, then we will add some buttons and hook up some actions to those buttons.

# Adding Interactivity to Your First App

# 5

This chapter is about storyboards, adding views, and making our app interactive. It explains how to hook up the UI components from the storyboard to the code. You will learn how to detect different user actions.

In this chapter, we will cover these topics:

- Storyboards
- Basic visual components in iOS
- How to add views
- How to link them to the code
- When to use storyboards or pure code

## Storyboards

A storyboard is a central place where all screens can be designed. It's not mandatory to use a storyboard to create a working iOS app, but with storyboards you can save a lot of time when defining a native UI. This is the official way of developing a UI in Apple's ecosystem of iOS, macOS, watchOS, and tvOS.

The storyboard editor is a special view of Xcode. It presents a visual editor for your application. Let's get back to our first empty app which has a single view. Do you remember that we had seen in the navigator that there is a special file named `.storyboard`? This is where we will start from and this is what your app renders initially:

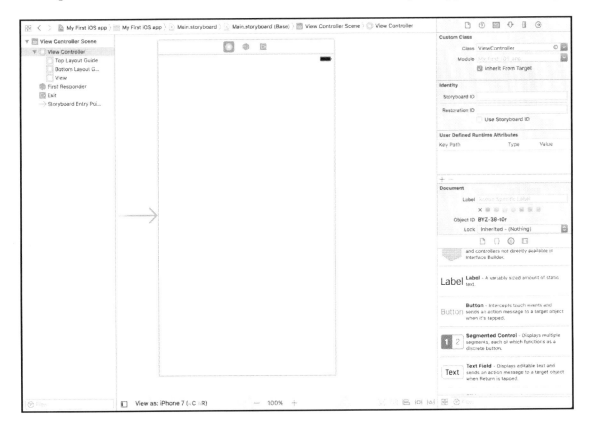

Initial screen of your app

This screen is the initial screen of your app. The UI components which you can add can be found at the bottom-right of the Properties panel. Simply, drag and drop items on the canvas and they will appear.

The storyboard is a nice way to define complex visuals without code. It can be used to visualize the connections between different app screens (called **scenes** in the storyboard). This makes the app easily understandable by developers and the storyboard provides a nice overview of the whole app. Working with different UI components, such as table view and custom cell, renders completely easily. The **Auto Layout**, which we will discuss later in the `Chapter 7`, *Developing a Simple Weather App*, allows you to define mathematical relations between a component position and a component size, thus the view fits nicely on different phone screens. In storyboards, you can describe the transitions between different screens and the transition between scenes.

There is an easy way to hook interactions to many view components. We will discuss this later in this chapter. Let's first start by adding a few visual components.

# Visual components

There are many different types of visual components which can be added. Let's see the default building blocks, which we can use when developing an iOS app:

- **Label**: Control to present a static text
- **Button**: Regular button, which handles touch interactions
- **Segmented Control**: Several buttons next to each other, but only one can be active at a time
- **Text Field**: Displays editable text and handles all interaction with the control
- **Slider**: Selects easily a single value from a range
- **Switch**: On or off switch, easily toggled
- **Spinner/Activity Indicator View**: Indefinite progress view
- **Progress View**: Presents the progress of a task over time
- **Page Control**: Displays dots for each page for easy navigation through pages

The next screenshot shows how the components look in Xcode. You can find them in the Utilities pane on the right. You have to activate the **Object Library** at the bottom:

Let's continue with the other controls:

- **Stepper**: View, which can increment or decrement a value
- **Horizontal Stack View**: View container, which arranges views horizontally
- **Vertical Stack View**: View container, which arranges views vertically
- **Table View**: Powerful control to display data in a list format; could have groups or sections for easy visual separation of the data
- **Table View Cell**: Single building block in a table view
- **Image View**: View in which an image or images could be rendered
- **Collection View**: Presents data in a collection of cells; works nicely with different screen sizes
- **Collection View Cell**: Single view item, part of a collection view
- **Collection Reusable View**: Special view, which is part of a collection view, but displays a section, header, or footer

Here are the next items which you should see (probably some of them) in the **Object Library**:

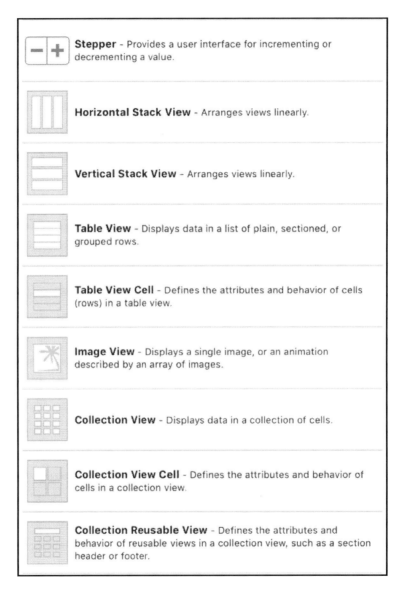

Here is the last part of default visual items, which we can use:

- **Text View**: Displays multilines of text; the text is scrollable and sends various events to a delegate
- **Scroll View**: View, which can display content bigger than its size; pretty handy when something huge should be displayed
- **Date Picker**: Control, which allows the user to select a date using spinning wheels
- **Picker View**: Spinning wheel full with values; only one can be selected
- **Visual Effect View with Blur**: Blur effect
- **Visual Effect View with Blur and Vibrancy**: Advanced blur effect with vibrancy
- **Map Kit View**: Displays map and gives a nice interface to navigate the map
- **MetalKit View**: Default Metal view, which uses Metal technology
- **GLKit View**: OpenGL ES view, which could be used to render OpenGL scenes
- **SceneKit View**: A view which can render a 3D scene
- **Web View**: Renders an embed web content and provides nice navigation
- **View**: Basic rectangular building item, which reports interaction; every subclass of UIView could be housed in this component
- **Container View**: Region of a view controller, which could include a child view controller

Here are the controls which you see in the object browser. They are easily distinguishable because of the icons. You can see a short explanation next to each item:

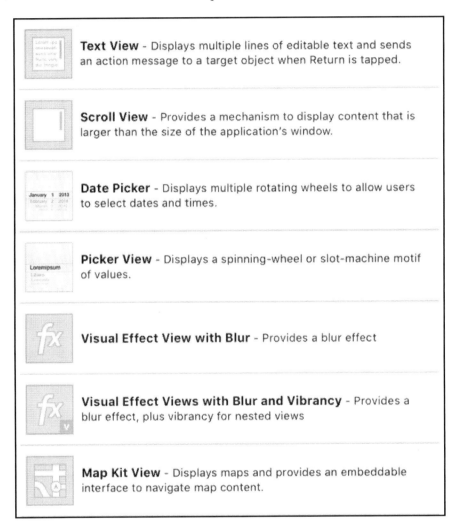

**Text View** - Displays multiple lines of editable text and sends an action message to a target object when Return is tapped.

**Scroll View** - Provides a mechanism to display content that is larger than the size of the application's window.

**Date Picker** - Displays multiple rotating wheels to allow users to select dates and times.

**Picker View** - Displays a spinning-wheel or slot-machine motif of values.

**Visual Effect View with Blur** - Provides a blur effect

**Visual Effect Views with Blur and Vibrancy** - Provides a blur effect, plus vibrancy for nested views

**Map Kit View** - Displays maps and provides an embeddable interface to navigate map content.

The list is long and you can see the rest here. In Xcode, scroll and the other views will appear in the list:

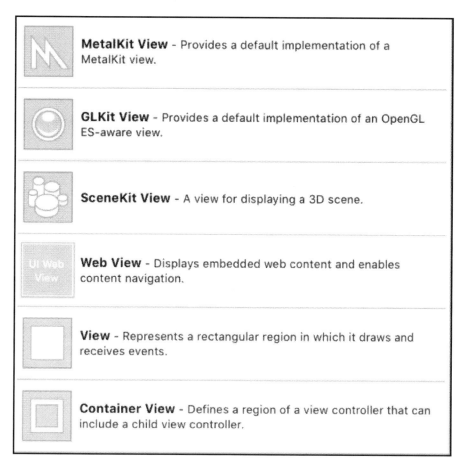

This is just the standard set of visual components which you can use in your apps. Each component can be customized and extended based on the app needs.

In the real world, if you need a special visual component, then you better check whether such a component exists before diving into development.

There are many places where developers share components for free or you can buy a license to use them in your apps.

Let's see some of the items in action, being part of our app.

# Adding items to the storyboard

Almost every app needs to present textual information. To do so, we need a label or a TextView to render the content in the app. Follow these steps to add a simple label on the screen:

1. Open the Utilities pane (*alt* + *cmd* + *0*).
2. Activate the **Object Library** tab. Simply click on the **Object Library** button shown here:

3. Click on the filter field at the bottom:

4. Type `lab`. The list of components will filter.
5. You should see just a single component. In this case, the **Label** view:

6. Start dragging the label to the storyboard in the center.

7. Drop it in the center:

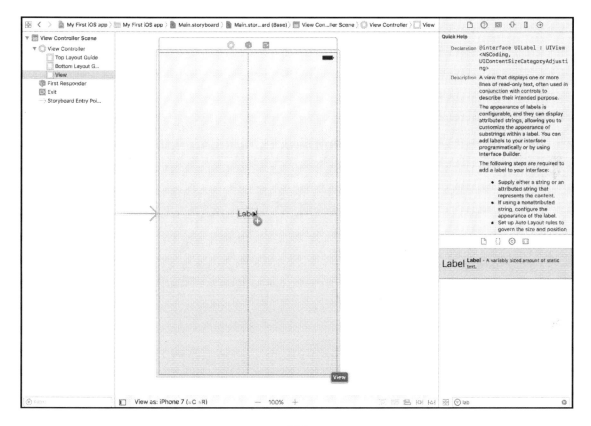

Label

 The designer will help you to center the label easily with guidelines.

8. Now, double-click on the label to enter your message, which should be displayed to the user. For example: `Click on the button below, please.`

9. Let's add some formatting to put this text in the center of the screen:
   1. Open the Attribute inspector.
   2. Set the **Lines** to **2**. (The label should be selected.)
   3. Edit the text in the **Text** field at the top, move after the word button and press *alt + enter*. This will insert a new line and the label will be broken into two lines:

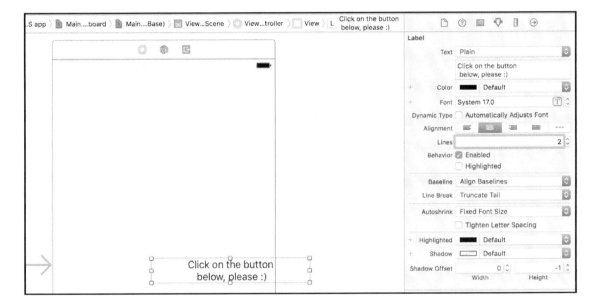

10. Center the label with the mouse.
11. Let's drag a button.
12. First, select the filter field and write `button`:

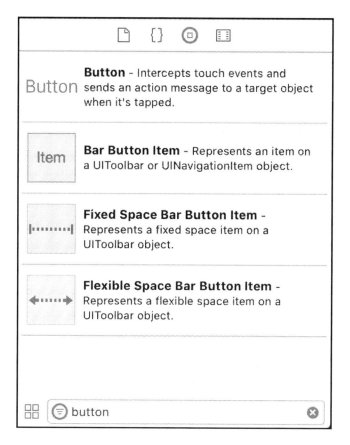

12. Then drag the button below the label.
13. Then change the text of the button to `Action`. Use double-click.

This is how easy it is to add visual items from the library to a scene. We have a pretty rich set of different basic UI components. We can use them in our apps. All users of the iOS ecosystems are already familiar with these controls, so they know how they are working.

You can customize each view in different ways. We will discuss possible ways of doing that.

 Pick the visual component which fits you for the particular case or app.

In this section, we discuss how to trigger the code of the app when the user interacts with the UI. Let's begin with our first button.

# Linking the UI with the code

Storyboards provide a nice way to link the user actions with functions (code) in the app. Here is what you should do:

1. Open `Main.storyboard`. To do it, you can use *cmd + shift + O* and start typing `Main`. Then select the file and hit *return/enter*.
2. Select the button on the screen.
3. Activate the Assistant Editor using the Assistant Editor button:

You should see the storyboard on the left, and the code of `ViewControler.swift` on the right:

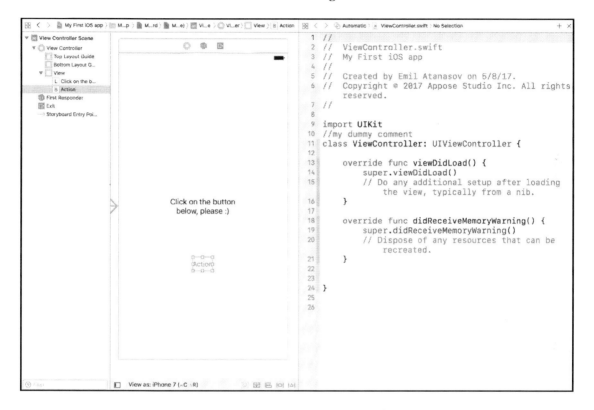

4. Right-click on the button in the storyboard. An action list should appear:

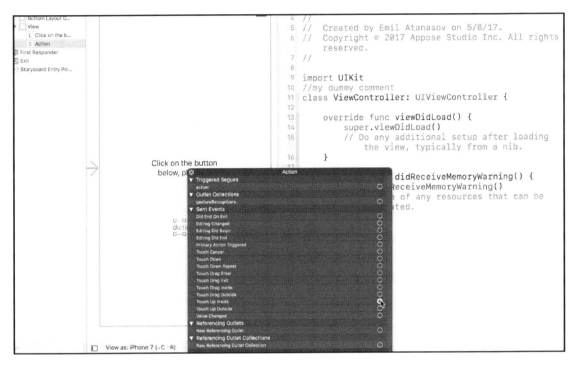

Action list

5. Position the mouse on the right part of the **Action** panel (on **Touch Up Inside** – a small plus sign will appear, as shown).

6. Start dragging it on top of the right panel:

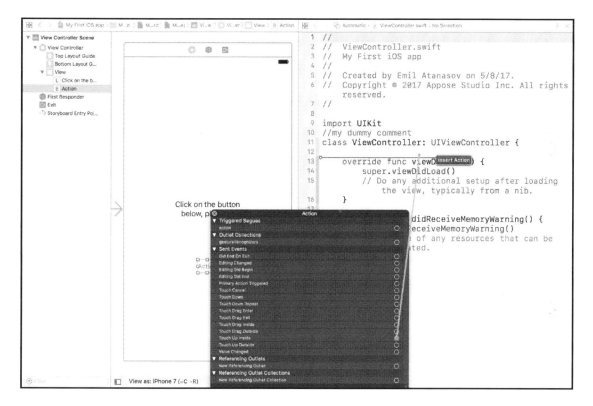

Dragging the action panel

7. A blue guideline will show you possible positions where to drop it. The only difference between these positions is where the code generated from Xcode will appear. If you keep the source code clean and tidy, then you will have a choice; otherwise, there is no difference between those places.

8. When you drop it on the right panel, the following popup is displayed:

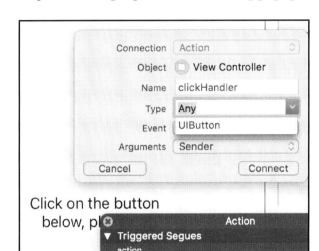

9. Enter the name of the function. You can use `clickHandler`.

> Use names which identify the action; generic names are not helpful.

10. You can change the type to `UIButton`, because the button will trigger the code, but it's not a problem to keep it as Any.

11. Click on **Connect**. The following code has been generated:

```
10  //my dummy comment
11  class ViewController: UIViewController {
12
13      @IBAction func clickHandler(_ sender:
            UIButton) {
14      }
15      override func viewDidLoad() {
16          super.viewDidLoad()
17          // Do any additional setup after loading
                the view, typically from a nib.
18      }
19
```

12. The gray outlet on the left shows that this function will be triggered by some action. If you position the mouse on top of it, you can easily see which visual item is linked:

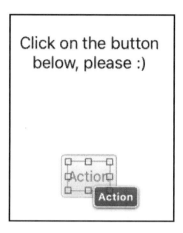

13. Now you have to enter the following code in the body of the hooked function, namely @IBAction func clickHandler(_ sender: UIButton):

```
let red:CGFloat = CGFloat(drand48())
let green:CGFloat = CGFloat(drand48())
let blue:CGFloat = CGFloat(drand48())
//change the background color
self.view.backgroundColor = UIColor.init(red: red, green: green,
blue: blue, alpha: 1)
```

The code generates three random values from 0 to 1.0 inclusive. These values are then used to generate a color at random. This color is set as a background color.

The expected result of the execution of this handler is to change the background color of the view.

14. Run the app in the simulator, using *cmd + R* or the Play button:

15. Check the simulator and press the button. The background should change once you press the button.

It's possible to have the same colors from time to time, so don't panic that the button doesn't work.

The following screenshot shows the app working:

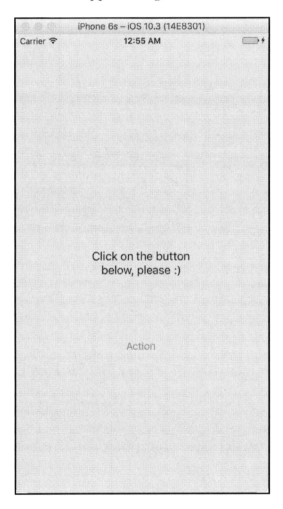

We've learned how to hook actions to a visual component using the Assistant view. Simply using the mouse and the Xcode, we were able to invoke a function (handler) when a certain user action is detected. It's not a secret what we have done with a mouse what we could do in pure Swift code. Let's try to do the same thing with another button:

1. Add another button below this one.
2. Label it `Fire!`.

   To do steps 1 and 2, you should switch back to **Standard Editor,** then open the Utilities pane and open the **Object Library**.

3. Now open `ViewController.swift`.
4. Add the following code to the top:

   ```
   @IBOutlet var fireButton:UIButton!
   ```

   With this line of code, we declare that the `ViewController` class will have a property of the `UIButton!` type, whose name will be `fireButton`. Unfortunately, this property is `empty`. We have to link it to our visual component, we can do it by following the further steps.

5. Open the `Main.storyboard`.
6. Select the **New** button.

7. Then open the Utilities pane and the Connections inspector:

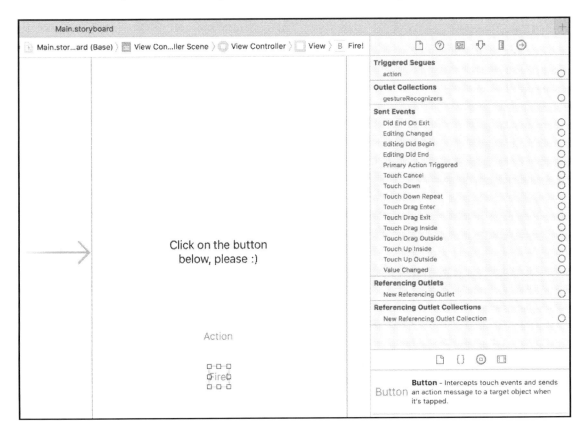

The Connections inspector is the same as the **Action** menu, which appears if we right-click on the button (see the previous section).

8. Start dragging the outlet (the small circle) at the very right of the **New Referencing Outlet** row.

9. Drop it on top of the top yellow circle (which denotes the current view controller).

Here are two possible places where you can drop the link:

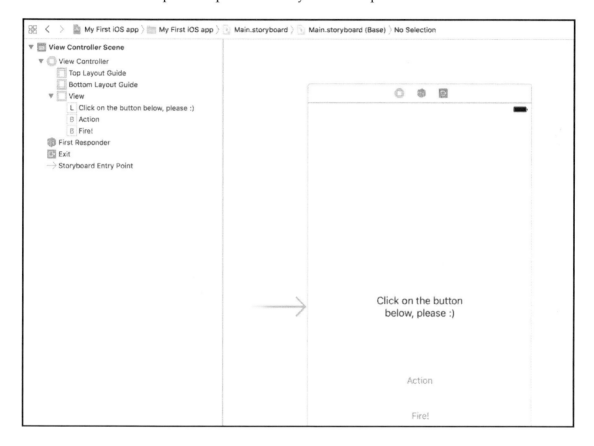

Here is how a proper linking should be done:

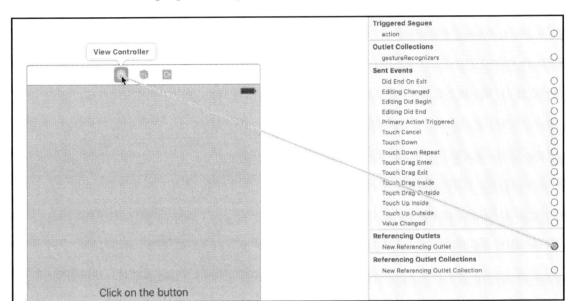

10. Once you drop it, the following menu will appear:

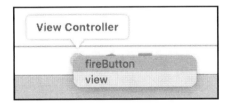

11. You have to select **fireButton**. This is exactly the same property, which we had defined earlier. With these actions, we managed to hook up this property with this exact visual component. You could do it with any item which you had added to the scene.

12. The result will appear in the Connections inspector:

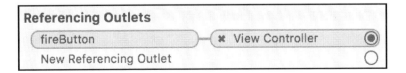

13. Open `ViewController.swift`.

    If you check the outlet in front of the **fireButton**, it shows that it's connected. If you click it, Xcode displays which button is linked to this property:

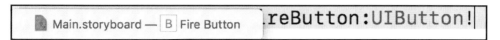

14. Add the following code. This should be included in the `ViewController` class (after the end of the last function):

    ```
    func fireClickHandler(_ sender: UIButton) {
        print("Fire button was pressed!")
        self.view.backgroundColor = UIColor.red
    }
    ```

    This should be inserted at the end of the `viewDidLoad` function:

    ```
    fireButton.addTarget(self, action:
    #selector(ViewController.fireClickHandler(_:)), for:
    UIControlEvents.touchUpInside)
    ```

15. Run the application.
16. Click on the **Fire!** button.

The result you should see is that the background becomes red. If you check the Xcode, then you should see the Debug Area opened at the bottom:

```
37          print("Fire button was pressed!")
38          self.view.backgroundColor = UIColor.red
39      }
40
41  }
42
43
```

My First iOS app

```
Fire button was pressed!
Fire button was pressed!
Fire button was pressed!
```

In the console, you should see the text **Fire button was pressed!** several times. It depends how many times you have activated the button.

To sum it up, we learned how to link visual components to a property in the code. We can hook a function, which will be triggered when the user interacts with the app. This could be achieved in two different ways: with pure code or through the **Action** menu in the storyboard.

Note that the event that we have used is called `UIControlEvents.touchUpInside`. This event gets triggered once the user lifts his finger inside a visual element. There are many other events, which could be used to react to different actions. For example, `UIControlEvents.touchDown` will be triggered when the finger initially touches a control.

iOS provides a neat mechanism for handling complex user interactions with the visual components. The classes responsible for detection of different user actions are called **gesture recognizers**. We will get familiar with them later on in the book.

If you need better touch handling, you have to explore the touch event life cycle in depth. See (`https://developer.apple.com/library/content/documentation/General/Conceptual/Devpedia-CocoaApp/EventHandlingiPhone.html`).

Let's practice what we have learned and add a cool feature to our app—a button which shows an image when it's on and hides it if it's off.

1. First of all, we need a switch, which has an on and off state. Of course, iOS has a perfect control for that. Now we can drag it to the scene. Then we need a label. You already know the storyboard view quite well, so go and add those to the scene.

Here is what it should look like:

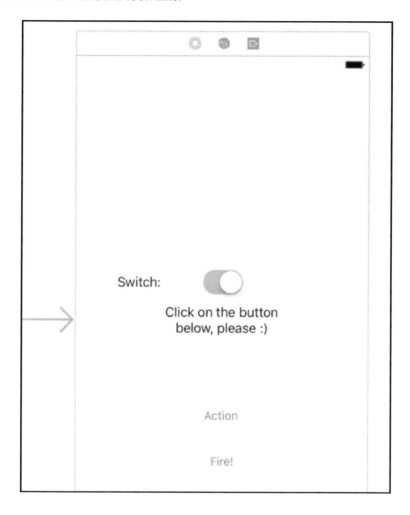

2. Now we need a place where the image will be displayed. This control is called Image View. Drag one to the scene and position it properly. Here is what it should look like:

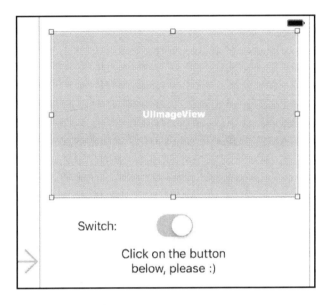

3. Now is the time to add some code. Open the `ViewController.swift` class and add the following:

```
@IBOutlet var imageView:UIImageView!
```

4. Then you have to link the `imageView` with this new property. Open the storyboard and right-click on the `imageView`. This opens the **Action** window. Start dragging the **New Referencing Outlet** plus and drop it on top of the view controller (the yellow circle). Then pick `imageView`. Now is the time to use the Assistant Editor. Select the switch. You can close the Navigation pane (*cmd + 0*).

5. Open the **Connections** tab in the Utilities pane. Locate the **Value Changed** row and drag the plus sign, to create a handler, to the code on the right. Once the blue guide appears, simply drop it and fill in the details. Here is what we have used:

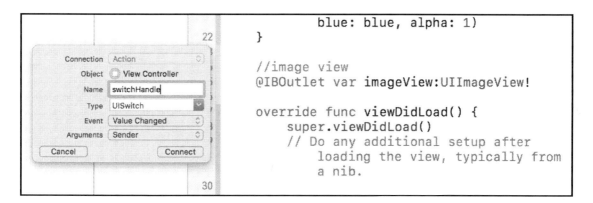

```
                                     blue: blue, alpha: 1)
                    22           }

    Connection  Action            //image view
        Object   View Controller  @IBOutlet var imageView:UIImageView!
         Name   switchHandle
          Type   UISwitch          override func viewDidLoad() {
         Event   Value Changed         super.viewDidLoad()
     Arguments   Sender               // Do any additional setup after
     Cancel            Connect             loading the view, typically from
                                           a nib.
                    30
```

6. Open the Navigation panel. Find an image, which you want to be part of your app and simply add it to your project (*alt + cmd + A* or **File** | **Add** files to **My First iOS App**). You can download any image using your favorite browser. Open the storyboard. Select the image view control and open the Attributes inspector in the Utilities pane. Pick an image from the **Image** box, use the list in which you should see the file (the image) you added earlier. Change the content mode to **Aspect Fit** to fit the image in the control.

There are different content modes, which change the way an image is rendered in an imageView.

7. We need the last bit: a code which will hide and show the image. We already have a handler, so let's open the source code (`ViewController.swift`). Locate the function, which was generated by Xcode and paste the following code:

```
imageView.isHidden = !sender.isOn
```

8. Then you can run the app. If you turn off the switch, it will hide the image. If you turn it on, the image will appear.

9. It looks nice, but what if we don't want to show the image initially? This shouldn't be hard. We have to hide the image initially. We can do this using code. We should add the following line as a last action in `viewDidLoad`:

```
imageView.isHidden = true
```

All the code that is in `viewDidLoad` will be executed, once the view is created. This guarantees that the outlets will be initialized and the object will be accessible to be configured properly.

We are almost there. We should set the initial switch state to **off**. Let's select the switch. Then we have to open the Attributes inspector. Then simply change the value to **off**. Voilá! You can run the app. The switch should be off initially and the image should be hidden.

# General discussion

We know how to use Xcode and storyboards to define UI. iOS has a pretty powerful tool set to define a slick and easy-to-use (native) user interface. You just need to drag and drop the appropriate visual components and order them as you want on the screen. (We will discuss how to use auto layout, so that your UI looks good on any screen—iPhone, iPad, AppleTV.) The next key part is to link them with a specific property. This way, each component can be accessed in the code. Hooking up handlers is not hard at all. A storyboard helps you by generating some part of the code for you; you just have to provide the name and the type of the parameter. Everything that you can do using storyboard can be developed in pure code. Usually, you pick the pure code solution when you need a much deeper control of your visual components.

You should use storyboards when possible. The pure code approach should be taken if you go above the limits of the storyboards.

If you decide to develop the app UI using code, you will need much more time. Even the simplest tasks, such as changing the size of the label font, would take extra time. Don't use this approach if you don't have really strong motivation to do so. Storyboards save a lot of time when developing. Under the hood, they are used to generate the view and to define the relations between different scenes. This saves a lot of time and, so far we know, only part of the functionality which they provide. Later in the book, we will discuss how we can use them to define auto layouts and transitions between scenes.

# Summary

In this chapter, we learned some details about storyboards. We will explore these later in the book. Adding a visual item to a storyboard turned out to be easy. We discussed two different ways to hook up a code to user interaction, and then we showed a nice way to manage other views. After this chapter, you should be able to add basic interactivity to different visual components. Also, everything which is done through a storyboard can be achieved with pure code, but it takes a lot more code.

In the next chapter, we will discuss different data structures that should be used while working with data. We will focus on experimenting with different protocols and the presentation of the data in iOS apps.

# 6
# How to Use Data Structures, OOP, and Protocols

In this chapter, we will begin with a short introduction of the primary collection types—array, set, and dictionary. Then, we learn how to visually present a collection. Finally, we will finish with a real application that displays information using a list. In the implementation, we will use OOP and protocols to handle the visualization of the data in an elegant fashion.

In this chapter, we will cover the following topics:

- Primary collection types
- List of items in a playground
- Table view in iOS app
- Protocols

# Primary collection types

In Swift, there are three collection types (for simplicity, we will discuss only mutable collections):

- **Array**: An ordered (indexed) list of values which are from the same data type
- **Set**: An unordered collection of **unique** values from the same data type
- **Dictionary**: An unordered collection map (key -> value), which links a key with a value, and the keys should be unique and from the same data type

Each collection has a fixed data type and there is no way to store values from different data types in the collection. This will become clear later in the chapter.

Array, dictionary, and set are implemented using generics and are called **generic collections**.

# Generics

Generics is a pattern approach to defining custom types or functions. They can work with any type that meets the desired requirements. This is a really powerful feature of Swift. The Swift standard library contains many classes, structures, enumerations, and functions which are defined as generic types.

This is why you can create different collections which contain either string or int, and Swift handles this without a problem. There is one robust generic implementation of the array structure which handles all different cases.

To illustrate the generics, we will define a generic structure which contains a raw data field and description, which is a string:

```
struct Item<T> {
    var raw: T
    var description: String

    init(raw: T, description:String = "no description") {
        self.raw = raw
        self.description = description
    }
}
var itemInt:Item<Int> = Item(raw: 55, description: "fifty five")
print("This is an int \(itemInt.raw) with description -
\(itemInt.description)")

var itemDouble:Item<Double> = Item(raw: 3.14, description: "Pi")
print("This is an int \(itemDouble.raw) with description -
\(itemDouble.description)")
```

This shows that we can create different concrete classes, where the template classes listed in brackets (like < T >) are linked with real data types.

Similar to structures, classes and enums can be defined in the same generic manner. Every generic type can be used only if the template types are linked with an exact data type that fulfills the requirements.

Let's get familiar with the details of some data collections that saw earlier in the book. The first collection type is array.

# Array

If you want to store values of the same type in an ordered list, then you have to use an array collection. The collection is part of Swift and it is implemented as a structure. There is an easy way to access each value—using its index (it should be valid). The same values can appear many times at different indices.

The array type is generic, which is why we can create arrays which hold different types of data such as strings, ints, doubles, and custom data types. Here is how you can define an array of string values:

```
var words = Array<String>(arrayLiteral: "one", "two", "three")
// short syntax using literals
//var words = ["one", "two", "three"]

for word in words {
    print(word)
}
```

Swift is pretty clever and can easily figure out the type of an array, which is declared using an array literal (list which is enclosed with [ ]). (The previous example contains an example in the comments.)

To create an empty array (of ints), you can use one of the following approaches:

```
//empty array of int-s
var emptyArrayOfInts = [Int]()
//empty array of int-s
var emptyArrayOfInts2 = Array<Int>()
//the variable type is Array<Int> and the value is empty Array
var emptyArray:[Int] = []
```

Also, you can use the handy constructor to create a list of repeating values from a certain type:

```
var tenZeros = Array(repeating: 0, count: 10)
print("The number of items is \(tenZeros.count).")
```

Be careful when using the aforementioned initializers. When you create an array of repeating objects, the passed object will be shared and will be used in the array.

If you have two arrays, the default operator + works like a concatenation of the two arrays in a new one. For example:

```
var even = [2, 4, 6]
var odd = [1, 3 ,5]
var concatenated = even + odd
print(concatenated)
```

When working with arrays, you will need some pretty handy functions, which are part of the array interface. Let's check some of them out:

- `.count`: A property, which is read-only and returns the number of items in the concrete array instance
- `.isEmpty`: A property, which is read-only and returns `true` if, and only if, the array instance has no items
- `.append(_:)`: A function which appends an item to the array instance (add the new item to the end of the list); an alternative option is to use the `+=` operator
- `.insert(_:at:)`: A function which inserts an item at a specific position in the array instance
- `.remove(at:)`: A function which removes an item at the specific positions, but the position (index) should be correct; the removed item is returned

Subscripts are a pretty neat way to access particular item(s) using the correct position in the array. The positioning starts from 0. Subscripts with ranges can be used to get a slice of the items without any trouble.

The minimal index in an array is 0. The maximal valid index for any non-empty array is `array.count - 1`:

```
//the concatenated array contains [2, 4, 6, 1, 3, 5]
var part = concatenated[2...4]
print(part)
//prints [6, 1, 3]
```

Range types are used to define sets of indices. They could be half-opened ranges or closed ranges—2..<4 includes 2 and 3; in contrast 2...4 contains 2, 3, and 4.

There are many ways to iterate over items in an array. We can use the `for...in` loop like so:

```
for value in concatenated {
    print("Item: \(value)")
}

for (index, value) in concatenated.enumerated() {
    print("Item #\(index + 1): \(value)")
}
```

The first `for` loop goes through all values in the array. The second one does the same, but we have assigned indices to all items and we can use those to enumerate each item.

Now, let's get familiar with a set collection, which stores only unique values and there is no order.

# Set

Set is a collection which stores values of the same type, but just a single copy of it. There is no order in this collection. The set can be used instead of an array, if the item order is not taken into account. The benefit when using set is that each value will appear only once.

The types which can be stored in a set must be hashable (must implement the Hashable protocol—for more information, read about protocols later in this chapter). A hash value (we can think of a corresponding int) can be calculated for each hashable object. For equal objects, the same hash value is assigned.

 A hash value shouldn't be stored, because it might differ between different executions of a program.

For example:

```
let a = 5
let b = 5

if a.hashValue == b.hashValue {
    print("a == b")
} else {
    print("a != b")
}
```

A custom type can be used in a set if you implement the Hashable protocol.

Here is how we can create a set of strings:

```
var phrases = Set<String>()
phrases.insert("hello")
phrases.insert("world")
phrases.insert("hel" + "lo") //"hello"

for item in phrases {
    print(item)
}
```

There is no short way to create a set, like `[]` for array. But we can use an array to initialize a set:

```
var cars:Set = ["Tesla", "Ferrari", "Audi"]
for item in cars {
    print(item)
}
```

The order of strings in the array is not the same when they are printed in the console. This is because there is no order in the set.

The type of the set could be specified like `Set<String>` but as you can see, Swift is smart enough to infer the type, because the right part is `[String]` and then it can be converted to `Set<String>`.

The set provides a pretty similar interface to the array. It has the following methods and properties, which are similar or completely identical:

- `.count`: A property which is read-only and returns the number of items in the concrete set instance
- `.isEmpty`: A property which is read-only and returns `true` if, and only if, the set instance has no items
- `.insert(_:)`: A function which inserts an item in the set instance
- `.remove(_:)`: A function which removes an item and returns it; if the item is not part of the set, then `nil` is returned

When we are working with two or more sets, we can effectively execute the fundamental operations:

- **Intersection (of two sets, a and b)**: This returns the items which are part of both sets
- **Union (of two sets, a and b)**: This returns a set of all items whose items are part of the first or the second set
- **Substracting (of two sets, a - b)**: This returns all items which are part of the first set, but are not part of the second set
- **Symmetric difference (of two sets, a and b)**: This returns all items which are not part of the intersection but are part of either the first or the second set

The following diagram sketches the two sets, a and b, and the results of all operations:

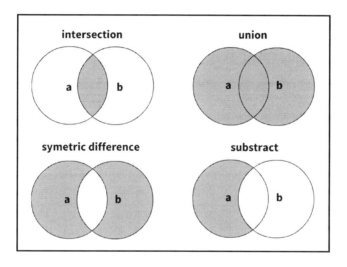

Here is the code which shows the same operations in Swift:

```
var cars:Set = ["Tesla", "Ferrari", "Audi"]

var electricCars:Set = ["Tesla", "Volkswagen"]

var intersection = electricCars.intersection(cars)
print("Intersection: \(intersection)")
//Intersection: ["Tesla"]

var union = electricCars.union(cars)
print("Union: \(union)")
//Union: ["Ferrari", "Volkswagen", "Audi", "Tesla"]
```

```
var substract = electricCars.subtracting(cars)
print("Substract: \(substract)")
//Substract: ["Volkswagen"]

var symetricDifference = electricCars.symmetricDifference(cars)
print("Symetric difference: \(symetricDifference)")
//Symetric difference: ["Ferrari", "Volkswagen", "Audi"]
```

We can also check some other basic relations, such as:

- `isSubset(of:)`: This is true if all items of the first set are part of the second one
- `isSuperset(of:)`: This is true if all items of the second set are part of the first one
- `isDisjoint(with:)`: This is true if two sets don't have intersections

The previous example could be continued like this to demo the new functions we discussed earlier:

```
if electricCars.isSubset(of: union) {
    print("Each set is a subset of the union of all sets.")
}

if union.isSuperset(of: cars) {
    print("The union is super set of all sets.")
}

if electricCars.isDisjoint(with: cars) {
    print("The two sets doesn't have common items.")
} else {
    print("The two sets have at least one common item.")
}
```

The functions are pretty handy when working with sets of data. They have strict versions such as `.isStrictSubset(of: )` and `.isStrictSuperset(of: )`.

With the collections which we know so far (`array` and `set`), we can keep track of values, but there is no easy way to associate a certain value with a specific key/ID. The array has indices, but they are not very expressive. The problem which is hard to solve is that if we need a value that fulfills certain requirements, then we have to go through all values and find the one which fits. Of course, in Swift there is a special type of collection called **dictionary**, which can help us solve similar problems. In the next section, we will dive into the detail, of what a dictionary is and when we should use it.

# Dictionary

A dictionary stores a set of keys of a specific type, which are associated with values from a specific type (keys and values may have the same type, but this is not the case in general). The key feature of the dictionary collection is the association. The data is not ordered like in the set, but we have a powerful way to find data based on its key. Usually, a dictionary is a map which keeps all relations between the keys and the data items.

The key type should conform to the Hashable protocol. (See the *Sets* section from this chapter.)

Here is how we can define a dictionary in Swift:

```
var animalsDictionary = Dictionary<String, String>(dictionaryLiteral:
("dog", "🐶"), ("cat", "🐱"))
var animalsDictionaryLiteral = ["dog": "🐶","cat": "🐱"]
//adding a new association
animalsDictionary["bird"] = "🐦"
for association in animalsDictionary {
 print("\(association.key) -> \(association.value)")
}
```

We can construct a dictionary using the default construction, defining the type of the key and the type of the values in < >, as in the preceding example as `Dictionary<String, String>()` or the short type `[String:String]`. There is a short literal syntax for creating a dictionary. It's close to defining an array but every value is preceded by a key. For example: `["dog": "🐶","cat": "🐱"]`. If you want to create an empty dictionary, you have to define its type and you can use the empty dictionary literal `[:]` or `[<key_type>:<value_type]()`:

```
var emptyDict:Dictionary<Int, String> = [:]
var emptyMap = [Int: String]()
```

The dictionary object has a similar public interface to the array:

- `.count`: A property, which is read-only and returns the number of items in the concrete dictionary instance
- `.isEmpty`: A property, which is read-only and returns true if and only if the dictionary instance has no items

- `.updateValue(_:forKey:)`: This function can be used to assign a specific value to a specific key

Only a single value can be stored per unique key.

- `.removeValue(forKey:)`: A function which removes a key-value pair and returns the value, if such a key exists; if the key is not part of the dictionary, then `nil` is returned

Using subscripts, we can easily add, update, and check if a value is associated with a specific key. Thus, the type returned when accessing a specific key is the optional version of the type of the values.

We can use `for...in` to iterate over the dictionary data. Here are some examples:

```
//all pairs
for (animalName, animalEmoji) in animalsDictionary {
    print("\(animalName) -> \(animalEmoji)")
}

//all keys
for animalName in animalsDictionary.keys {
    print("\(animalName)")
}
//all values
for animalEmoji in animalsDictionary.values {
    print("\(animalEmoji)")
}
```

We have easy access to all keys and all values. We can easily convert those to set or array collections:

```
var allEmojis = [String](animalsDictionary.values)
var allAnimals = [String](animalsDictionary.keys)
```

The following section discusses the data structure in general and their good and bad sides. There are some nice examples showing where each one should be used.

# How to choose the best collection type

When solving real-life problems, you can start using the default data collections. These collections have strong sides, but they have weak sides as well. We will scratch the surface of the different data structures here, but there are many other books which discuss pretty complex data structures in detail. When you are developing an algorithm in which every second matters, then you have to pick the best data structures which could do the job in no time.

Each data structure has a specific interface and many actions (operations with the data), such as:

- Insert an item
- Look up (search) for an item
- Remove an item
- Sort all items
- Check whether some values exist, and so on

Each operation is taking a different amount of time based on the collection's internal implementation.

Based on the mostly used operations (`search`, `insert`, `remove`, and `sort`), we can prefer certain collections for some specific common tasks. Here are a few helpful tips which you can follow. For example:

- If you have to search for an item by some key, then the correct collection is dictionary. Everything else won't be that fast. If you are looking for a particular value in an array, then you have to go through all the items (if they are not sorted) until you find what you are looking for.
- If you need sorted values in the end, then all the structures will work with similar speed. Simply store the sorted values in an array.
- If you need a sorted structure, which is always sorted after insert or remove actions, then the best option here is beyond the basic collection types. For example, you can achieve this with a heap data structure or a B-tree. But be careful when you are using a specific data structure. Each one has strengths and weaknesses and you have to pick the best one that fits your needs.

In the next section, we will render a list of items using `UICollectionView` in a playground. We will discuss some tips on how to do this easily.

# List of items in a playground

In this chapter, we will get familiar with different collections of data. They are pretty useful for storing data in memory and to work with, but in many cases we should present a collection of the data to the user. In the previous chapter, we discussed some nice UI iOS components which can be used in our app. Now, we will learn how to present an array of values in a simple collection view. To show this, we will use a playground and do some experiments with the view.

# UICollectionView

UICollectionView is a visual component which presents ordered collections of data items using custom layouts. By default, iOS comes with one pretty robust layout—UICollectionViewFlowLayout which orders all items in a grid. But the underlying hierarchy gives an abstract class—UICollectionViewLayout which could be used as a basis for new layouts. We will discuss that later in this section. Now, let's create a basic UICollectionView:

1. Create an empty playground.
2. Add the following imports:

```
import UIKit
import PlaygroundSupport
```

3. Create a basic view controller class, which will be displayed:

```
class CollectionViewController : UICollectionViewController {
    var data:[String]

    init(data:[String], collectionViewLayout layout:
      UICollectionViewLayout) {
        self.data = data
        super.init(collectionViewLayout: layout)
    }
    //this is required and we simply delegate
    required init?(coder aDecoder: NSCoder) {
        self.data = []
        super.init(coder: aDecoder)
    }

    override func viewDidLoad() {
        super.viewDidLoad()
        self.collectionView?.backgroundColor = .white
```

```
        self.collectionView?.register(UICollectionViewCell.self,
          forCellWithReuseIdentifier: "Cell")
    }

    //how many items we have in each section
    override func collectionView(_ collectionView:
      UICollectionView, numberOfItemsInSection section:
      Int) -> Int {
        return self.data.count
    }

    override func collectionView(_ collectionView:
      UICollectionView, cellForItemAt indexPath:
      IndexPath) -> UICollectionViewCell {
        let cell = collectionView.dequeueReusableCell(
        withReuseIdentifier: "Cell", for: indexPath)
        cell.backgroundColor = .green

        return cell
    }
}

var animals = ["Cat", "Dog", "Bird", "Mouse", "Elephant"]

var flowLayout = UICollectionViewFlowLayout()

var controller = CollectionViewController(data:animals,
collectionViewLayout: flowLayout)

PlaygroundPage.current.liveView = controller
PlaygroundPage.current.needsIndefiniteExecution = true
```

4. Then, switch to the Assistance Editor using the Assistant button ( ⬭⬭▾ ) or use the menu, **View** | **Assistant Editor** | **Show Assistant Editor**. Then, you will see the code of the playground on the left and the interactive visual component on the right (if you don't see anything on the right, try to close and reopen the Xcode app):

```
Chapter6.playground                                                          Timeline    Chapter6.playground (Timeline)
 72    override func viewDidLoad() {
 73        super.viewDidLoad()
 74        self.collectionView?.backgroundColor = .white
 75        self.collectionView?.register(UICollectionViewCell.
               self, forCellWithReuseIdentifier: "Cell")
 76    }
 77
 78    //how many items we have in each section
 79    override func collectionView(_ collectionView:
           UICollectionView, numberOfItemsInSection section:
           Int) -> Int {
 80        return self.data.count
 81    }
 82
 83    override func collectionView(_ collectionView:
           UICollectionView, cellForItemAt indexPath:
           IndexPath) -> UICollectionViewCell {
 84        let cell = collectionView.dequeueReusableCell
               (withReuseIdentifier: "Cell", for: indexPath)
 85        cell.backgroundColor = .green
 86
 87        return cell
 88    }
 89
 90
 91  }
 92
 93  var animals = ["Cat", "Dog", "Bird", "Mouse", "Elephant"]
 94  //animals.append("Bear")
 95
 96  var flowLayout = UICollectionViewFlowLayout()
 97
 98  PlaygroundPage.current.liveView = CollectionViewController
         (data:animals, collectionViewLayout: flowLayout)
 99  PlaygroundPage.current.needsIndefiniteExecution = true
100
```

The collection view displays five green rectangles. Now, we have to customize the look and feel of each cell, so we can see the emoji representing each animal. If we append another animal such as a bear to the collection before passing it to the view controller, then we will see another green rectangle or six in total.

The data which we passed to the view collection is not visible yet. We have to create a custom `ViewCell` which will be used to render the data on the screen.

# UICollectionViewCell

To render something more than solid color rectangles, we need a custom cell view that will be used to display the data. With that in mind, we have to create a custom cell class which inherits from `UICollectionViewCell`. Because we will construct those cells with code (not using a storyboard layout), then we have to implement a specific constructor. If we have to use a storyboard, then we should implement the `init(coder:NSCoder)` method. It's called once the storyboard is rendered on the screen.

Here is how we can start:

```
/**
 * Custom UICollectionViewCell which has a label on top.
 */
class AnimalCollectionViewCell :UICollectionViewCell {
    private var _label: UILabel

    override init(frame: CGRect) {
        let fr = CGRect(x: 0, y: 0, width: frame.size.width,
                        height: frame.size.height)
        _label = UILabel(frame:fr)
        super.init(frame: frame)

        _label.text = "?"
        _label.textAlignment = NSTextAlignment.center
        addSubview(_label)
    }
    // used when the UI is initializes from storyboard
    required init?(coder aDecoder: NSCoder) {
        _label = UILabel()
        super.init(coder:aDecoder)
        _label.text = "?"

        addSubview(_label)
    }

    public var emoji:String? {
        set {
            _label.text = newValue
        }

        get {
            return _label.text
        }
    }
}
```

With the preceding code, we have defined a custom cell, which has a label with the same size as the cell. The text is centered.

Now, we should let our `CollectionView` know about this new cell which we want to use. We should register the new cell class:

```
self.collectionView?.register(AnimalCollectionViewCell.self,
forCellWithReuseIdentifier: "Cell")
```

We are simply replacing our current default cell class with this new, much powerful one. In general, we can register more than one cell type and mix those, but for simplicity, we will stick to only one.

Then, we have to replace the function which is invoked when a new cell should be displayed:

```
override func collectionView(_ collectionView: UICollectionView,
cellForItemAt indexPath: IndexPath) -> UICollectionViewCell {
    let cell:AnimalCollectionViewCell =
collectionView.dequeueReusableCell(withReuseIdentifier: "Cell", for:
indexPath) as! AnimalCollectionViewCell
    cell.backgroundColor = .green

    let animal = self.data[indexPath.row]
    cell.emoji = animal
    return cell
}
```

The key changes here are:

1.  The type of the cell is changed to **AnimalCollectionViewCell**.
2.  We fetch the current data from the collection:

    ```
    let animal = self.data[indexPath.row]
    ```

3.  We update the cell's content using its interface:

    ```
    cell.emoji = animal
    ```

4.  When we run the example, we will see that each cell displays the animal's name:

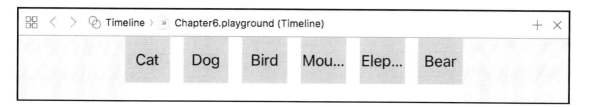

This is cool, but let's try to make our example a bit fancy. Why not try to display the emoji instead of regular text? Yes, we can achieve this pretty easily.

1. Let's create a dictionary, next to our controller instance:

```
var animalsToEmoji = ["Cat": "🐱", "Dog": "🐶", "Bird": "🐦" ,
"Mouse" : "🐭", "Elephant" :"🐘","Bear":"🐻"]
```

2. Then store that map (dictionary) in the `UICollectionView`. First, add a property to the `CollectionViewController`:

```
var dataMap:[String:String]?
```

3. Then, assign the dictionary to our controller instance:

```
controller.dataMap = animalsToEmoji
```

4. Use the data from the map. Add the following rows before the `return` statement in the `collectionView(_ collectionView: UICollectionView, cellForItemAt indexPath: IndexPath)` method:

```
if self.dataMap != nil {
    cell.emoji = self.dataMap?[animal]
} else {
    cell.emoji = animal
}
```

5. Here is the final result:

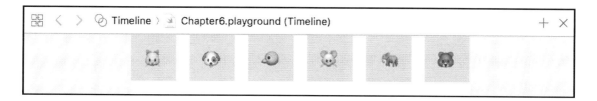

It's good to know when an item has been selected. To do so, we have to set a delegate to the `UICollectionView` and when an item is selected (touched), then a specific method from that delegate will be invoked.

The delegation is a design pattern which is used when specific duties should be delegated to an unknown type. The only restriction is that this type should implement a specific protocol (fulfill certain requirements). Usually, the class which delegates some actions defines a protocol, which will be used when those actions are activated. The delegate will be invoked when an action is triggered.

In our particular example, we need a `UICollectionViewDelegate`. We can create a new instance which conforms to the `UICollectionViewDelegate` protocol (we will see protocols later in this chapter) or we can use `CollectionViewController`, which already conforms to this protocol. The only thing is to override the function as follows:

```
override public func collectionView(_ collectionView: UICollectionView,
didSelectItemAt indexPath: IndexPath) {
    let animal = self.data[indexPath.row]
    print(animal)
}
```

Once you see a working example, if you click on certain cells, the name of the animal will be printed in the console.

# Reusing cells

The current implementation reuses the cells which are leaving the screen. This means that only a minimal number of cells are stored in memory and they are reused. This speeds up the scrolling experience because there is no need to create new visual objects when the user scrolls. The benefit is visible only in cases when the data that should be visualized can't fit on one screen.

All visual collections such as `UITableView` and `UICollectionView` use the same way of optimization and cell reuse. Here are the steps which you should do to use this optimization.

First, the cell class should be registered in the collection view. In our case, this happens in the `viewDidLoad` method:

```
self.collectionView?.register(AnimalCollectionViewCell.self,
forCellWithReuseIdentifier: "Cell")
```

There is an alternative method which can be used to register a visual component defined in a storyboard or a `.nib` file using the following function:

```
func register(_ nib: UINib?, forCellWithReuseIdentifier identifier:
String)
```

With this method, later you will be able to reuse all cells from the same type. The collection view will know which class to use when a new cell is created or reused.

The key magic happens in the following method:

```
override func collectionView(_ collectionView: UICollectionView,
cellForItemAt indexPath: IndexPath) -> UICollectionViewCell {
    //reuse a cell or create a new ine
    let cell:AnimalCollectionViewCell = collectionView
      .dequeueReusableCell(withReuseIdentifier: "Cell",
      for: indexPath) as! AnimalCollectionViewCell
    cell.backgroundColor = .green

    let animal = self.data[indexPath.row]
    cell.emoji = animal

    if self.dataMap != nil {
        cell.emoji = self.dataMap?[animal]
    } else {
        cell.emoji = animal
    }

    return cell
}
```

The code returns a view cell that is marked as reused. (A cell is marked for reuse when it leaves the screen and is not visible anymore.) This call may return `nil` if the identifier is not correct or there is no view cell registered yet:

```
collectionView.dequeueReusableCell(withReuseIdentifier: "Cell", for:
indexPath)
```

In the function `func collectionView(_ collectionView: UICollectionView, cellForItemAt indexPath: IndexPath) -> UICollectionViewCell,` you should get a cell view and update its presentation based on the data which corresponds to the `indexPath` parameter. This method should be optimized because it's called many times while the user is scrolling through the data. It does the magic and simulates a long collection, but in fact, only a couple of views are scrolled on the screen (a few more than the visible ones).

When you have to present really long collections of data, be careful using this technique. Your application will be butter smooth and your users will find it slick and cool.

In the next section, we discuss different layouts which define the internal arrangement of all items.

# Layouts

The layout object is responsible for positioning the items in the collection view. It can be used to customize the appearance of each cell inside the `UIViewCollection`. There are different cell types (decorators) which can be specified. Now, we will discuss the default layout implementation, `UICollectionViewFlowLayout`.

This layout arranges all items in a grid. It's a perfect solution for the multi device apps because it uses the whole screen estate and it's different for different iOS devices. The algorithm positions all items on the screen using the whole available space, starting from top to bottom. Based on the scroll direction, the next cells are populated with views. The class provides a neat delegate object of type `ICollectionViewDelegateFlowLayout` through which you can control the item size and the spacing between them. You can define the header and the footer sizes for a particular section. Details about the naming of each specific method can be found in the official iOS documentation: `https://developer.apple.com/documentation/uikit/uicollectionviewdelegateflowlayout`

The layout class stores default values which are used if no delegate is assigned. Let's try to experiment slightly with some values for `itemSize` to show how powerful the layout is:

```
flowLayout.itemSize = CGSize(width: 200, height: 200)
```

We can change the padding between items:

```
flowLayout.minimumLineSpacing = 50.0
```

We can also change the direction of scrolling:

```
flowLayout.scrollDirection = UICollectionViewScrollDirection.horizontal
```

If you want to define a custom layout you have to inherit `UICollectionViewLayout`. Your class should provide the default attributes of each view. The attributes are stored in instances of `UICollectionViewLayoutAttributes` or a custom class which inherits from this one.

First, we have to create a new subclass of `UICollectionViewLayout` with the name `PuzzleViewLayout`. The following methods should be implemented:

- `prepare()`: This method is called before the initial layout operation. In this function, your class should calculate the content's view size (approximately if exactly is not possible) and all items should be positioned.
- `collectionViewContentSize : CGSize`: The property should return the width and height of the whole content of the collection, not only on the visible part.
- `layoutAttributesForElements(in rect: CGRect) -> [UICollectionViewLayoutAttributes]?`: This method will be called several times and you should return the attributes for all items in the collection which are part of the given rectangle.

Here is what a custom layout may look like:

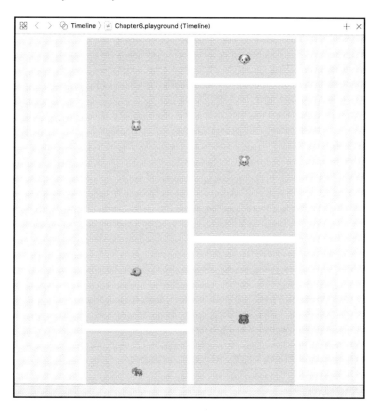

Here is the code that achieves something basic:

```
class PuzzleViewLayout : UICollectionViewLayout {
    // number of columns in the layout
    var columns: Int = 2
    var padding: CGFloat = 6.0
    //collection of all attributes
    var layoutAttributes = [UICollectionViewLayoutAttributes]()
    //size of the content
    var contentHeight: CGFloat  = 0.0
    var contentWidth: CGFloat  = 0.0

    //prepare function is in the next code block

    //return size of the whole view collection
    override var collectionViewContentSize : CGSize {
        return CGSize(width: contentWidth, height: contentHeight)
    }
    override func layoutAttributesForElements(in rect: CGRect)
      -> [UICollectionViewLayoutAttributes]? {
        var attrs = [UICollectionViewLayoutAttributes]()
        //send all items which are visible in the current rectangle
        for itemAttributes in self.layoutAttributes {
            if itemAttributes.frame.intersects(rect) {
                attrs.append(itemAttributes)
            }
        }
        return attrs
    }
}
```

In the preceding code, we extend the `UICollectionViewLayout`. The `prepare` function of the class is given here:

```
//should be part of the class above
override func prepare() {
    layoutAttributes.removeAll()
    let insets = collectionView!.contentInset
    self.contentWidth = collectionView!.bounds.width -
      (insets.left + insets.right)
    let columnWidth = self.contentWidth / CGFloat(columns)
    var column = 0
    //vertical offset
    var topOffset = [CGFloat](repeating: 0, count: columns)
    //horizontal offset
    var offset = [CGFloat]()
    for column in 0 ..< columns {
```

```
            offset += [CGFloat(column) * columnWidth]
        }
    //consider only the first section
    let section = 0
    for item in 0 ..< collectionView!.numberOfItems(inSection: section)
{
            let indexPath = IndexPath(row: item, section: section)
            //pick the height of each cell at random
            let height:CGFloat = 70 + CGFloat(arc4random_uniform(25) * 10)
            //use the precalculated values from the previous items
            let frame = CGRect(x: offset[column], y: topOffset[column],
                width: columnWidth, height: height)
            let insetFrame = frame.insetBy(dx: padding, dy: padding)
            let attributes = UICollectionViewLayoutAttributes(
                forCellWith: indexPath)
            attributes.frame = insetFrame
            self.layoutAttributes.append(attributes)
            //stretch the content view bounds
            self.contentHeight = max(frame.maxY, contentHeight)
            //move to the next y position
            topOffset[column] = topOffset[column] + height
            //move to the next column and always stay in valid index
                [0 .. columns - 1]
            column = (column + 1) % columns
        }
    }
}
```

The prepare method calculates the positions of each cell and caches the result in the layoutAttributes collection.

If you want to use it in real products, then you can tweak it a bit, so that it works for more than one section. The layoutAttributesForElements method might be optimized if you pick the correct data structures.

In the next section, we will discuss another view controller which presents many records vertically. The user is able to scroll through the data, filter it, select records, and do other actions. Without further discussion, let's try to implement a single view app, which displays UITableViewController, which lists cities in Europe.

# Table view in iOS app

First, let's create a new single view Xcode project with the default language Swift and target OS—iOS. We already know how to do this from previous chapters:

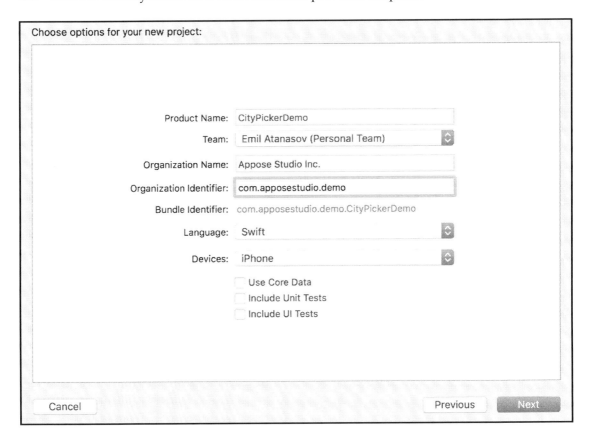

Open the storyboard and add a new table view controller. (Use the Utilities panel and the object library. If you filter the controls, you will find the **Table View Controller** in no time.) You should see two view controllers on the screen:

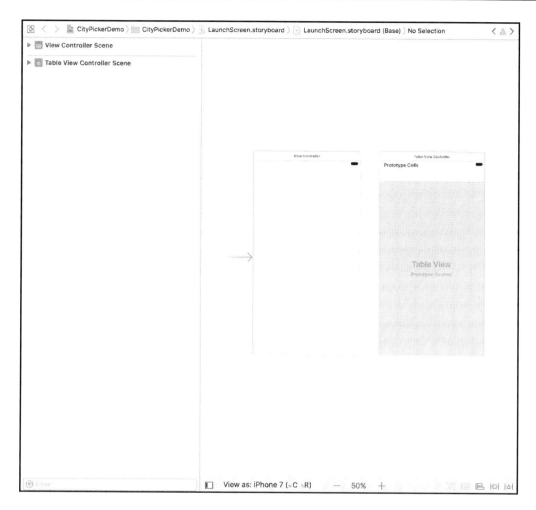

Two view controllers on the screen

Use a different scale level so that you can see more scenes at once.

Drag the gray/blue arrow (the one on the left) from the default view controller to the new view controller. This arrow defines which scene (screen) is the app's initial view controller. You can remove the other view controller, which we won't use.

Before defining the table cells, which should be used to render each item in the table, we need to sort out where the data will come from. For simplicity, the app will use a hardcoded list of countries. Each of them will have one or more cities and exactly one of those cities, will be the capital of that country.

# Model list of cities

Let's create a file that stores the hardcoded data. Then, we will define the model classes which will be used in our app.

We need a class that represents a country, another that defines a city, and a special class that represents a capital. It will inherit from the `City` class.

Here is the Swift code that defines this hierarchy:

```swift
class Country {
    var name = "No name"
    var cities:[City] = []
    init(name:String) {
        self.name = name
    }
    init(name:String, cities:[City]) {
        self.name = name
        self.cities = cities
    }
}

class City {
    var name: String
    var population: Int
    init(name:String, population:Int) {
        self.name = name
        self.population = population
    }
}

class Capital: City {
    var isActive = true
}
```

All the building blocks are already implemented. In a separate extension, we will define a static function that returns a list of countries. The data here can be extended:

```
extension Country {
    static public func getHardcodedData() -> [Country] {
        var countries:[Country] = []
        //add some european countries
        let germany = Country(name:"Germany")
        germany.cities += [Capital(name: "Berlin", population: 3_426_354)]
        germany.cities += [City(name: "Hamburg", population: 1_739_117)]
        germany.cities += [City(name: "Munich", population: 1_260_391)]
        germany.cities += [City(name: "Cologne", population: 963_395)]
        countries.append(germany)
        let italy = Country(name: "Italy")
        italy.cities += [Capital(name:"Rome", population:2_648_843)]
        italy.cities += [City(name:"Milan", population:1_305_591)]
        italy.cities += [City(name:"Naples", population:1_046_987)]
        italy.cities += [City(name:"Venice", population:297_743)]
        countries.append(italy)
        let france = Country(name:"France")
        france.cities += [Capital(name:"Paris", population: 2_152_000)]
        france.cities += [City(name:"Marseille", population: 808_000)]
        france.cities += [City(name:"Lyon", population: 422_000)]
        countries.append(france)
        let uk = Country(name:"United Kingdom")
        uk.cities += [Capital(name:"London", population: 7_074_265)]
        uk.cities += [City(name:"Birmingham", population: 1_020_589)]
        uk.cities += [City(name:"Leeds", population: 726_939)]
        uk.cities += [City(name:"Glasgow", population: 616_430)]
        countries.append(uk)
        let spain = Country(name:"Spain")
        spain.cities += [Capital(name:"Madrid", population: 2_824_000)]
        spain.cities += [City(name:"Barcelona", population: 1_454_000)]
        spain.cities += [City(name:"Valencia", population: 736_000)]
        countries.append(spain)
        return countries
    }
}
```

Open `ViewController.swift` and replace the current implementation with the following code:

```
class ViewController: UITableViewController {
    var countries:[Country] = []
    override func viewDidLoad() {
        super.viewDidLoad()
        countries = Country.getHardcodedData()
    }
}
```

We have our hierarchy and a static function that returns the test data that we want to display in our app.

Now, we should update the code, so we can see the name of the cities on the screen.

## Displaying all cities

First, we have to update the storyboard. Then, we should write some code to feed the data into the `UITableViewController`:

1. Open the `Main.storyboard`.
2. Then, select the **Table View Controller**.
3. Open the **Identity Inspector** (cmd + *Alt* + 3).
4. Select the class value to be `ViewController`. This visual component will use our previous table's implementation.

 In the Interface Builder, we can associate a custom class with any visual component. The only limitation is that the class should be derived from the default component class.

5. Expand the **Table View** and select the **Table View Cell**. Open the Utilities panel (cmd + *Alt* + 4) and select the **Attributes Inspector**.

You have to set the cell identifier so that we can create as many copies as we need in the future. Set it to **Cell**. Then, change the cell style to **Subtitle**. We will display the city name at the top and its population:

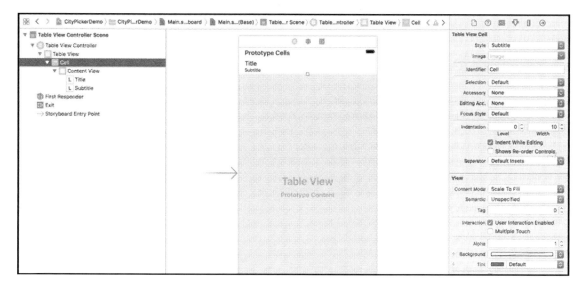

Cell

It's good to add a title to the `TableViewController`. To do that, we will add a navigation view controller. This can be easily achieved like this:

1. Select the view controller.
2. Then, click on **Editor | Embed In | Navigation Controller**.

After this step, our storyboard should look like this:

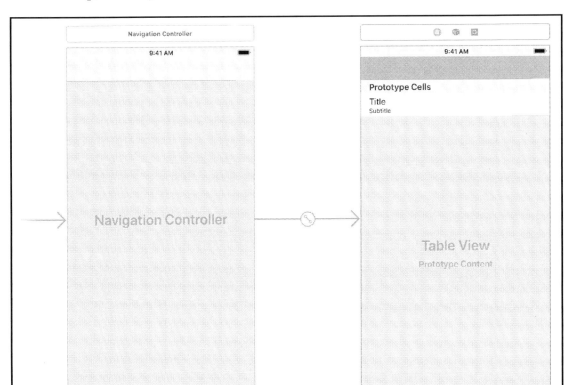

Then, we have to set a title for the `TableViewController`. We have to select the Navigation toolbar and change the title text to `Cities`.

To start serving the real data, we need a couple of extra functions. First, we should define the number of all sections—this is equal to the number of all countries. Here is the function which you should add to the `ViewController`:

```
override func numberOfSections(in tableView: UITableView) -> Int {
    return countries.count
}
```

Then, every section should know how many items are in it. Thus, we should return the number of cities in each country object:

```
override func tableView(_ tableView: UITableView, numberOfRowsInSection
section: Int) -> Int {
    return countries[section].cities.count
}
```

Each section should have a name. This name will be the name of the country. The string returned by the following function will be used to label the separators of each section:

```
override func tableView(_ tableView: UITableView, titleForHeaderInSection
section: Int) -> String? {
    return countries[section].name
}
```

We have to update the content of each cell. To make the scrolling like butter, it's good to keep the execution of `func tableView(_ tableView: UITableView, cellForRowAt indexPath: IndexPath) -> UITableViewCell` pretty short and not CPU/GPU intensive. Thus, we will reuse our cells, similar to what we learned for the `UICollectionView`:

```
override func tableView(_ tableView: UITableView, cellForRowAt indexPath:
IndexPath) -> UITableViewCell {
    let cell:UITableViewCell =
self.tableView.dequeueReusableCell(withIdentifier: "Cell", for: indexPath)

    let country = self.countries[indexPath.section]
    let city = country.cities[indexPath.row]

    cell.textLabel?.text = city.name
    cell.detailTextLabel?.text = "Population: \(city.population)"

    return cell
}
```

If you have used another identifier (not `Cell`) in the `Main.storyboard`, then you have to use it when asking for a reusable cell with `dequeueReusableCell(withIdentifier:, for:)`. Besides that, the method is pretty simple—it just fetched the city and updated the cell's title and subtitle labels. The current cell template has those two labels because we had changed its style earlier.

If we execute the code, we will see a list of all cities, separated by country. Here is what it should look like:

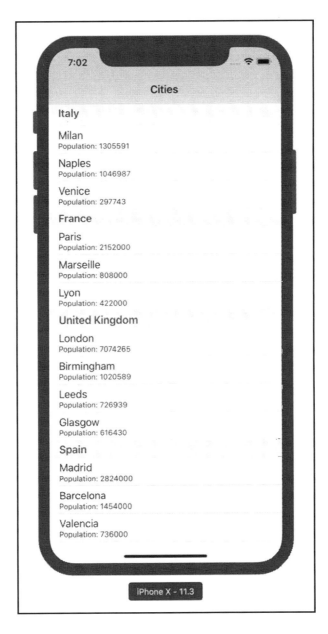

We will print the selected city into the console. To do so, we should override a method which is implemented by the table controller, because it confirms the UITableViewDelegate:

```
override func tableView(_ tableView: UITableView, didSelectRowAt indexPath:
IndexPath) {
    let country = self.countries[indexPath.section]
    let city = country.cities[indexPath.row]
    print("City \(city.name) was selected.")
}
```

The current data is not that huge. In general cases, the number of records will be far more, which makes it pretty hard for the user to find a particular record. It's good to implement a solution which can help the user. Searching through lengthy collections is something mandatory for a great app.

# Adding search

In this section, we will try to upgrade the latest on-screen app to support a search.

1. Let's define a UISearchController property in our ViewController:

    ```
    let searchController = UISearchController(searchResultsController:
    nil)
    ```

2. Then, we should update the viewDidLoad function to display the search UI in the table. It should contain the following code:

    ```
    override func viewDidLoad() {
        super.viewDidLoad()
        countries = Country.getHardcodedData()
        //search
        searchController.searchResultsUpdater = self
        searchController.dimsBackgroundDuringPresentation = false
        definesPresentationContext = true
        tableView.tableHeaderView = searchController.searchBar
    }
    ```

3. The final step is to implement func updateSearchResults(for searchController: UISearchController), but we should declare that the view controller conforms to the UISearchResultsUpdating protocol. (You can read more about the protocols later in this chapter.) To keep our implementation clean, we will add this functionality in a separate extension:

```
extension ViewController: UISearchResultsUpdating {
    func updateSearchResults(for searchController:
UISearchController) {
        let searchText =
searchController.searchBar.text!.localizedLowercase
        if searchText.count > 0 {
            var filteredCountries:[Country] = []
            for country in countries {
                if let filteredCountry = filteredCities(in:
country, searchText: searchText) {
                    filteredCountries.append(filteredCountry)
                }
            }
            countries = filteredCountries
        } else {
            countries = Country.getHardcodedData()
        }
        tableView.reloadData()
    }
    //helper function for proper filtering
    func filteredCities(in country:Country, searchText:String) ->
Country? {
        let c = Country(name: country.name)
        c.cities = country.cities.filter {
            $0.name.localizedLowercase.contains(searchText)
        }
        return c.cities.count > 0 ? c : nil
    }
}
```

The function is triggered when the text in the search box is updated. Based on the text, we should provide a different country list. This is why we need a helper function, which creates a new country object that contains only the cities which match the search text:

You can verify that our click handler here is working properly with the new filtered collection. In fact, the new collection and the old collection are the only sources that are used from the table view.

Keep the table view as simple as possible. Just render a single data collection (model). If you need to filter it, then update the model and the view will reflect it.

The following section discusses the protocols and where they can be used. We have seen them in action in so many places, but it's good to get familiar with their basics.

# Protocols

A protocol defines a set of methods, properties, and requirements which should be fulfilled by a class, structure, or enumeration type. The interface defined by the protocol should be implemented by the types, which conform to the protocol. The interface is a public one because all methods and properties in the protocol are `public`, even though there is no explicit visibility modifier. (For more information, read more about the visibility levels.)

We can think of protocols as types of contracts to be followed. Once you sign a contract (conform to a protocol), then you meet certain requirements and then you can be picked for certain actions.

The definition of a protocol is pretty close to what we know when defining a class, structure, or enumeration type:

```
protocol CustomContractProtocol {
    // list of all requirements (methods or properties)
}
```

When picking a name for a protocol, start with capital letters like the names of classes, structs, or enums.

When a type conforms to a protocol, the protocol should be listed after the type. Here is how it should look for classes and structures:

```
struct MyStruct : CustomContractProtocol {
    //all properties

    //all protocol requirements
}

class BaseClass {
    //empty base class
```

```
    }

    class MyClass : BaseClass, CustomContractProtocol {
        //all properties

        //all protocol requirements
    }
```

Here is how we can use the protocol to add some properties and/or method requirements:

```
    protocol GeoLocationProtocol {
        var long: Double { get set }
        var lat: Double { get set }
        var name: String { get }
        //function which calculates distance to specific geo point
        func calculateDistance(to: GeoLocationProtocol) -> Double
    }
```

When conforming to this protocol, the type should provide an implementation of all requirements. The getter properties required by the protocol could be implemented as regular properties (with or without setters).

Static methods and properties can be added to the protocol without any problem. If you use a *mutating* modifier when defining a protocol, then when implementing this protocol in a class, you must omit it.

All the initializers which are defined in a protocol, when implemented, should be preceded by `required`. Here is an example:

```
    protocol InitProtocol {
        init(from: Int)
    }

    class MyInt : InitProtocol {
        var value:Int

        required init(from: Int) {
            //code goes here
            self.value = from
        }
        //failable init
        init?(from: Double) {
            self.value = Int(floor(from))

            if(Double(self.value) != from) {
                return nil
            }
```

```
        }
    }
```

It's worth mentioning that typical initializers are responsible for constructing a valid object, but we can define failable initializers, which result in a `nil` if they fail. They are used when an optional version of a type is required:

```
var myInt = MyInt(from: 3)
var myDouble = MyInt(from: 3.2)

if myDouble != nil {
    print("The value is \(myDouble?.value)")
} else {
    print("The object is nil.")
}
//prints The object is nil.
```

We saw how we can define protocols and how they can be connected with other types. The protocols are types on their own and they can be used to work with objects which conform to them.

# Protocols and inheritance

Once a protocol is defined, then it is immediately converted to a type. Even though the protocols do not implement any functionality, they can be used in many places:

- For a type of a constant, variable, or property
- For a type of values in different collections
- For a type of parameters or return types in functions, methods, or initializers

An arbitrary type can conform to a protocol using an extension. This is really handy when you want to extend a type and make it work with your current hierarchy. To conform to a protocol, you have to explicitly declare that either when defining the class or when using an extension. If your type contains all methods and properties required by a protocol, this doesn't mean that the type conforms to the protocol.

Protocols can be inherited much like classes. A protocol can inherit more than one protocol and the final result is the union of all requirements:

```
protocol A {
    var a:Int {get}
}

protocol B {
```

```
        var b: Int {get}
}

//protocol inheritance
protocol C: A, B {
        var c: Int {get}
}

class MyTuple : C {
        var a: Int = 0
        var b: Int = 0
        var c: Int {
            get {
                return 7
            }
        }
}
```

Sometimes, when you want a parameter to conform to two or more protocols, you can use protocol composition. Protocol composition is to list several protocols with &. For example, if we want to comply with protocol A and B, then we can define the following function:

```
func isSpecial(object: A & B) -> Bool {
        return object.a % object.b == 7
}
```

Protocol composition doesn't define a new protocol. It simply uses a local protocol, which combines all requirements.

When working with protocols, we need a mechanism to check if a certain protocol has been implemented. There are two operators to do so:

- is: Returns true if an instance implements a protocol.
- as: With its two forms, as? and as! can be used to downcast to a specific type. If as? is used and the casting is not successful, the result could be nil, otherwise, its result is an optional type of the protocol's type. If as! is used, then the result is the protocol's type or runtime error, if the cast is not successful.

 You can use a combination of is and as! to secure your code from runtime errors.

We have optional requirements for protocols if we mix the Swift code with Objective-C. We won't dive too much into detail, but it's good to know that such options exist only because Swift should be compatible with Objective-C.

Protocols can be extended as well, and in the extension, you can provide a default implementation of some methods. These implementations will be used if a class conforms to a protocol and doesn't provide an implementation for this particular method.

A protocol's extensions can use constraints (with where clause) to limit the classes which should have access to the default implementations.

For example:

```
extension Collection where Element : A {
    func toPrettyString() -> String {
        var s = ""
        for a in self {
            s += "\(a.a) :)"
        }

        return s
    }
}

var arrayTuples = [MyTuple()]
print(arrayTuples.toPrettyString())

//prints 0 :)
```

Any other collection which doesn't contain items which conform to protocol A won't have access to this method.

We have discussed a lot of details about protocols, some of which are pretty handy and will be used in our applications.

# Summary

In this chapter, we refreshed our knowledge of the default data structures *array*, *dictionary, and set.* We understood how to model real data and present it in using `UICollectionView`. We saw a working example in a playground and we created a single view which shows a list of cities and countries in an iOS app. In the end, we decided to add search functionality to this single screen.

After reading this chapter, you will have a deeper understanding of OOP and data structures. Each structure should be used when certain constraints are met. There are many other structures that may fit better when solving a particular problem. The best solution is to explore the problem and then pick the best match.

In the next two chapters, we will apply what we have learned so far. Namely, we will implement a small weather app, which consumes data from a public API, visualizes it in a nice way, and keeps track of favorite locations. We will spend some extra time in the storyboard and some time writing models, defining controllers and relations between them.

# Developing a Simple Weather App

# 7

In this chapter, we will develop a `Weather` app. First, we will define all the screens in the storyboard, and learn how to open different view controllers and how to create custom animations between them. Finally, we will understand how to define constraints, and discuss how to pass information between two view controllers. This chapter covers the following topics:

- Designing an application screen in the storyboard
- Defining the model
- Showing different screens when a button is pressed
- Passing data between view controllers
- Constraints and auto layout
- Refreshing what we know about `UITableView` and `UICollectionView`

Let's begin the development of the `Weather` app with a definition and what the app should look like.

# Defining the app screens

Usually, a `Weather` app displays the weather forecast for a week for a particular location. We will develop a version that works for a single city and later, we will expand it to fetch data from the internet. For that reason, here are the screens that we will develop in this chapter:

- **The loading screen**: Every app has a starting screen, which is displayed while the app is loading. By default, every project comes with a separate storyboard, where this can be defined. We will use something pretty plain here and will allow further customization once we want to make our app a bit slicker.

- **Main forecast screen**: This scene will be our entry point. It will display the forecast for a particular place. Once we support many locations, this screen should provide easy navigation to the other locations. For example, the default weather app that comes with iOS allows us to swipe left or right on the first screen to reach the next location. We will implement a similar interaction once we deliver the core functionality of the app.

- **Favorite locations screen**: This screen presents a list of all of the user's favorite cities. They will be easily reachable from the home screen, and a weather forecast will be presented for them.

- **Adding a location screen**: The user should be able to pick a city a list. The selected one will become part of the favorite locations screen.

The number of scenes is pretty limited at the beginning. Later, we can add extra ones and try to improve the user experience. The app will start simple and we will add new user interactions one by one, getting familiar with iOS specifics.

Let's share initial prototypes, which will be used later when defining the scenes and their relations in the storyboard:

The preceding screenshot shows the splash screen, which presents minimal information about the app. To make it nicer, we can add images of the sun, rain, and snow:

On this screen, the user should see the current date and temperature, and the name of the location/city. A list of temperatures per hour for the date should follow (or for the next 12 hours). The forecast for the next 5 or 7 days should be placed below. A nice idea is to use different images and icons, reflecting the weather conditions. We need a button to go to the favorite locations screen, too, as shown in the following screenshot:

The list of favorite locations stores all of the user's favorite places. The list can be expanded by using the **Add a location....** button. The button should open the **Add a Location** screen, which we will define next. Each item from the list can be removed if the user doesn't need that location. If there is no location in the list, then a default location is used. In the app, we will stick to **New York** as the default location. The following screenshot shows how the user can pick a location/place:

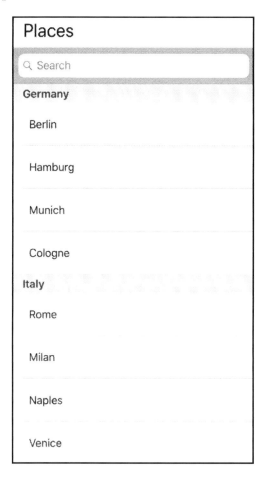

The preceding screenshot presents a list of all the available locations in the app with a search functionality at the top for easy navigation through the data. When a specific location is selected, it will be added to the **Favorites** screen (the previous one).

First, you have to create a new project with a single view. Our app will have more than one screen, but we will learn how to display other scenes later in this chapter. We will define custom transitions between different `ViewControllers` that should be displayed on the screen.

By now, you should be able to create a new `Weather App` project with the default language Swift. Xcode is pretty helpful and will generate all of the starting files for us. Please open the `Main.storyboard` file and then we can dive into developing each scene. The next step is to stitch them together, creating a fully functional app.

We learned how to create an iOS project in `Chapter 5`, *Adding Interactivity to Your First App*. Please follow the steps there and you will have a new project with a local Git repository ready to be shared through GitHub. Don't forget to commit your changes from time to time to save your progress.

Before diving into the app's details, we can warm up with the splash screen. This is the very first screen that is presented once the application is launched. We have full control over it in `LaunchScreen.storyboard`. Open this file and add two labels. One should be placed in the middle of the scene and the other at the bottom in the middle. The final result should look similar to the following screenshot:

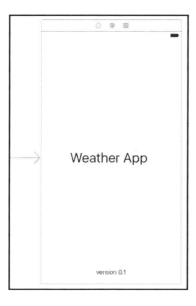

The next section describes the basic version of the starting scene. We have called this home, because the user will see this starting screen every time the app is started.

# The home screen

There is a single view controller that is visible on the screen if you run the empty project app. We have to add the key features from the prototype in order to depict the home screen. Let's start with the name of the place and the weather underneath. The following is the result that we are looking for:

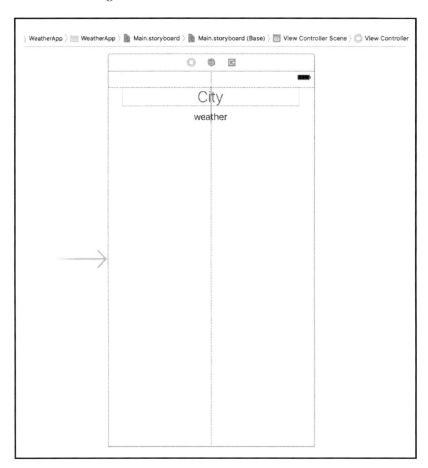

To achieve this, you have to add two labels and change their font size. Position them correctly.

Later in this chapter, we will discuss how to make the layout flexible so that it looks nice on different iPhone screens. For now, we will focus only on standard iPhone 6/7/8 devices.

Let's tale a look at the following steps:

1. We have to add a label that shows the temperature. It should be centered. We also need a degree sign. To insert it, you can navigate to **Edit** | **Emoji & Symbols**. Then, simply start typing `degree` in the search box at the top and it will appear. The following screenshot shows what it should look like:

2. Next, we should add `UICollectionView`, which will display the weather forecast on each hour, starting from now. When we drag `UICollectionView`, we set the place where the data will be rendered, but we should provide a cell for each piece of data. We need a cell to display the information. The cell should have a label to display the time and an image to display the current weather. This will save us space and allow us to enter another label to display the temperature at this very moment:

 Don't worry if the UI of your app is not perfect. We will have another iteration to polish it. Right now, we are putting together all of the main pieces. Later, we will focus on the look and feel.

3. Don't forget to set the scroll direction of the `UICollectionView` item to `Horizontal`. You can do that from **Attributes Inspector**, which is the fourth tab (left to right).

4. Next, we want to display the forecast for the next 5 days, but not in such detail. We can use `UITableView` to display the next 5 days with the necessary information. The storyboard should look like this:

5. One last bit; add a button called **Favorites**. We will use it to pick different locations. Later, we can support a list of favorite locations and then we can have easy access to any of those. But for now, let's keep the app simple.

You can see all of the items in the Document Outline (the left panel  ) panel.

You can use the button at the bottom to open or close the Document Outline panel.

We have the home screen structure created in the storyboard file. The process that we followed was to convert our initial idea to visual components, which are shallow. Now, we will move on to the other screens. Later, we will link all of the screens together and we will add some stub data to see our components in action.

Let's focus on the list of favorite locations. This is the only screen that we can open from the home screen.

# Favorite locations

On this new screen, all of the user's favorite locations will be listed. We need to define a collection that will allow us to display all of the favorite locations. This list of locations has to be preserved between application starts. We should be able to add and remove items from this list. The topmost item will be the target of our weather forecast on the home screen. The final UI that we have to implement should be close to the following screenshot:

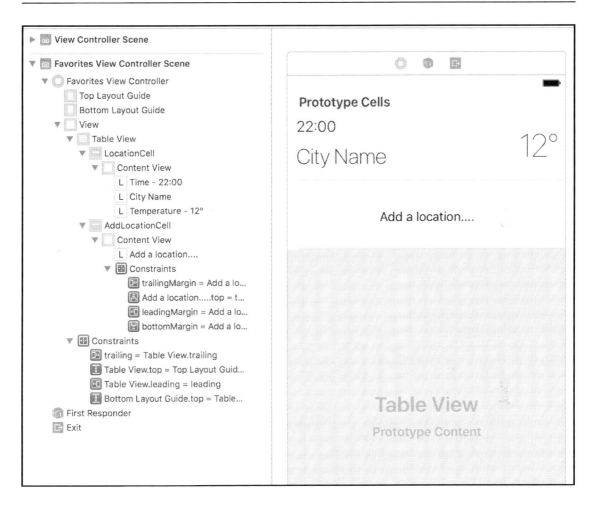

Here is a short list of steps to explain how to achieve this. First, we have to add a new view controller to the storyboard. We can drag in a new one from the **object library**. You should be pretty comfortable with the Xcode interface already, because we have discussed it in Chapter 2, *Getting Familiar with Xcode and Playgrounds*. If you don't feel comfortable, then you should spend some time with the IDE to understand the most important parts of it. We need a table view (UITableView), which should fill the whole screen estate. Then, we need two different types of UICellView. The first one will be used to list all the favorite items and the other one will be used as a button to open the screen from where we can add other locations to the favorite ones.

Let's create first `UICellView` inside `UITableView`. We need three labels—one to show the current time where the location is, another one to show the location name, and one to show the current temperature. Here is what it looks like:

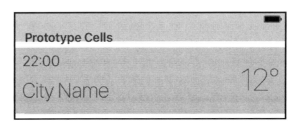

The other one is pretty simple. Don't forget to add another `UICellView` view to the table. You will just need a single label that should be centered in the cell. This can be achieved with constraints. The constraints are rules, which can be defined to ease the layout of visual components (`UIView`) on different device screens.

# Constraints

There are a few different ways to create constraints in the **interface builder** (**IB**) in Xcode. One way is to use the mouse and *Ctrl* key and to drag from one view to the next. This way gives you control and you can add constraints one by one. Here is what it looks like:

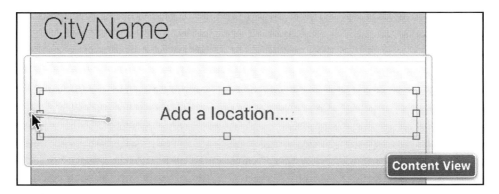

The preceding screenshot shows how a leading constraint is added. You have to select its type in the following window:

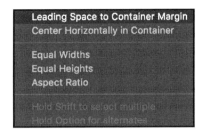

In the preceding screenshot, you can see that all of the constraints are ready, but you have to add them manually. Don't panic if you see some red lines in the view. They show the missing constraints. Once you add all of them, they will be removed:

Another option for adding constraints is to use the handy menu at the bottom of the IB.

First, select the view, and then click on the button 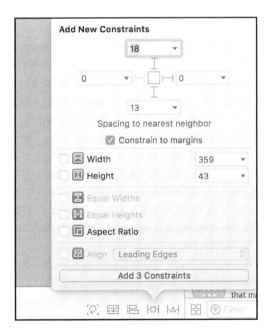 . Then, you should see the following window:

The red lines show which constraints to the parent view will be added. The number in the box denotes the distance from each edge. Once you click the button at the bottom of the window, it will add all of the constraints. The next screen, where you can pick a location, which should be added to the favorites list, is pretty similar.

# Picking a location

The Weather app should allow the user to pick a location and check what the weather forecast is for that particular place. To keep our example attractive enough, we will start with a predefined list of several locations. Later in the book, we will discuss a way to extend this feature and load many locations. Right now, let's focus on this simple version of the app.

We need a collection of locations to be displayed. It would be nice if we could add a search functionality as well. This should remind us of the previous chapter in which we created a table view with a search functionality. Now, we have to recreate that in the Weather app. The following the UI that we could use. You can define something more complex if you wish:

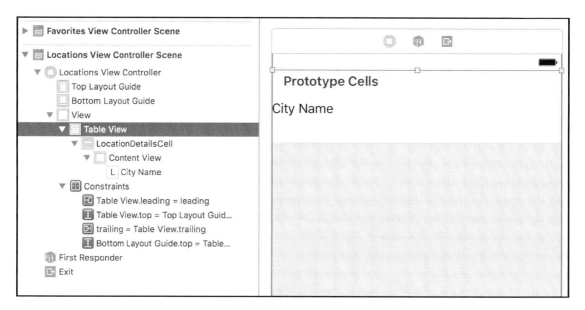

We have UITableView, which takes the whole screen estate. We have implemented that with constraints. Sometimes, if you create your constraints, you may see a warning sign in the Document Outline panel (on the right-hand side). The layout tree of the **Favorites View Controller** panel is presented in the following screenshot:

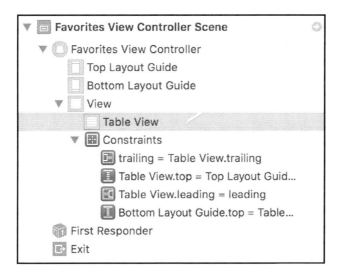

Don't panic! You can use the Xcode suggestion to solve the problem and update all the constraints as shown in the following screenshot:

The IB option can be used to check what the UI will look like on different screens. This is a good validation of the constraints if they are used. Also, you can see if something doesn't look correct on a certain screen size without executing the application on different devices/simulators:

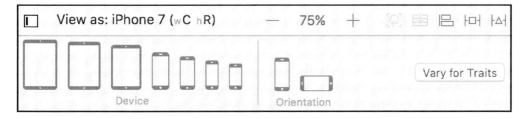

Simply pick different screen sizes using the bottom menu in the IB.

 Always double check the app's look and feel on a simulator and on the actual device. This way, you might catch something that has slipped through during development.

The app version is pretty important when building a release version that should be passed to quality assurance. Usually, when having a build, it's good to see which version is the app—when running (tested) on a device. Thus, adding a label to display the app version is neat and will ease the process of testing.

Let's try to define a model that fits in with our app's needs. Later, we will improve it and make it work with external data fetched from a server that provides a weather forecast.

# Model

The app needs a model that stores all of the information about the home screen. This model should contain a location, the current weather, and a detailed forecast for every hour until the end of the current day. It should also contain a forecast for the next 4 or 5 days. It's as simple as that. The model classes that follow fit these requirements. We could use a structure, not a class; it might have different fields, but this is our solution. This is the beauty of software development: many different classes, structures, and abstractions could lead to the same result:

```
public struct Location {
    var name: String
}
public class Forecast {
    var date:Date
    var weather:String = "undefined"
    var temperature = 100
    public init(date:Date, weather: String, temperature: Int) {
        self.date = date
        self.weather = weather
        self.temperature = temperature
    }
}
public class DailyForecast : Forecast {
    var isWholeDay = false
    var minTemp = -100
    var maxTemp = 100
}
```

```
public class LocationForecast {
    var location:Location?
    var weather:String?
    var forecastForToday:[Forecast]?
    var forecastForNextDays:[DailyForecast]?
    // create dummy data, to render it in the UI
    static func getTestData() -> LocationForecast {
        let aMinute = 60
        let location = Location(name: "NewYork")
        let forecast = LocationForecast()
        forecast.location = location
        forecast.weather = "Sunny"
        //today
        let today = Date().midnight
        var detailedForecast:[Forecast] = []
        for i in 0...23 {
            detailedForecast.append(Forecast(
              date: today.addingTimeInterval(TimeInterval(
              60 * aMinute * i)), weather: "Sunny",temperature: 25))
        }
        forecast.forecastForToday = detailedForecast
        let tomorrow = DailyForecast(date: today.tomorrow,
          weather: "Sunny",temperature: 25)
        tomorrow.isWholeDay = true
        tomorrow.minTemp = 23
        tomorrow.maxTemp = 27
        let afterTomorrow = DailyForecast(date:
          tomorrow.date.tomorrow, weather: "Sunny",temperature: 25)
        afterTomorrow.isWholeDay = true
        afterTomorrow.minTemp = 24
        afterTomorrow.maxTemp = 28
        forecast.forecastForNextDays = [tomorrow, afterTomorrow]
        return forecast
    }
}
```

Create a swift file—`LocationForecast.swift`—and declare your models.

 If you go with different fields or different names for the structure and classes, be aware that you should update the code, which you will see later in the chapter.

We have created the `getTestData` function to return a testing data. This testing data will be used to fill the home screen with data and to verify that everything is working as expected. We can start the app to verify that we see an empty screen, only with the default data. To add some data to `UICollectionView` or `UITableView`, you have to set the `datasource` property to a special class that implements a certain interface.

We will keep the model data in the view controller class, so this means that the view controller should implement the `UICollectionViewDataSource` and `UITableViewDataSource` interfaces. First, let's create outlets in `ViewController.swift`, which will help us to control the following two collections:

```
//details outlet
@IBOutlet weak var details: UICollectionView!
@IBOutlet weak var nextDays: UITableView!
```

Now, we should link the UI with the corresponding outlets. Here is how you can do it (we have already practiced this in previous chapters):

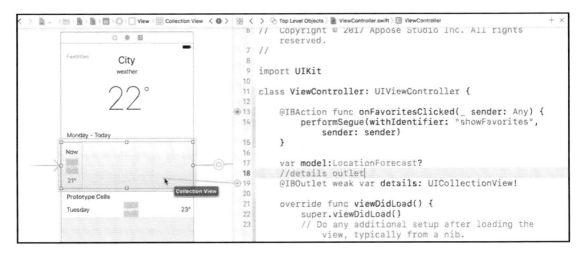

We should create cell classes and link all the cell items (for both collections, respectively.) Here are the classes:

```
class DailyForecastViewCell: UITableViewCell {
    @IBOutlet weak var day: UILabel!
    @IBOutlet weak var icon: UIImageView!
    @IBOutlet weak var temperature: UILabel!
}
class WeatherViewCell: UICollectionViewCell {
    @IBOutlet weak var time: UILabel!
```

```
    @IBOutlet weak var icon: UIImageView!
    @IBOutlet weak var temperature: UILabel!
}
```

Each cell prototype should be linked with its corresponding class. This can be done using the Identity Inspector pane:

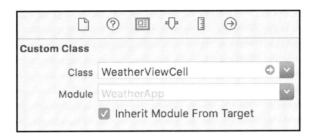

Here is how you can link the cell prototypes with their outlets:

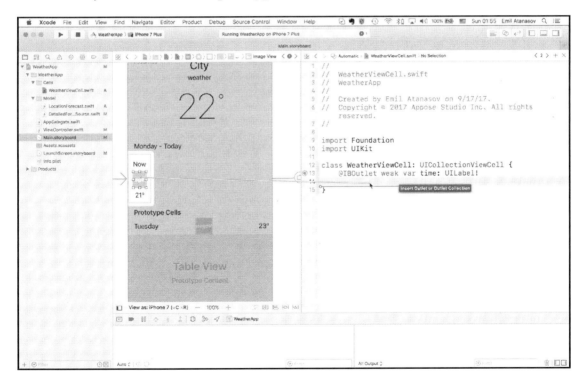

Linking cell prototypes with their outlets

This is how we improve the starting view controller class, which is responsible for the home screen:

```
class ViewController: UIViewController {
    var model:LocationForecast?
    //details outlet
    @IBOutlet weak var details: UICollectionView!
    @IBOutlet weak var nextDays: UITableView!
    var forecast:[Forecast] = []
    var degreeSymbol = "°"

    let collectionViewFormatter = DateFormatter()
    let tableViewFormatter = DateFormatter()
    override func viewDidLoad() {
        super.viewDidLoad()
        //fill the model with mock data
        model = LocationForecast.getTestData()
        collectionViewFormatter.dateFormat = "H:mm"
        tableViewFormatter.dateFormat = "EEEE"
        //out class implements the correct protocols in extensions
        details.dataSource = self
        nextDays.dataSource = self
    }

    // MARK: private
    fileprivate func getIcon(weather:String) -> UIImage? {
        return nil
    }
}
```

The preceding code outlines the overall behavior of the view controller. Here is the implementation that will load the data into the `UICollectionView` and `UITableView` instances:

```
extension ViewController: UICollectionViewDataSource {
    public func collectionView(_ collectionView: UICollectionView,
      numberOfItemsInSection section: Int) -> Int {
        return model?.forecastForToday?.count ?? 0
    }
    public func collectionView(_ collectionView: UICollectionView,
      cellForItemAt indexPath: IndexPath) -> UICollectionViewCell {
        let cell:WeatherViewCell = collectionView
          .dequeueReusableCell(withReuseIdentifier:
          "WeatherCell", for: indexPath) as! WeatherViewCell
        let forecast:Forecast = (model?.forecastForToday?[indexPath.row])!
        cell.time.text = collectionViewFormatter.string(
          from: forecast.date)
```

```
        cell.icon.image = getIcon(weather: forecast.weather)
        cell.temperature.text = "\(forecast.temperature)
          \(self.degreeSymbol)"
        return cell
    }
}
```

The preceding snippet shows the implementation of the `UICollectionViewDataSource` protocol. The following code snippet is the extension, which defines our view controller as `UITableViewDataSource`:

```
extension ViewController: UITableViewDataSource {
    public func tableView(_ tableView: UITableView, numberOfRowsInSection
      section: Int) -> Int {
        return model?.forecastForNextDays?.count ?? 0
    }
    public func tableView(_ tableView: UITableView, cellForRowAt
      indexPath: IndexPath) -> UITableViewCell {
        let cell:DailyForecastViewCell = tableView
          .dequeueReusableCell(withIdentifier: "FullDayWeatherCell",
          for: indexPath) as! DailyForecastViewCell
        let forecast:DailyForecast = (model?.forecastForNextDays?
          [indexPath.row])!
        cell.day.text = tableViewFormatter.string(from: forecast.date)
        cell.icon.image =  getIcon(weather: forecast.weather)
        cell.temperature.text = "\(forecast.maxTemp)
          \(self.degreeSymbol)/\(forecast.minTemp)\(self.degreeSymbol)"
        return cell
    }
}
```

With that extension, we can use the view controller instance to provide data for the items in the table. This will render the forecast for the next few days.

If everything is set as expected, then you should be able to see the following on your simulator (in this case, we are using the iPhone X simulator):

Not all fields are linked. To be able to set the city name and all other details, we need some extra outlets. You can create some in the code and then link them.

You can add images to the project (check the `Assets.xcassets` file in the sample project files) and update the source code a bit to start displaying those icons.

The app needs a helper function that maps text to `UIImage`. The following function should be added to the `LocationForecast` class:

```
static func getImageFor(weather:String) -> UIImage {
    switch weather.lowercased() {
        case "sunny":
            return #imageLiteral(resourceName: "sunny")
        case "rain":
            fallthrough
        case "rainy":
            return #imageLiteral(resourceName: "rain")
        case "snow":
            return #imageLiteral(resourceName: "snow")
        case "cloudy":
            return #imageLiteral(resourceName: "cloudy")
        case "partly_cloudy":
            return #imageLiteral(resourceName: "partly_cloudy")
        default:
            return #imageLiteral(resourceName: "sunny")
    }
}
```

And the updated version of the `getIcon(weather:String)` function in the `ViewController` class should be updated slightly:

```
fileprivate func getIcon(weather:String) -> UIImage? {
    return LocationForecast.getImageFor(weather:weather)
}
```

With this minor change, the Home screen looks rich and communicates the information to the user easily:

To see this screen complete, the **Favorites** button at the top should open another screen. We will find out what to add to the button handler to transition to a new screen soon. Before that, we have to develop the **Favorites** screen. Let's focus on its development and then we will stitch those together.

If you move the arrow that you can see on the storyboard (check the following screenshot) to point to another view controller, then it becomes the main view controller that will be displayed when the app is started. We have to make the second view controller application the starting point:

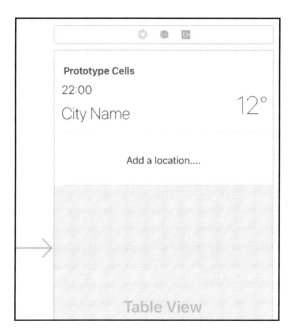

The app has to handle locations, because they are the core of our app model.

# Locations

To keep our app implementation understandable and clear, each location used should be related to a city. It's good to have a name and country to easily identify the city. Because our data is initially filtered, we will assume that there won't be any repetitions in the data. Simply, it means that each city will be unique for each country. This is enough for the current version of the `Weather` app.

In the previous chapter, we developed a similar model. We displayed countries and cities. We are about to use that model as a basis and will expand it slightly to fit our needs.

The location structure should be related to a specific city. Each city should contain its time zone (daylight time won't be taken into account):

```
//city & country model
class Country {
    var name = "No name"
    var cities:[City] = []
    init(name:String) {
        self.name = name
```

```
        }
        init(name:String, cities:[City]) {
            self.name = name
            self.cities = cities
        }
    }
    public class City {
        var name: String
        init(name:String) {
            self.name = name
        }
        static var NewYork: City = {
            return City(name: "New York")
        } ()
    }

    public struct Location {
        var city:City
        init(city: City) {
            self.city = city
        }
        var name: String {
            get {
                    return self.city.name
            }
        }
    }
```

 We have updated the home screen because it uses the old version of the location structure.

In `LocationForecast.swift` you will see the following line of code:

```
let location = Location(name: "New York")
```

It should be replaced with the following content:

```
let location = Location(city: City.NewYork)
```

We have a nice model, which we will use to list all the favorite locations. Now, we should hook up the UI with the model. We have done that a few times so far.

First, we need a variable, which will keep a reference to our table view. We have to link it with the actual UI on the storyboard:

```
@IBOutlet weak var favoritesTableView: UITableView!
```

We need a collection that will hold all the items rendered on the screen:

```
var favorites:[Location] = []
```

Here is the minimal number of methods that should be implemented, so that we see something on the screen in `UITableView`:

```
public override func viewDidLoad() {
    super.viewDidLoad();
    formatter.dateFormat = "H:mm"
    loadFavorites()
    if favorites.count == 0 {
        //New York is a default location
        var loc = Location.init(city: City.NewYork)
        // or -4 * 3600 if in DST
        loc.timeZone = -5 * 3600
        favorites.append(loc)
    }
    favoritesTableView.dataSource = self
    favoritesTableView.delegate = self
}
```

The next step is to implement the following interfaces—`UITableViewDataSource` and `UITableViewDelegate`. These will be implemented in the same file in separate extensions:

```
extension FavoritesViewController: UITableViewDataSource {
    public func tableView(_ tableView: UITableView,
      numberOfRowsInSection section: Int) -> Int {
        //1 for the last special cell
        return favorites.count + 1
    }
    public func tableView(_ tableView: UITableView,
      cellForRowAt indexPath: IndexPath) -> UITableViewCell {
        let index = indexPath.row
        if index < favorites.count {
            let location = favorites[index]
            let cell:FavoriteViewCell = tableView
              .dequeueReusableCell(withIdentifier: "LocationCell",
              for: indexPath) as! FavoriteViewCell
            cell.city.text = location.name
            cell.temperature.text = location.temperature +
LocationForecast.degreeSymbol
```

```
            let date = Date()
            formatter.timeZone = TimeZone(secondsFromGMT:
location.timeZone)
            cell.time.text = formatter.string(from: date)
            return cell
        }

        //last cell is a static one
        let cell:StaticViewCell = tableView
          .dequeueReusableCell(withIdentifier:
          "AddLocationCell", for: indexPath) as! StaticViewCell
        return cell
    }
}
```

We will provide a stub implementation of the click delegate, which we can redefine in the future:

```
extension FavoritesViewController: UITableViewDelegate {
    public func tableView(_ tableView: UITableView,
      didSelectRowAt indexPath: IndexPath) {
        if indexPath.row == favorites.count {
            //TODO: open a new view controller
        } else {
            selectedItem = favorites[indexPath.row]
            //TODO: pick this location and save all locations
            saveFavorites(favorites: favorites)
        }
    }
}
```

There are two functions that handle saving and loading of the favorites collection. When the view controller is presenting the data, we load the favorites. If the collection is empty, we add a single item to it (New York). Saving is done once an item is selected, because we will close this view and update our home screen. Later, we can improve the saving if we change the application workflow. The functions are as follows:

```
// MARK: save favorites
func saveFavorites(favorites:[Location]) {
    let encoded = try? JSONEncoder().encode(favorites)
    let documentsDirectoryPathString = NSSearchPathForDirectoriesInDomains(
      .documentDirectory, .userDomainMask, true).first!
    let filePath = documentsDirectoryPathString + "/favorites.json"
    if !FileManager.default.fileExists(atPath: filePath) {
        FileManager.default.createFile(atPath: filePath, contents: encoded,
          attributes: nil)
    } else {
```

```
        if let file = FileHandle(forWritingAtPath:filePath) {
            file.write(encoded!)
        }
    }
}
```

The `save` function converts the model to a **JavaScript Object Notation (JSON)** and then creates a file in which the whole JSON is saved.

 When working with files on an iOS device, you have to use the `FileManager` class and its default instance, `FileManager.default`. If you have to read, write, or update a file, then you have to use `FileHandler`.

Here is the `loadFavorites` function:

```
func loadFavorites() {
    let documentsDirectoryPathString = NSSearchPathForDirectoriesInDomains(
        .documentDirectory, .userDomainMask, true).first!
    let filePath = documentsDirectoryPathString + "/favorites.json"
    if FileManager.default.fileExists(atPath: filePath) {
        if let file = FileHandle(forReadingAtPath:filePath) {
            let data = file.readDataToEndOfFile()
            let favs = try? JSONDecoder().decode([Location].self,
              from: data)
                favorites = favs!
        }
    }
}
```

The `load` function tries to load the content of the model file. If the file exists, then it is opened. We use `JSONDecoder` to convert the string representation to an array of locations. The next screen that should be opened, once the **Add a location....** items are selected, should allow the user to pick a new location, which then should be added to the **Favorites** screen. We implemented something similar in the previous chapter with a neat search functionality. We will leave this part as a little exercise for the user, to convert the code from the previous chapter and to make it work in this project.

 A full working solution could be found in the source code, which you can download from our Git repository.

We have defined different pieces of our app. Now is the time to learn how to stitch them together in a working application.

# Controllers and segues

Every controller takes care of a visual component on the screen. Some controllers are responsible for the whole screen estate; some take care of only a part of it. We will focus on the ones that are taking up the whole screen, because we are working on small devices, but in general what is applicable to them can be easily transferred to more complex hierarchies of view controllers.

The key concept in presenting new screens is a **segue**. This is a transition without interruption from one view controller to another. Using the segues, we can link together different scenes in our app and we can even transfer information between view controllers. Each segue can define different animations when transiting from once scene to another.

 Segues are tightly coupled with the storyboard.

Now, let's create our first segue between the home screen and the **Favorites** view.

# The first segue

We will learn how to create segues using the storyboard and how to trigger them using the code. Each segue is a relation (transition) between different screens in your app, and those transitions can be fired upon a user's action or by using any other trigger (time trigger, or an action from a server):

1. The easiest way to create a segue is to hold *Ctrl* and then drag it from the view controller or button to the view controller, which should be presented on the screen. In our case, we can start with the home screen. Let's start a *Ctrl* drag from the **Favorites** button and then drop it on the next view controller (the favorites). The following screenshot shows what this should look like:

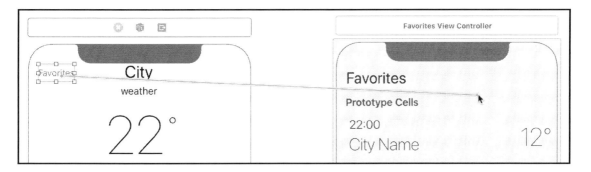

2. Once you lift the mouse, a small popup is displayed, asking you to pick the action to be used. This action will define how the new view controller will be presented on the screen. We will use the **Push (deprecated)** option, but in other cases, some other options are better:

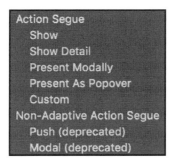

3. Once we pick an action, a connection between our two view controllers will be added on the storyboard:

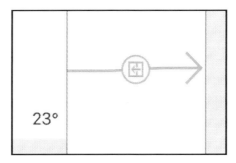

This link represents a relation between those two screens. If we add another segue, which will lead to another view controller, then we will have another link between these view controllers.

You can select the segue and add an identifier in the properties panel on the right. This identifier can be used to trigger a segue with code. For example, the selected segue has the following ID—showFavorites:

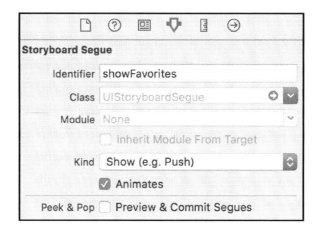

The segue that we created is tightly coupled with the button and it will be activated when the button is touched:

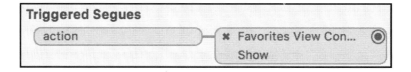

Another way to activate a segue is to use code and then add an action that will be fired upon using the Touch Up Inside event. Then in the function, you can activate the segue with the following code:

```
@IBAction func onFavoritesClicked(_ sender: Any) {
performSegue(withIdentifier: "showFavoritesAlternative",
   sender: sender)
}
```

You should create a segue with the showFavoritesAlternative identifier on the storyboard. A generic segue, which will be started from the code, can be defined with a *Ctrl* drag from a view controller to the next view controller:

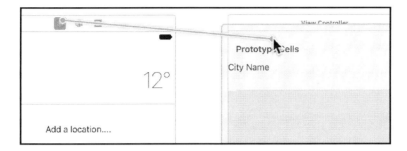

This is an example in which we link the next two view controllers, but you can define as many segues as you need. They will be displayed on the storyboard and this will help you visualize the complex flows in your applications.

Now, we know how to transition from one scene to another, but we should pass data and make the user believe that those scenes are related. We define each screen as a template, which could present specific information. We have to pass that information, and the view controller will handle it from there.

# How to pass data

First, when designing each screen, we make it dependent on some model (data). This model should be passed when the transition happens and once the view controller is presented, the data should appear. This way, the user thinks that the two screens are linked together. An example is a collection view and the details view, which displays extra info. These two screens can work independently, but when we pass data from one to the other, they are perceived as the same thing.

Well-developed scenes (view controllers) can appear in many places in the app.

In our simple application, each scene has a particular role and we won't be able to reuse a view controller in different places, but well-designed apps should reuse them.

Now, let's open the code and jump straight to the view controller that we want to send data, when a specific segue is fired. In that controller, we have to override the following method:

```
override func prepare(for segue: UIStoryboardSegue, sender: Any?) {
    if let id = segue.identifier {
        switch id {
```

```
        case "showFavorites":
            print("transfer the data");
        default:
            break;
        }
    }
}
```

In the preceding code, we detect which segue will be performed. We know which screen will be next. The new view controller that will be presented on the screen should accept the data. Usually, the view controller has a `public` property (properties) which should be set. You have two arguments. The first one is the `segue` object, which contains both view controllers. The `sender` object identifies the item that has triggered the segue. Both arguments are needed to distinguish between different logical scenarios and we can develop the app to act differently in different cases. Here is what the code should look like if we want to pass some data to the favorites view controller:

```
override func prepare(for segue: UIStoryboardSegue, sender: Any?) {
    if let id = segue.identifier {
        switch id {
        case "showFavorites":
            guard let favVC: FavoritesViewController =
                segue.destination as? FavoritesViewController else {
                    return
            }
            favVC.receivedData = 42
        default:
            break;
        }
    }
}
```

The `receivedData` property can be used freely in the `viewDidLoad()` method. We can pass a lot of information, which can be used in the next view controller. There is no limitation as to what type it should be. When the next view controller is activated, it will have access to the passed bits.

A slightly different problem is to pass data in the reverse direction. Let's try to understand why we need it first. When we do some actions in a child view controller, its nice to pass the data to the parent view controller. This approach will improve the module's design. Every view controller does it's own job and passes the model after some updates.

# Passing information in the reverse direction

Passing information from a view controller to a parent view controller is a bit tricky. There is no easy way to know which view controller has opened the current view controller, thus when we want to define a segue back to a specific view controller, we should create a special function in that particular view controller.

In our case, we want to pass the selected item to the home screen. To do so, we have to add a new function that will handle the reverse transition:

```
@IBAction func unwindToHomeScreen(sender: UIStoryboardSegue) {
    if let favoritesVC = sender.source as? FavoritesViewController {
        model = LocationForecast()
        model?.location = favoritesVC.selectedItem
    }
}
```

This function will be triggered when the unwind segue is fired. We have to pass the data from the source view controller to the current view controller. To create this unwind segue, you have to start creating a segue with a *Ctrl* drag from the view controller and drop it to the exit point:

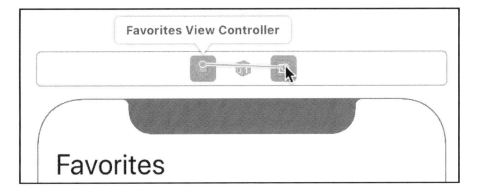

Then, we have to pick the exact function that should be triggered. The functions in the list are part of the other view controllers:

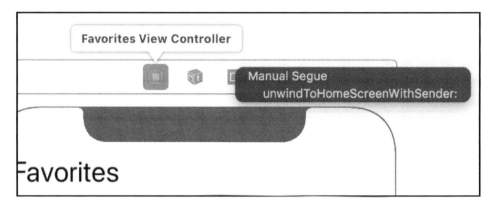

functions

We know how to define a segue, which will replace our visible view controller and go back to a specific one. Now, we will discuss how we can provide custom segues, which will animate the transition back and forth.

# Defining a custom segue

We can create custom segues to perform the animation. Each one is used for either activation or deactivation. Here is how we can define a custom transition.
First, you have to create a new class which extends from UIStoryboardSegue:

```
class ZoomInSegue : UIStoryboardSegue {
    override func perform() {
        zoomIn()
    }

    func zoomIn() {
        let superView = self.source.view.superview
        let center = self.source.view.center
        self.destination.view.transform = CGAffineTransform.init(scaleX:
0.05, y: 0.05).rotated(by: 90 * .pi / 180)
        self.destination.view.center = center
        superView?.addSubview(self.destination.view)
        UIView.animate(withDuration: 0.5, delay: 0, options: .curveEaseIn,
animations: {
            self.destination.view.transform = CGAffineTransform.identity
        }, completion: { success in
```

```
            self.source.present(self.destination, animated: false,
completion: nil)
            })
    }
}
```

In this class, you have to override the `perform` method, which is activated once the segue is triggered. In the preceding example, we are using a separate help function, but all the code could be in the `perform` method. The key is to create an animation using `UIView.animate` and to present the view of the new controller without animation (we defined the animation manually). The animation interpolates the initial state (the view is tiny and rotated) and the final state (the view is positioned in the center and fills the whole screen). The best way to create slick animations is to experiment with different values and transformations.

In the next section, we will briefly discuss a few ideas on how to improve the app.

# Further improvements

What about an easier way to switch to other locations? At the moment, our application displays only one favorite location. It would be better if the user could easily reach other locations and see the forecast for them. Side scrolling between forecasts for different locations sounds intuitive. Just with an easy swipe gesture, the user would be able to check the next favorite location. If the favorite locations are rearranged in the list, that should be reflected and the home screen should reorder too.

To do so, we have to check if our current design of the app (code + UI) allows us to introduce such improvements. Here is what we need:

- The home screen should be expanded to use a list of views and all the interactions should be passed to a delegate. The controller that we have is really abstract, but it uses a single home screen. We have to create a home view that can be used easily with other locations.
- We need a special control which should allow a horizontal swipe. The iOS provides a perfect match for this (hint: check `UIScrollView`).
- The app should use models only, so it could rerender everything once the models are updated. The current model needs slight changes, but those can be figured out on the go.

The discussed improvement of the app will reflect on the current app model and structure, but it can be easily achieved with the current level of understanding of the iOS framework. You should have been using Git until now; if not, now is the perfect moment to do so. Create a local repository and commit the current version. Then, create a separate branch in which you will do your experiments. Call it `side-scrolling`. You can experiment with the app without being concerned about the old version. It's in a safe place—Git—and you can always switch to the master branch and start over.

A picture is worth a thousand words. To make the app better looking, we should add some nice assets/pictures that will hint at the current weather conditions at the selected location. This way, it's much easier to associate the forecast with the weather outside. If we want to develop this idea one level further, try to implement some of the proposed ideas.

# Summary

The reader knows how to create an app that solves real-world problems. He/she can develop the initial idea on paper and then try to create the UI in the storyboard. This version is called the **early prototype**. The reader can experiment with different screen sizes and make the UI work on different screens. We've practiced a nice way to add interactivity and link together different screens. Transition and passing information between screens is a technique that is used in all apps and we have discussed this in detail. We have used the standard iOS toolkit and sample data. The data used here simulates how our app will behave once real data is loaded.

The next chapter discusses modern software development using open source projects. It will show how easy it is to link together several projects using CocoaPods, one of the most popular dependency managers for Swift and Objective-C. We will learn how to use other frameworks in our projects. We should stop trying to reinvent the wheel; a better approach is to look for open source projects that might fit our needs, this will save us a lot of time in development and debugging.

# 8
# Introducing CocoaPods and Project Dependencies

This chapter presents external popular tools for code integration and project distribution. We will learn how to use terminal tools and external projects to extend our own Swift projects. At the end of the chapter, we will know what's needed if we have to develop a library or component that can be shared with the iOS community.

The following topics will be discussed:

- Building software the modern way
- CocoaPods
- Carthage
- Swift Package Manager
- Popular third-party libraries
- GitHub and how to distribute our own libraries/frameworks

Without further ado, let's dive into the problem of modern software development and its solution using different dependency management tools, such as **CocoaPods**, **Carthage**, and **Swift Package Manager**.

# Software – the modern way

Every piece of software begins as a small application and grows with time. New features and functions are added. Some old functions are deprecated or removed. It's a live product, which evolves with time. The process is pretty similar to how a building is built. It's small at first with only the base. Afterwards, windows, doors, and bricks are added. Then, the roof is constructed. Later, the internal parts are finished. The whole process takes a lot of time if everything is designed from scratch. There is no need to reinvent the wheel every time and to build windows or doors from scratch. We can go and buy standardized working components, which can be easily installed in the right place in a building. This saves resources and significantly reduces the time for execution of the whole project. Later on, it's even easier to replace those third-party building blocks with newer versions—lighter, durable, modern—because they follow some specific standard.

In the same way, there are software components which solve different, well-known problems. We will call these components software libraries or frameworks.

 A software library is slightly different from a framework. For example, a framework could contain one or more libraries. (It's possible to have a few frameworks in a library, but it's not common.)

When we are building complex software apps, we will have to overcome recurring issues, such as playing sound/music, applying filters to images, detecting device connections, and so on.

The underlying frameworks in iOS provide a solid foundation for such routine problems, but this is not always the case. Thus, the community builds different software solutions (some of them really robust) which are published as open source projects. These solutions are based on the iOS base layer, but solve a common problem well. The solution is then shared with the whole community. Each library or framework is distributed under a specific license agreement. It can be integrated in a software product if it meets the software and business requirements.

A few years back, the only way to integrate an external framework/library was to copy the code and link it manually to your project. This is a tedious task and takes a lot of time. Once a new version of that software is released (similar to the buildings, when a new version of different components appear) the whole process of integration should be repeated. This is a lot of repetitive work for each version and each library that could be automated.

In short, when the software becomes more complex, the need to manage different subcomponents grows. Such a need leads us to the invention of different package management software.

In the next section, we will discuss when CocoaPods appeared and why it's so popular.

# Ruby and CocoaPods

Ruby is the programming language behind the CocoaPods implementation. It comes bundled with your macOS and it's a no-brainer to install CocoaPods on your machine. This is the main reason why CocoaPods is so popular and widespread.

 The Ruby language is part of macOS by default and can be used without any hassle.

Here are the simple steps which you should follow to install CocoaPods on your machine:

1. Open the Terminal (use Spotlight and type `Terminal`).
2. You should see a window, similar to this one, but the colors may be slightly different (they can be easily configured from the app's preference screen—*cmd +* ,):

3. Type the following command:

   ```
   sudo gem install cocoapods
   ```

4. Now, let's understand what this command does:

   - It uses `sudo` and will ask you for your admin password so that it is able to install this package
   - It calls `gem` (RubyGems command tool) with the `install` option
   - The final argument points to which Ruby package should be installed

5. You should enter the admin password in the same window. CocoaPods should now be installed on your machine. If you don't have admin rights on your machine, then you can use the following alternative to install CocoaPods for your current user:

```
gem install cocoapods --user-install
```

The preceding setup shows us that `cocoapods` is a package, which can run on systems where Ruby is presented. Unfortunately, it is tightly coupled with Xcode and thus it's working only on macOS at the moment.

 There are rumors that CocoaPods might start supporting Linux in the near future.

CocoaPods is a dependency manager for iOS projects written in Swift and/or Objective-C. It has more than 36,000 libraries (and growing) and is being used in more than 2.5 million apps (not all of them are published on the App Store).

We will be using it to add some extra functionality to our projects, but before that, we should understand how to add it to a regular project.

## How to use it

CocoaPods should be integrated in your project. You can do this by simply adding a single file in the project root folder. In this special file, you should describe all dependencies that you need. Under dependency, we will understand an external framework (set of classes). Then, the rest will be handled by the dependency tool. It will fetch the referenced classes and assets and will link those versions to your project. The configuration file is called `Podfile`.

Open your project and add a new empty file, whose name is `Podfile`.

 The file doesn't have any extension.

You can use Xcode to create this file. Just click on **File** | **New** | **Empty** and name this new file Podfile, as shown in the following screenshot:

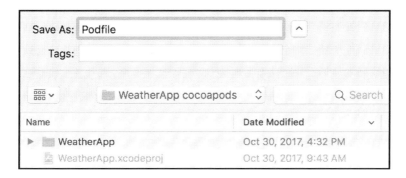

 We are using Swift in our projects, so we will only discuss this particular case. Don't forget that CocoaPods is working pretty fine with Objective-C.

Instead of creating the file manually, we can use CocoaPods to create it for us by performing the following steps:

1. Open the Terminal.
2. Navigate to the project folder using the following command:

   **cd /path/to/your/project**

3. Generate the Podfile file using the following command:

   **pod init**

4. That's it. You can verify that Podfile was generated in the root project folder with the ls -all command in the Terminal.

 Don't panic if you can't see the Podfile file in your Xcode project. This is normal, because the file is not part of your app. To be able to see it, you have to add it manually.

Here is what a very basic (empty) Podfile file should look like:

```
platform :ios, '9.0'

target 'WeatherApp' do
```

```
# Comment the next line if you're not using Swift and don't want
to use dynamic frameworks
use_frameworks!

# Pods for WeatherApp

end
```

All lines which start with # are comments are skipped by CocoaPods. Usually, developers use comments to clarify what framework it is and why it is part of the Podfile file.

All dependencies should be listed in a target. We can create different targets, and different sets of dependencies could be part of them.

5. When you have a Podfile file and all dependency projects listed, then it's time to install them. It's a piece of cake to do this. You have to open a Terminal window in the project root file—the same place where the Podfile file is located and execute the following command:

    **pod install**

The installation was successful, because there are no dependencies, as shown in the following screenshot:

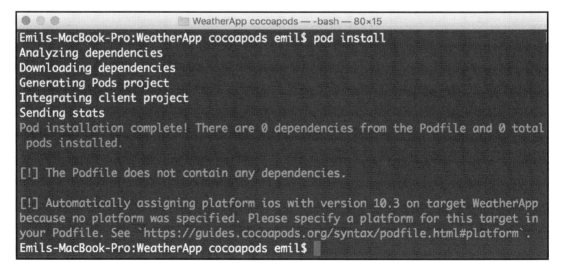

CocoaPods complains about the lack of dependencies and that the project has no default platform version.

6. You should remove the # symbol from the following line, `platform :ios,` `'9.0'`. Now, let's add our first dependency, `Alamofire`. We will discuss it in detail later in this chapter. To add your first dependency, which helps us to implement a remote communication with a public web service, we have to add the following line to our `Podfile` file:

   ```
   pod 'Alamofire', '~> 4.4'
   ```

7. Then, we should reinvoke the `pod install` command. This time, the output is different and we can understand that the new dependency was installed:

```
●  ●  ●                    WeatherApp cocoapods — -bash — 80×10
Emils-MacBook-Pro:WeatherApp cocoapods emil$ pod install
Analyzing dependencies
Downloading dependencies
Installing Alamofire (4.4.0)
Generating Pods project
Integrating client project
Sending stats
Pod installation complete! There is 1 dependency from the Podfile and 1 total po
d installed.
Emils-MacBook-Pro:WeatherApp cocoapods emil$
```

Our project was transformed slightly from CocoaPods. A workspace file was created. It includes our project and all dependencies, which are part of a pods project.

From now on, the workspace should be opened. The file which shows that there is a workspace from several projects is the `.xcworkspace` file. Instead of the well-known `.xcodeproj` file, we have to get used to open the workspace file that includes our project and additional project file, which includes all dependencies.

Don't forget to commit `Podfile.lock` to the repository. This is the correct way if you want everyone who will be working on the same project to have the same dependencies version.

Each dependency declared in the `Podfile` file has a version rule next to it. Based on the version rules of all dependencies, CocoaPods decides what should be fetched and added to our projects. The following is a short explanation of the rules:

- You can specify a particular version, for example, "2.0"
- You can use logical operators (>,>=,<,<=), for example, > 0.2 which means a version higher than 0.2

- You can use the optimistic operator ~> 0.2—this means that any version higher than 0.2 and lower than 1.0 can be used

If CocoaPods can't find a resolution, then it will let you know that there is a problem when fetching the dependencies.

Now is the time to check a few commands which we should memorize when using CocoaPods.

# CocoaPods useful commands

The first command creates a common workspace (if one is not set beforehand), then it fetches all the dependencies and creates a `./Pods/` project with them. Your current project and this new one are added to one workspace:

```
pod install
```

This command should be invoked when we check out a new project locally, which has a `Podfile` file or when we have added some new dependencies.

 When you have a workspace, then you will need an extra line in your `Podfile:` file: `workspace 'MyWorkspace'`

The `install` command is using `Podfile.lock` to fetch the same versions of all dependencies.

The following command is used to update all dependencies (based on the versioning rules) or to update a specific one if we pass its name:

```
pod update
```

If you are looking for all outdated pods, then you should invoke the following command to see the list of dependencies which could be updated:

```
pod outdated
```

If you feel that you don't need CocoaPods in your project, you can use `pod deintegrate` to remove any traces of CocoaPods and any dependencies from your project. Then, you can easily switch to an alternative dependency manager which matches your taste.

Let's discuss an alternative to CocoaPods and Carthage and then we will get you familiar with the new kid on the block—which comes along with the Swift language—Swift Package Manager.

# Carthage

Similarly to CocoaPods, Carthage is a tool which is used to manage external dependencies. But its idea is not to modify the project file and add all dependencies, neither is it here to support a central place where all dependencies are listed. Don't panic. Carthage does the heavy lifting for you. Namely, it downloads the source code and compiles a framework, which should be manually added to the project.

Again, you have a file where all dependencies are described. Carthage uses that file to fetch all dependencies one by one and builds those. Then, it's up to you if you want to include the libraries in your project. When you update the dependency descriptor file, a new version will be fetched and built, but you have to manually update the linked framework. The update could be automated though; you just have to link the output file and once a new version is built, it will replace the old one.

The name of the descriptor file is `Cartfile`. The structure is really simple compared to the `Podfile` file. There is a list of dependencies in the following format:

```
type web-address version
```

The type could be one of the three values such as `github`, `git`, or `binary`.

The address should be a corresponding web address or the name of the GitHub repository, where the resource could be found. For example, take a look at the following command:

```
github "Alamofire/Alamofire" ~> 4.5
git "https://path.to/the/git/repo.git" => 1.0
```

The final part of the definition could define a version rule or exact commit hash. You have to know the following common rules:

- At least version x can be written as `>= x.0`
- Compatible with version x can be written as `~> x.0`
- Exactly version x.1 can be written as `== x.1`

If no version is specified, then any version is allowed and the best one which matches all other rules will be picked.

You may be wondering which dependency manager is better for your project. It depends on what you want to use. If all the dependencies are supported by CocoaPods, you can use it. For the rest, you can use Carthage. If you feel that you need to do a little manual work, then Carthage is a better match; the best solution is to try one. If you need something that's not supported from one dependency manager, you can always use both in the same project.

The third dependency manager which comes with Swift is Swift Package Manager.

# Swift Package Manager

Every new language comes with a package manager for easy dependency support. **Swift Package Manager** (**SPM**) is a tool that is integrated with the Swift system for distributing your Swift projects and using shared ones. It works on Linux and macOS, which makes it the best choice for developers writing backend applications using Swift.

We already know that the code in Swift is organized in modules. Sharing modules which solve common tasks is a breeze with SPM. We need to define which modules we want to use in our project and then they will be cooked for us.

In `Package.swift`, we describe all dependencies (where the source code is located, external dependencies) and what kind of project we are building. Here is an example of a manifest file:

```
// swift-tools-version:4.0
import PackageDescription

let package = Package(
 name: "Weather Service",
 products: [
 .library(name: "WeatherServiceLib", targets: ["WeatherServiceLib"]),
 ],
 dependencies: [
    .package(url: "https://github.com/Alamofire/Alamofire.git",
            from: "4.0.0")
 ],
 targets: [
 .target(
 name: "WeatherServiceLib",
 dependencies: ["Alamofile"]),
 ]
)
```

It describes a library project with a single target. That target has one external dependency—`Alamofile`. The difference between SPM and other dependency managers is that the SPM file uses Swift syntax to describe the project structure and all dependencies.

Each dependency has a URL and a version. These are used to fetch the correct version. The SPM is trying to find the best version which matches all the version rules declared in your project and all sub dependencies. This step is really important when working with many dependencies, but it's automatically done for you. The only problem which you can face is that if there are rules which can't be satisfied and the exact submodules will be pointed to this. Then, unfortunately, you will have to find a workaround—either by updating some modules or just switching to a newer version.

Let's get familiar with the basic command that we will need to work easily with SPM.

# Useful commands

The list of commands for this is not that broad like other dependency managers. An important command is as follows:

```
swift build
```

It automatically downloads all dependencies defined in the manifest file. Then, they are compiled and linked to the current module, but to use it, you need a working manifest file—`Package.swift`.

If you want to develop an executable Terminal project from scratch, then you have to use the following command:

```
swift package init --type executable
```

We can use `--type library` if we want to develop a Swift library and get the following output:

```
swift-executable — -bash — 80×9
Emils-MacBook-Pro:swift-executable emil$ swift package init --type executable
Creating executable package: swift-executable
Creating Package.swift
Creating README.md
Creating .gitignore
Creating Sources/
Creating Sources/swift-executable/main.swift
Creating Tests/
Emils-MacBook-Pro:swift-executable emil$
```

The following command will generate an empty executable project which can be executed with:

```
swift run
```

If everything is working, then you should see Hello World! printed in the Terminal, similar to the following screenshot:

```
swift-executable — -bash — 80×12
Emils-MacBook-Pro:swift-executable emil$ swift run
Compile Swift Module 'swift_executable' (1 sources)
Linking ./.build/x86_64-apple-macosx10.10/debug/swift-executable
Hello, world!
Emils-MacBook-Pro:swift-executable emil$
```

The name of the project is the same as the folder name.

With the following command, you can generate an Xcode project which can be used to develop the app:

```
swift package generate-xcodeproj
```

The generated project includes all the files which are described in the manifest file. The actual project structure is simple as shown in the following screenshot:

```
swift-executable
├── Package.swift — the manifest file
├── README.md — a markup file where you put description and helpful information
├── Sources — a folder in which all source files will be located
│    └── swift-executable — a folder which contains the source files
│         └── main.swift — the main source file
└── Tests — a folder in which all test will be located
```

You have to add other source files in the correct Sources subfolders. By convention, the Sources folder should contain all the source files.

Now, let's try to create a library module in Swift. We can create a new folder—swift-lib—on the disc and open the folder in the Terminal. Then, by executing the following command which we already know:

```
swift package init --type library
```

We end up with the following project structure:

```
swift-lib
├── Package.swift – main manifest file
├── README.md – simple description of the library project
├── Sources – the source folder
│   └── swift-lib
│       └── swift_lib.swift – the library main source file
└── Tests
├── LinuxMain.swift – linux specific test file
└── swift-libTests
└── swift_libTests.swift – file which contains the test
```

The SPM supports testing of the code. This modern approach ensures the higher quality of the code if tests are developed with the library. To start the tests, you have to run the following command:

```
swift test
```

Here is an example of the output after a successful execution:

```
Emils-MacBook-Pro:swift-lib emil$ swift test
Compile Swift Module 'swift_lib' (1 sources)
Compile Swift Module 'swift_libTests' (1 sources)
Linking ./.build/x86_64-apple-macosx10.10/debug/swift-libPackageTests.xctest/Con
tents/MacOS/swift-libPackageTests
Test Suite 'All tests' started at 2017-11-16 01:09:14.766
Test Suite 'swift-libPackageTests.xctest' started at 2017-11-16 01:09:14.766
Test Suite 'swift_libTests' started at 2017-11-16 01:09:14.766
Test Case '-[swift_libTests.swift_libTests testExample]' started.
Test Case '-[swift_libTests.swift_libTests testExample]' passed (0.237 seconds).
Test Suite 'swift_libTests' passed at 2017-11-16 01:09:15.003.
        Executed 1 test, with 0 failures (0 unexpected) in 0.237 (0.237) second
s
Test Suite 'swift-libPackageTests.xctest' passed at 2017-11-16 01:09:15.003.
        Executed 1 test, with 0 failures (0 unexpected) in 0.237 (0.237) second
s
Test Suite 'All tests' passed at 2017-11-16 01:09:15.004.
        Executed 1 test, with 0 failures (0 unexpected) in 0.237 (0.237) second
s
Emils-MacBook-Pro:swift-lib emil$
```

Let's add a structure to the library and a few tests. We can generate an Xcode project:

```
swift package generate-xcodeproj
```

Then, we will open the `swift_lib.swift` file and we add the following structure:

```swift
//public to be accessible from other modules
public struct Toy {
    public var name    = "Unknown"
    public var age     = 1
    public var price   = 1.0
    public init(name:.String, age:Int, price:Double) {
        self.name = name
        self.age = age
        self.price = price
    }
}
```

Then, we open the test file, `swift_libTests.swift`. In that file we add two new tests, which are checking the default construction of a toy instance:

```swift
func testToyDefaultValues() {
    let toy = Toy()
    XCTAssertEqual(toy.name, "Unknown")
    XCTAssertEqual(toy.age, 1)
    XCTAssertEqual(toy.price, 1.0)
}

func testToy() {
    let toy = Toy(name: "Rex", age: 2, price:99)
    XCTAssertEqual(toy.name, "Rex")
    XCTAssertEqual(toy.age, 2)
    XCTAssertEqual(toy.price, 99.0)
}
//update this for Linux
static var allTests = [
    ("testExample", testExample),
    ("testToyDefaultValues", testToyDefaultValues),
    ("testToy", testToy),
]
```

Everything looks clean and neat in the Xcode:

```
88  <  >  🗂 swift-lib  >  📁 Tests  >  📁 swift-libTests  >  🗋 swift_libTests.swift  >  🗋 swift_libTests
1   import XCTest
2   @testable import swift_lib
3
◈   class swift_libTests: XCTestCase {
◈       func testExample() {
6           // This is an example of a functional test case.
7           // Use XCTAssert and related functions to verify your tests produce the correct
8           // results.
9           XCTAssertEqual(swift_lib().text, "Hello, World!")
10      }
11
◈       func testToyDefaultValues() {
13          let toy = Toy()
14          XCTAssertEqual(toy.name, "Unknown")
15          XCTAssertEqual(toy.age, 1)
16          XCTAssertEqual(toy.price, 1.0)
17      }
18
◈       func testToy() {
20          let toy = Toy(name: "Rex", age: 2, price:99)
21          XCTAssertEqual(toy.name, "Rex")
22          XCTAssertEqual(toy.age, 2)
23          XCTAssertEqual(toy.price, 99.0)
24      }
25      //update this for Linux
26      static var allTests = [
27          ("testExample", testExample),
28          ("testToyDefaultValues", testToyDefaultValues),
29          ("testToy", testToy),
30      ]
31  }
32
```

Don't forget to add every test case to the static property—`allTests`—these tests will be executed on Linux.

We have two different modules which are living next to each other on the filesystem. In your case, it depends where you have created both folders. Now, we will show you how to integrate the library module in the executable application. To achieve this, we have to open the library project and create a Git repository. We should execute the following commands in the Terminal:

```
git add .
git commit -m "Initial Commit"
git tag 1.0.0
```

If you have other commits or you have been using Git, you need at least one version tag, like 1.0.0. The local Git repository will be used to fetch the dependency, but first, we have to update the manifest file of the executable project:

```
let package = Package(
    name: "swift-executable",
    dependencies: [
        // update the url if your folders are located on different place
        .package(url:"../swift-lib/", from: "1.0.0"),
    ],
    targets: [
        // Targets are the basic building blocks of a package. A target can
define a module or a test suite.
        // Targets can depend on other targets in this package, and on
products in packages which this package depends on.
        .target(
            name: "swift-executable",
            dependencies: ["swift-lib"]),
    ]
)
```

Now, we can update the executable file and try to use our structure defined in the module. Here is the new version of `main.swift`:

```
import swift_lib

let toy = Toy(name: "Rex", age: 2, price: 99)
print("Hello, \(toy.name)!")
```

Then, to run the new example, you have to execute the following command:

```
swift run
```

Here is the result which you should see in the Terminal:

```
Emils-MacBook-Pro:swift-executable emil$ swift run
Fetching /Users/emil/Documents/Swift 4/Chapter 8/swift-lib
Cloning /Users/emil/Documents/Swift 4/Chapter 8/swift-lib
Resolving /Users/emil/Documents/Swift 4/Chapter 8/swift-lib at 1.0.0
Compile Swift Module 'swift_lib' (1 sources)
Compile Swift Module 'swift_executable' (1 sources)
Linking ./.build/x86_64-apple-macosx10.10/debug/swift-executable
Hello, Rex!
Emils-MacBook-Pro:swift-executable emil$
```

We have learned how to use the Swift Package Manager from the Terminal. It's not limited to macOS, so we can use it when we are working on the Linux platform. We can create empty library projects and executable projects, and we can use Git and link together many projects.

> Keep the executable project minimal. Implement the solution in a separate library module(s) and reuse it in different projects.

We have said that there are many open source projects, which we can use in our apps. Let's discuss some popular ones and the easiest way to find others.

# Popular third-party libraries

There are many pretty useful frameworks which can boost your development. Some of them are visual ones, while some help you build the solid foundations of your application. But do you know where to find them?

The first place where we could start from is the CocoaPods official site—`https://cocoapods.org/`. Yes, CocoaPods is a centralized dependency manager and there is a central place where all of pods are listed. And yes, you can search through all of these solutions and find the best one that suits your needs:

You can filter by platform or language—Swift or Objective-C.

All of these projects are hosted on the CocoaPods servers, but many of them are living on GitHub. GitHub is a web service provider that has free and paid Git hosting services. If you use the free tier, then your project should be open to the community. This means that anyone with internet access can see its code, but can't use it (it's protected under copyright license). You can always pay and use the private plan, that allows you to keep the code of your project a secret.

The developers from different communities such as Swift, iOS, and so on are using this awesome free tier to share their projects. This is how open source became really popular—GitHub is a perfect channel that helps you build and support open source projects. It's not the first such service, but today it's the most popular one worldwide.

Back to the question—where do you find a possible solution to a problem? Yes, GitHub. You can try to search for something which is close to your problem.

 Swift is an open source language. Its source code is hosted on GitHub. The actual address is `https://github.com/apple/swift`.

There are plenty of open source projects. Some are pretty popular and the community around them has spent an enormous amount of time to build really robust solutions. We will present a few really cool projects which you might find interesting and that you can try to use in your very next iOS project.

Again, don't forget to check the license information of each project before blindly integrating it into your app. This might lead to a problem in the near future, so be cautious.

Here are some really useful frameworks, which are part of many projects. We will start with the one used for simple communication with servers—`Alamofire`.

# Alamofire

At some point, you will need a nice and easy way to consume web resources, for example, to download images, read data from a remote location, or to upload data to a Swift backend. These are all valid problems which need a good solution. We can develop everything from scratch using the tools part of iOS—`NSURLDownload`, `CFHTTPStream`, `NSURLSession`, or `NSURLConnection`. Each of these should be used in different situations, but you will need to write the very same boilerplate code to prepare everything and to handle all resources. Is this necessary every time? No. You can simply use `Alamofire`. This is an HTTP networking library which is really popular. It is written in Swift and is pretty easy to use. There is a huge community around this particular project and a group which is responsible for its further development—`https://github.com/Alamofire/Foundation`. There are many articles which explain how to use this framework. If you decide to implement networking, don't waste your time reinventing the wheel. Use this powerful project in the following cases:

- For making requests, response handling, and response caching

- For supporting different HTTP methods (`PUT`, `GET`, `POST`, `PATCH`, `DELETE`)
- Parameters encoding, HTTP headers, and authentication
- Routing requests, adapting, and retrying
- Session management
- Uploading and downloading big files
- Security and reachability

Before jumping into the deep waters of the networking layer in iOS, you must check if `Alamofire` can help. If the answer is no, then check again. There are too many people who are using the layer and the probability of finding working solutions with `Alamofire` is higher.

The next stop is AsyncDisplayKit or, as referred to under its new name—**texture**.

# Texture

If you want your application to be smooth and slick, then you should be careful and keep the frame rate close to 60 fps. This is not that easy, because each render cycle should take less than 16.67 milliseconds. What does this mean? It means that our code to be executed shouldn't last too long. This way, the frame rate will be high and the rendered content will look smooth. The default UIKit implementation provides the foundations, but there are pretty common problems when developing mobile applications that should be solved. For example, how do you load many items in `UITableView` and how do you keep the higher frame rate? Well, AsyncDisplayKit or texture is an abstraction over `UIView` and `CALayer` (the inner parts of UIKit) that will help us to achieve butter-smooth animations.

If you bet on texture, you will get the following results:

- Good, smooth scrolling
- Pre-fetching of items and pre-buffering
- A clear architecture
- Shorter classes
- A higher frame rate
- Performance

Get familiar with this framework before you start working with it. The learning curve is not flat and mastering it will take time. Evaluate all the benefits and what is really important in your app for your users.

Then, the next stop is a completely alternative universe or reactive development. This is a completely different approach to what we know so far, and a fresh functional approach to telling the app what it should do.

# RxSwift

Functional programming is a programming style. It avoids state change and considers computing to be similar to function evaluation. It's a declarative paradigm in which statements such as assignment are not tolerated. In short, if you have a function, its result depends on the input arguments and there are no side effects.

Next, the observer pattern is a design pattern in which we have a collection of observers and if there is a change, every observer receives a notification that something has happened. We can use the ideas from functional programming, observer patterns, and iterator patterns to define the **ReactiveX programming**. It's a modern read of the asynchronous programming using observable streams.

The good sides are as follows:

- It handles complex cases with ease
- The code is declarative and clear
- It can be used with streaming information to handle huge volumes of data
- It's something new and working

Don't switch everything to RxSwift. It's not a silver bullet, but it's a different approach which is pretty powerful. You can use this concept in many different programming languages. RxSwift is the Swift implementation of the Rx API. The code is really readable and simple, without bugs.

Such interesting frameworks and ideas exist on GitHub. Take your time to explore what's there. If you feel that you can build something worth sharing, then you already know how to work with Git. GitHub is not that much different. Go, register there, and share your invention with the whole world.

We have discussed a lot of new technologies in this chapter, starting from dependency managers to some very popular frameworks.

# Summary

Modern software development uses different solutions to build complex applications. Such libraries are hard to manage, and thus dependency managers (third-party programs) appeared. They help developers manage different, complex building blocks in their projects.

We discussed the most popular ones used when developing an iOS and pure Swift project: CocoaPods, which is based on Ruby and works only on iOS, Carthage, the manual solution, which simplifies the management of external dependencies, and the new fresh solution which comes bundles with Swift—Swift Package Manager. We explored how to use every single tool and we should know the basic commands to use any of them.

Finally, we discussed what an open source project is and where they can be found. In the end, we got familiar with three projects which are quite popular and can be used in our next project.

Before diving into development, check the open source places for a solution which might do what you need to implement. If its license matches your business goal, then you can use it in your solution.

Now that we know how to integrate open source projects in our project, let's see what we can do next to make our applications better.

In the next chapter, we will improve our Weather app. First, we will start with the integration of `Alamofire` (you should know what it does), and then we will try to fetch real data from a live web service. Next, we will add some slick animations to the app and some cool effects to make our app stand out. This should give us the final touch to make this project close to a real-world app that it could be used on a daily basis.

# Improving a Version of a Weather App

# 9

By showing you how to consume an external API, we will make our application a working one. It could be used on a daily basis and will add value to the users. We should know that many applications rely on complex backend APIs to do the heavy lifting, and communication through the internet is a key part of modern mobile development.

In this chapter, we will discuss the following topics:

- How to fetch data from a real weather forecast API
- How to add Alamofire to our project
- How to make a request
- How to parse a response
- How to present the data from the server
- Other different improvements using third-party libraries

In the following section, we describe an open weather forecast API, which we can use in our application.

# Weather forecast API

There are many web services which provide weather forecasts. Some of them are paid, while some of them are free. To learn how to consume one, we can use a free access one and later, when we are sure what exactly we need, we can decide to use the best provider on the internet.

# What's an API?

**API** stands for **Application Public Interface**. In terms of the web, this is a set of functions which are hosted and can be accessed by different users through the global network. These functions provide certain data or they can transform data.

For example, there could be a mathematical API which implements different mathematical functions. To consume it, we should know the server address and the name of the functions. Then, we have to make correct requests to the server and it will respond to our queries. This communication is done through different internet protocols—HTTP and HTTPs. Usually, every API (free or paid) needs a specific user ID to be sent with every request. This way, it knows who is doing the request and minimizes the chance of an internet attack.

If many people are making requests and the API can't respond in a certain time, then we can say that the API is down or it's not working. Attacks on API servers are possible, but if the API requires registration, then there won't be many.

When it's time to pick an API for your next mobile app, you have to be sure that it can scale—or that it can simply serve enough users. The reason why it should scale is that are developing a mobile application which will be distributed to many people (millions, if your application is awesome) and those people will make requests to the API when they are using your application. In short, that means millions of requests to the API from different places around the world.

We have picked a free weather forecast API—`http://openweathermap.org/appid`.

You should visit `https://home.openweathermap.org/users/sign_up` and register an account. This procedure doesn't take more than 10 minutes. First, start by registering for an account:

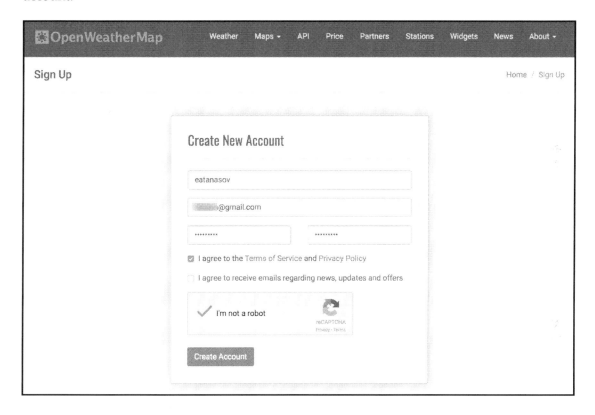

Upon successful registration, you should open the API section to see your API key:

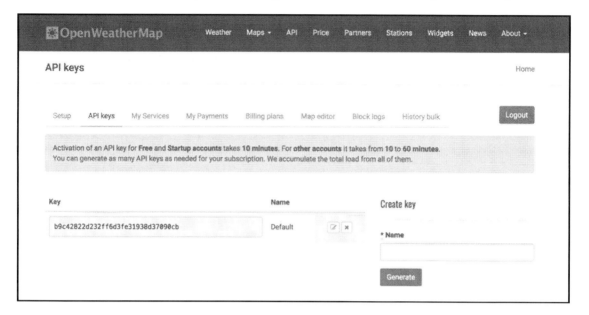

Why do we you need an API key? This key will be sent with every request to the API. This way, the server will identify who is making the requests; in general, which group of users are using the API.

In the next section, we will see which requests will fit us and a nice way to check the returned result.

# List of requests

Every API describes all endpoints which could be hit and what information will be returned. The one which we should request is:

```
http://api.openweathermap.org/data/2.5/weather?id=CITY-ID&appid=API-
KEY&units=metric
```

In this request, we should replace the API-KEY with our key—the one generated by the system. The CITY-ID should be replaced with a specific ID, which can be found in the file provided by openweathermap.com at: http://bulk.openweathermap.org/sample/city.list.json.gz.

The other request which we want to make is to fetch the forecast for the next five days:

```
http://api.openweathermap.org/data/2.5/forecast?id=CITY-ID&appid=API-KEY&un
its=metric
```

Let's try to make a request using the browser. We will use the first API call for Berlin, whose ID is 2950159:

```
http://api.openweathermap.org/data/2.5/weather?id=2950159&appid=ce7a971952c
7df04c4224435da5d818f&units=metric
```

The response is something like this:

```
{
    "coord": {
        "lon": 13.41,
        "lat": 52.52
    },
    "weather": [{
        "id": 803,
        "main": "Clouds",
        "description": "broken clouds",
        "icon": "04n"
    }],
    "base": "stations",
    "main": {
        "temp": 2,
        "pressure": 1000,
        "humidity": 96,
        "temp_min": 2,
        "temp_max": 2
    },
    "visibility": 10000,
    "wind": {
        "speed": 6.2,
        "deg": 260
    },
    "clouds": {
        "all": 75
    },
    "dt": 1516222200,
    "sys": {
```

```
        "type": 1,
        "id": 4892,
        "message": 0.0105,
        "country": "DE",
        "sunrise": 1516172827,
        "sunset": 1516202806
    },
    "id": 2950159,
    "name": "Berlin",
    "cod": 200
}
```

In the next section, we will define a model that could store the data sent from `openweathermap.com`. We should copy the project from `Chapter 7`, *Developing a Simple Weather App*. This will be our starting point, and from there, we will continue to build up.

# Creating new models

We have to create a model which should store this data once we fetch it from the server. The latest version of the app uses a model which we can improve to make it work. What should we do?

In Swift 4, a new feature has been implemented—**Codable** protocol (**Encodable** and **Decodable**). This is an easy way to make a class, enum, or structure easily convertible to and from different formats, and in particular, JSON.

We have to create the following structures which will store the data sent from the server:

```
public class City: Codable {
    var name: String
    var id:Int?
    init(name:String) {
        self.name = name
    }
    static var NewYork: City = {
            let newYork = City(name: "New York")
            newYork.id = 5128638
            return newYork
    }()
}
```

The preceding class defines a city. It has an ID and a name to identify the city. The ID is the same as the IDs which we get from the *openweathermap* service:

```
public class Location: Codable {
    var city:City
    init(city: City) {
        self.city = city
    }
    var name: String {
        get {
            return self.city.name
        }
    }
    var timeZone:Int = 0
    var temperature:String = "-"
}
```

The next class is the location, which contains a city, its time zone, and temperature:

```
struct WeatherResponse: Codable {
    var weather:[WeatherInfoVO]
    var visibility:Int
    var wind:WindVO
    var time:Int
    var name:String
    var id:Int
    var responseCode:Int
    var forecast:WeatherVO
    enum CodingKeys: String, CodingKey
    {
        case weather
        case visibility
        case wind
        case time = "dt"
        case name
        case id
        case responseCode = "cod"
        case forecast = "main"
    }
}
```

This structure represents the response from the API call which we make. It's tightly coupled with the format of the data returned by the server:

```
struct WeatherVO: Codable {
    var temperature:Double
    var pressure:Int
    var humidity:Int
```

```
var minTemperature:Double
var maxTemperature:Double
enum CodingKeys: String, CodingKey
{
    case temperature = "temp"
    case pressure
    case humidity
    case minTemperature = "temp_min"
    case maxTemperature = "temp_max"
}
}
```

The preceding structure defines the weather data. We are using the new `Codable` interface and the way to map fields from the JSON to our model:

```
struct WeatherInfoVO: Codable {
    var id:Int
    var main:String
    var description:String
    var icon:String
}
```

This is a weather details structure, which will be used to store details about the weather forecast for a particular time:

```
struct WindVO: Codable {
    var speed:Double
    var degree: Double
    enum CodingKeys: String, CodingKey
    {
        case speed
        case degree = "deg"
    }
}
```

In this structure, we define the information that describes the wind.

The preceding code should be added to `LocationForecast.swift`.

The code is using a handy technique to rename the fields from the JSON to something that fits our app better. This is achieved with the enum `CodingKeys`, that extends `String` and `CodingKey`. We should remember the following two important rules:

- The name of the fields should be matched exactly by all of the names of the cases.
- The properties which are missing should have a default value in order for our type to be conforming to `Codable`.

The model defined here will be used in the app to display information on the screen. At the moment, it's not hooked to the rest of the mock application, but we will link it soon.

Now, let's try to make a request, which fetches the information from the server. We will discuss the default way of making a web request to a server using the default classes which are part of iOS.

# Pure network requests

Now, we should try to make some requests to fetch information from the weather service. But where is the best place to make network requests?

The application has to display the data from the API on different screens. If we do all of the requests from a single controller, then we have to pass the stored data to the next controller. Wouldn't it be better if we have a shared place in the memory (forecast store) which could be accessed by every controller? Once a controller needs some data, it should ask for it and pass a closure (code block) that will be executed when the data is available. This way, the communication with the backend will be encapsulated and only the final result will be provided.

This is a pretty neat trick, but be careful—don't use it everywhere because everything will become dependent on it, which is bad, if you want to write reusable code.

 **Reusable code** is the code (classes, protocols, structures, enums, and so on) which can be used in different projects without any modification or with a really tiny one. A framework is well-designed if it can be used in several projects without being changed.

We have to create a new class, which should implement one of the really popular design patterns—**singleton**. This design pattern allows just a single instance of a class to be created. It can be accessed easily from anywhere. Here is how you can implement this design pattern in Swift:

```
class ForecastStore {
    public static let instance:ForecastStore = ForecastStore()
    private init() {
        print("initialization goes here")
    }
}
```

Create a new swift file called `ForecastStore.swift`. Then, you can add the preceding class. You can define its interface based on your needs. The key difference is that you can create any objects from this class on your own. The initializer is private. You can access the only instance which is stored in a `static` property.

Let's do our first request in a function called `loadForecast(for city: City, callback: @escaping (_ response:WeatherResponse?, _ error:LoadingError?)->())`. This function takes an argument, `city`, and a `callback` function, which will be fired once the server sends a response. If something goes wrong, the callback will have access to the error type and the app can communicate the problem to the user if this is appropriate.

Don't bother the user with meaningless messages such as: *Error #1234 server response has missing key "code".* Use the user language and communicate the general picture, which will make sense to the user. For example: *"Server is down, please excuse us and try again later."*

Don't forget that the internet is an unreliable medium and that the information could be corrupted or the connection couldn't be established. You have to handle all the edge cases so that the user knows if something goes wrong. The user needs feedback from the app.

Here is how we can handle the communication using the default set of classes provided by iOS:

```
public func loadForecast(for city: City, callback: @escaping (_
response:WeatherResponse?, _ error:LoadingError?)->()) {
        guard let cityId = city.id else {
            callback(nil, LoadingError.invalidCity)
            return
        }
        let configuration = URLSessionConfiguration.default
        let session = URLSession(configuration: configuration)
        let urlString = ForecastStore.WEATHER_API
            + ForecastStore.WEATHER_API_QUERY + "&id="
            + String(describing: cityId)
        if let url = URL(string: urlString) {
            //create a task and start it, please check the next
              code snippet
        }
    }
```

Here is the actual task creation and execution. The code should be placed in the preceding function, but for better understanding, we have separated it into logical pieces:

```
let task = session.dataTask(with: url) { (data, response, error) in
    if let _ = error {
        callback(nil, LoadingError.wrongResponse)
    } else {
        guard let data = data else {
            callback(nil, LoadingError.wrongResponse)
            return
        }
        do {
            //debug
            let rawData = String(data: data, encoding:
                String.Encoding.utf8)
            let decoder = JSONDecoder()
            let responseModel = try decoder.decode(WeatherResponse.self,
                from: data)
            callback(responseModel, nil)
        } catch let err {
            callback(nil, LoadingError.wrongResponse)
        }
    }
}
task.resume()
```

In the preceding code, we create a task object with a closure, which will be executed once the task fetches any data from the server. To start the task, we should call the `resume` function, where we have the following type defined:

```
enum LoadingError {
        case invalidCity
        case noConnection
        case invalidURL
        case wrongResponse
    }
static let WEATHER_API = "https://api.openweathermap.org/data/2.5/weather"
static let WEATHER_API_QUERY = "?appid=YOUR-API-KEY&units=metric"
```

Now let's dive into the detail. To handle the communication with a server, we have to make requests. Each request is a separate action. We should use `URLSession` to manage all HTTP requests.

HTTP protocol is the foundation of the WWW (or the internet, which we are using every day). It's used to serve web pages, send messages, and many other actions, which we do on a daily basis using our mobile phones, computer, or tablets.

To create a valid URLSession, we have to pass a valid configuration—URLSessionConfiguration. Based on the type of communication we want to implement, we can use one of the main three different configuration options:

- .default: This one is the default one. It's using the global disk cache, user, and credential storage.
- .ephemeral: This is the one which stores everything in the memory. After the app is closed, there is no trace left. It should be used when we want to keep the user's information private.
- .background: This is the option we should use when downloading huge files and in case we want to keep the application doing some action (uploading or downloading) after it's sent to the background.

The configuration object can be used for tweaking the HTTP parameters or for sending extra headers. These options may come in handy when you are implementing more complex APIs which force you to send special information with every request. More details can be found in the official URLSession documentation.

To update the URLSession configuration, you have to update the configuration object and create an entirely new URLSession object. There is no other way if you want to change the policies.

 The policies which are set in the URLSession can override the policies set in the URLRequest if they *are* restrictive. For example, if you set that the session shouldn't allow connections on cellular network, then it won't matter what the actual URLRequest policy is.

We should create specific instances of URLSessionTask using the URLSession methods. Each task belongs to a session. Based on the method which we call, the final task could be one of the following:

- URLSessionDataTask: A standard request call which is not supported in the background session.
- URLSessionUploadTask: The upload of data is easier if you are using this task. It's supported in the background session.

- `URLSessionDownloadTask`: Download and save the resource straight to a file on disk. This is supported in any session.
- `URLSessionStreamTask`: Used to establish a TCP/IP connection from a host and port.

Once you have created a task, then you have to call `resume()` to start it. Each task is executed asynchronously. This is perfect, because it won't hurt our performance. The UI of the app is always rendered on the main (UI) thread. There is one caveat: the handler is executed on the background thread as well.

Always update the UI components from the main thread. Some UI components could be updated from other threads, but some will cause the app to crash.

There is a way to configure the session: by using the main thread to execute the task handler, or the more generic option is to use **Grand Central Dispatch (GCD)** to execute a block of code on the main thread. We will stick to the latter option, because it can be used to update the UI from other async calls.

If you want to use the main thread for execution of the task handlers, then you have to use the other `URLSession` constructor, which takes three parameters:
`URLSession(configuration: .default, delegate: nil, delegateQueue: OperationQueue.main)`.

After constructing the `URLSession` object, we create the URL of the resource which should be loaded. To do that, we use the API and our knowledge of how to create a valid URL:

```
session.dataTask(with: url) {(data, response, error) in
//...
}
```

The completion handler is a block of code which will be executed once the request has been made and no matter what the actual result is. Based on the response from the server, we can receive different values in the `data` parameter or in the `error` parameter.

In our implementation, we check for an error. If there is an error, we report that the response from the server is wrong. Here, we can do detailed analysis of the error and break it down. It's good practice to distinguish, when the device has no active connection to the internet.

If there is no error, then we check the data parameter. It holds the actual response from the web service. It should follow a specific structure. The following code simply prints the actual response in the console:

```
let rawData = String(data: data, encoding: String.Encoding.utf8)
print(rawData)
```

 Such lines should be removed from the final version of the app once we are ready to release it. They are really handy when debugging, but in general, they are slowing down the app and might expose sensitive information.

The response which we receive is in JSON format. We should parse it. Parsing of a response means that we've received a text response from the server (in JSON or any other format) and then it will be converted to the appropriate model of objects. Those objects can be used in our app to render the received information and the user will be able to see the new data.

We declared our models to implement the decodable protocol. This will make parsing a breeze:

```
let decoder = JSONDecoder()
let responseModel = try decoder.decode(WeatherResponse.self, from: data)
callback(responseModel, nil)
```

The actual parsing is done by a `JSONDecoder` object. In the following data, the decoder should find a `WeatherResponse` object. Once the object is created, then it is passed to our `callback` function.

The parsing could fail, and thus we are using the `try` clause and a catch block. In the `catch` block, we are checking for errors. If something goes wrong, then we can trigger the callback with the appropriate error. In this case, the error is still the same—`LoadingError.wrongResponse`.

Once we have parsed the data, then we should use it to render it on-screen. Here is how we can do that in the main view controller:

```
let currentCity = City.NewYork
ForecastStore.instance.loadForecast(for: currentCity) { (response, error)
in
    if error != nil {
        print("there is an error")
    } else if let responseModel = response {
        DispatchQueue.main.async { [weak self] in
            self?.updateUI(city: currentCity, forecast:responseModel)
        }
```

```
    }
}
//and the following helper function
func updateUI(city aCity:City, forecast:WeatherResponse) {
    city.text = aCity.name
    if forecast.weather.count > 0 {
        cityWeather.text = forecast.weather[0].description ?? "???"
    }
    temperature.text = String(format: "%.0f",
      forecast.forecast.temperature)
}
```

We have implemented dummy error handling—simply print the error in the console. We can do that at this early stage of the app. Yes, it is still in development. Later in this chapter, we will discuss better error handling and how to present the information to the user.

The other case is when we have a valid response, which contains the forecast for the weather in the city, which is passed to the API. We have to update the UI. Unfortunately, the handler will be called on a background thread, which means that we shouldn't update the UI. To stay on the safe side, we should execute the block on the main thread:

```
DispatchQueue.main.async { [weak self] in
    //code that will be executed on main thread
}
```

We use [weak self] to avoid retain cycles in the code block. The helper function is just a simple interpretation of the data and it handles the exact update.

In the next section, we will discuss how to use one really popular network managing framework. It provides generic solutions to common problems and simplifies network handling.

# Alamofire implementation

We know that there are many open source libraries which could ease our app development. Knowing much about CocoaPods, we can try to integrate Alamofire—a library which many apps are using to solve their network problems.

Please refer to the Chapter 8, *Introducing CocoaPods and Project Dependencies*, to see how to set up a Podfile for the project. Once you have a Podfile, simply add the following line to include the Alamofire library:

```
pod 'Alamofire', '~> 4.5'
```

You have to execute the following to fetch the latest version of the added framework:

**pod install**

Don't forget to use the workspace project instead of the regular project.

Now, we will redo the API call using the Alamofire framework:

```
func loadForecastAlamofire(for city:City, callback: @escaping
(WeatherResponse?, LoadingError?) -> ()) {
    guard let cityId = city.id else {
        callback(nil, LoadingError.invalidCity)
        return
    }
    let urlString = ForecastStore.WEATHER_API
        + ForecastStore.WEATHER_API_QUERY + "&id=" + String(
        describing: cityId)
        //use of Alamofire, please check the next code snippet
}
```

Here is the code which should be added in the preceding function that uses the Alamofire framework :

```
Alamofire.request(urlString).responseJSON { response
    guard let data = response.data else {
        callback(nil, LoadingError.wrongResponse)
        return
    }
    do {
        let rawData = String(data: data, encoding: String.Encoding.utf8)
        let decoder = JSONDecoder()
        let responseModel = try decoder.decode(WeatherResponse.self,
          from: data)
        callback(responseModel, nil)
    } catch let err {
        callback(nil, LoadingError.wrongResponse)
    }
}
```

The code makes a request and the handling is done in a closure, similar to the preceding example (without `Alamofire`). There is not much difference in the closure which handles the data received from the server.

The `Alamofire` implementation looks slightly simpler. There is no configuration which should be set; just a simple call and then a handler that will be executed once the server's response is received:

```
Alamofire.request(urlString).responseJSON {
//
}
```

`Alamofire` is pretty powerful and it has different types of requests. Here, we are using the `responseJSON`. This is the one which we should use when the format of the response is JSON.

We can always use a classical `response`. It is pretty close to what we have done with `URLSession` in the previous section. The data is copied straight from the `URLSession` handler, using no other actions.

There are a few more:

- `responseString`: Converts the data sent to a String
- `responseData`: Converts the data to a data type
- `responsePropertyList`: Converts the data to a plist (object type)

All the different responses might be chained, which means they may be executed one after another. Those handlers will be executed on the main thread. This is the default behavior, but there is an easy way to change that.

The library provides an easy validation of the response. Here is an example:

```
Alamofire.request(url, method: .post)
    .validate(statusCode: 200..<300)
    .validate(contentType: ["application/json"])
    .responseData { response in
        switch response.result {
        case .success:
            print("Validation is successful")
        case .failure(let error):
            print(error)
        }
    }
```

It's pretty easy to make different requests. The method type is passed to the `request` function. Also, the parameters and encoding could be specified. The library provides a powerful way of customization. The final code is clean and concise.

We can discuss a lot of details, but the best place to dive into the detail is the official Alamofire page, which can be found here—`https://github.com/Alamofire/Alamofire`.

In the next section, we will analyze the best way to handle errors, which appear through the apps lifetime.

# Improvements using third-party libraries

We will discuss different styles to handle these errors in iOS. There are many ways that might fit your application. It's good to know the popular ones and to pick the best based on the case.

The first style is silent error handling. The errors are not presented to the user. This means that they are  handled appropriately, but there is no feedback from the app. This is good, because the user doesn't see any problems with the app and keeps a positive attitude. Unfortunately, if the user expects something to happen and it doesn't happen, then they feel a bit confused. This ruins the good impression.

In critical parts, where the user's action needs to be confirmed and there is an error, it's best to give any feedback. This leads us to the second style of handling—communicating the critical problems. To communicate an error, we can pick a different approach. The easiest one is to use the **Alert box** (`UIAlertController`), which steals the focus from the user and waits for the user's input:

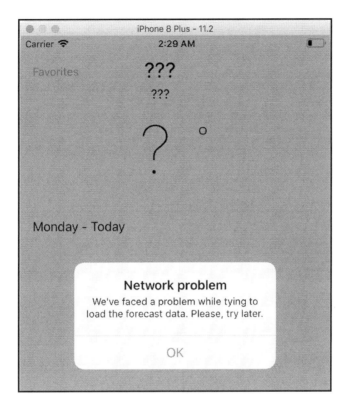

This is working fine if the problem is really major, but it's annoying. A better approach is to use an unobtrusive way to communicate the problems. Good solutions are the toast notifications which pop up for a short time at the bottom (or at the top), and then they disappear. The user has enough time to read them and to understand the problem. They don't need any action from the user and can be skipped freely.

The last style is to notify the user for everything. Such app behavior is not good. It's perfectly fine when developing the app, but later you have to filter which errors are good to be communicated and which are minor. It is really important to keep the user happy while using the app.

Let's show you how to present different notifications (not only for errors).

# Better error handling

The simplest way to handle an error is to display a message, which appears on top of everything. It blocks the rest of the UI and steals the user's attention. This is not the most elegant way, because it's very intrusive, but it's perfect in cases where we have to bring something really critical to the user. For example, when the weather app is trying to fetch the forecast from the server and there is a problem with the network or with the server's response, the app won't be able to receive any data and the user should know what the cause is.

 When presenting such important information, use the user's language. Don't use technical information such as the number of the error or something which is pretty specific. Try to address everyone who will be using your application.

Here is how we can create a simple alert that shows our message to the user:

```
let alert = UIAlertController(title: "Network problem", message: "We faced
a problem while tying to load the forecast data. Please, try later.",
preferredStyle: UIAlertControllerStyle.Alert)
alert.addAction(UIAlertAction(title: "OK", style:
UIAlertActionStyle.Default, handler: nil))
self.presentViewController(alert, animated: true, completion: nil)
```

This code brings a typical alert, which the user should dismiss by pressing the **OK** button. It's something pretty common.

 If you want to present `UIAlertController`, you have to be sure that it's executed in `viewDidAppear` or after that method was invoked.

Here is how we should change the code in `ViewController.swift`. We will move the loading of the information in the `viewDidAppear` function, so that the alert can be added on the screen:

```
override func viewDidAppear(_ animated: Bool) {
    super.viewDidAppear(animated)
    //we set the current city to New York
    let currentCity = City.NewYork
    ForecastStore.instance.loadForecastAlamofire(for: currentCity) {
      [weak self](response, error)  in
        if let error = error { //there is an error
            //actual error handling, please check the code snippet below
        } else if let responseModel = response {
```

```
            DispatchQueue.main.async { [weak self] in
                self?.updateUI(city: currentCity, forecast:responseModel)
            }
        }
    }
}
```

The error handling should be done correctly, thus we have put it in a separate place:

```
witch error {
    case .invalidCity:
        let alert = UIAlertController(title: "Network problem",
            message: "We faced a problem while tying to load the
            forecast data. Please, try later.", preferredStyle:
            UIAlertControllerStyle.alert)
        alert.addAction(UIAlertAction(title: "OK",
            style: UIAlertActionStyle.default, handler: nil))
        self?.present(alert, animated: true, completion: nil)
    case .noConnection://handle this case
        break
    case .invalidURL: //handle this case
        break
    case .wrongResponse: //handle this case
        break
}
```

There are several different types of errors which should be handled. For brevity, we have implemented the first case, .invalidCity, but it's good to handle all the cases in your code using the same approach.

The change of the code is a must, because there is no way to present UIAlertController from the viewDidLoad function. This way, the loading of the data from the server is shifted slightly in time. For more complex applications, this might be critical, so it's possible to start the loading and then delay the presentation of the UI.

There is a better approach to show the error to the user. Simply use a toast notification that appears for a short period of time on the screen in a visible place and then vanishes. There is no need for user interaction, but you can't be sure that the user has read it.

Unfortunately, there is no default mechanism for displaying a toast notification. Thus, we should use a third-party library. The one which we are going to integrate is called Toast-Swift. It can be found at: https://github.com/scalessec/Toast-Swift.

To add it, you can use your CocoaPods. Just add the following line:

```
pod 'Toast-Swift', '~> 3.0.1'
```

Don't forget to call `pod install` to install the new dependency. Here is how you can show a toast notification at the top:

```
self?.view.makeToast("We've faced a problem while trying to load the
forecast data. Please, try later.", duration: 1.5, position: .top)
```

This is the pretty neat, right? Just a single line, but don't forget to add the import at the top:

```
import Toast_Swift
```

Here is what the UI looks like:

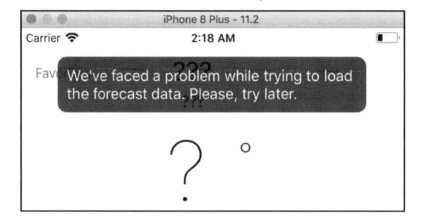

The toast notification is rendered at the top and it disappears after 1.5 seconds. You can always extend the time it should be on-screen, but it shouldn't be too long.

In the next section, we will design a pop-up screen which will display information about all external dependencies.

# About the screen

This screen will show extra information about the application, including who has developed the application, how to use it, and a list of all open source libraries. Each open source library comes with license information that should be accessible by the user within the app.

Don't forget to include the license information for all external libraries, otherwise you may have legal troubles.

Here is what we want to create:

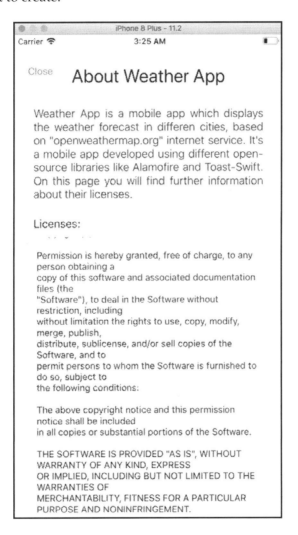

This screen will be opened from the main screen. Now, let's update the storyboard. We have to add a new view controller. This view controller should have a couple of static labels and a `UITextView`. The text view will be used to display all the license information for all external libraries used in the app. This **About** screen is a generic one and it can be used in many other applications which are using external applications:

About screen

Then, we need a `.swift` file to define the `AboutViewController` class, which extends `UIViewController`. We will need an outlet to the text view. Here is the code of the new controller:

```
class AboutViewController: UIViewController {

    @IBOutlet weak var licenses: UITextView!
    let licenseToastSwift =
"""
...paste the whole license...
"""
    let licenseAlamofile =
```

```
"""
...paste the whole license...
"""
    override func viewDidLoad() {
        super.viewDidLoad()

        licenses.text = licenseToastSwift + "\n\n\n" + licenseAlamofile
    }
    @IBAction func onCloseClicked(_ sender: Any) {
        self.dismiss(animated: true, completion: nil)
    }
}
```

The `onCloseClicked` function dismisses the view controller. This function should be triggered once the user activates the **Close** button. The `UITextView` instance is used in the `viewDidLoad` function to load the whole license.

> You can use an arbitrary long text (including empty lines) which is surrounded with """ (triple quotes).

Don't forget to add a segue from the Home screen and activate it once the **About** button is clicked.

About screens are a tiny part of each app, but they are mandatory screens for all apps, because this is the place where you can add all the necessary information telling your users that your app is using third-party software under specific license.

> Double-check which licenses are fine with your application and your business model. Don't try to use libraries without giving credit.

We have been through so many things in this chapter, so let's recap.

# Summary

In this chapter, we have learned what an API is, the easiest way to consume one, and what we should do to start integrating a working backend in a mobile app. We improved the previous version of the Weather application and filled the UI with real data, which is fetched from `openweathermap.org`. The user can extend it by adding the five-day forecast for each city. The list of the cities should be loaded from a structure and all IDs should be in sync with the data provided from `openweathermap.org`. This is out of this scope of the book, but with the knowledge which we already have, it can be implemented easily.

We have used a standard way of communication and the more robust library—`Alamofire`. If you are creating a small app, you can stick to the pure iOS approach. But when you need a much more powerful solution straight out of the box, then `Alamofire` is what you are looking for.

We spent some time discussing different styles of handling errors. The best solution is to handle all major errors and communicate those to the user. We know how to do this using toast notifications and alert boxes. Both can be used, but it depends on the current situation.

Finally, we discussed that each app should contain an **About** screen and information about all open source libraries that are used in the app.

We gained a lot of experience by using the basic `UIComponents`. We practiced how to integrate external APIs in our application. Now is the time to learn how to integrate local frameworks, such as `CoreImage` or `CoreGraphics`. In the next chapter we will try to build a copycat application that is similar to Instagram. We are going to build it from scratch with all the key features without integrating a real backend. Then, we will extend the mock up with Firebase services—a free backend solution—which will simulate the backend of the real app.

# 10
# Building an Instagram-Like App

It's time to build a working app that uses a backend service to handle various user activities such as login, uploading and downloading images, adding comments, and sharing images using other applications. For such an app, you will need a robust backend service. We won't dive into many details on how to build such a service application; instead, we will develop a free solution that is powered by Google's web service: Firebase.

## Tabbed app project

Open Xcode and start a new tabbed app project. Give it a nice name. You can always use `InstagramLikeApp`. Update the organization identifier `com.packtpublishing.swift4`. Set the language to be Swift if it's something else. Then, pick a folder where the project should be saved. You can add a local Git repository to keep all changes under control. The next step is to add a **Podfile**. You just have to open the Terminal window and write:

```
pod init
```

Then, you have to edit the new Podfile. We will start by adding the bare minimum to integrate Firebase:

```
pod 'Firebase/Core'
```

Then, we should call:

```
pod install
```

Don't forget to open the workspace file, where we will have the Pods project linked to the initial project.

 In the future, we will list only the `pod` module that should be added to the Podfile. This means that you will update the Podfile, close Xcode, call `pod install`, and then open the workspace again in Xcode.

Now, we have a project that has the core classes of **Firebase** or Firebase SDK (software development kit, or set a of handy classes to consume Firebase services). We will expand the app a lot by adding different features from the SDK. Now, let's learn more about Firebase.

# Firebase

**Firebase** is a platform that includes many products that solve real problems in software development. It has a free version that has some limitations, but it fits perfectly fine when starting a mobile app from scratch. Once you have gained enough users, Firebase allows you to easily scale and support your product.

You can open the Firebase console (`https://console.firebase.google.com/`), where you have to create your project:

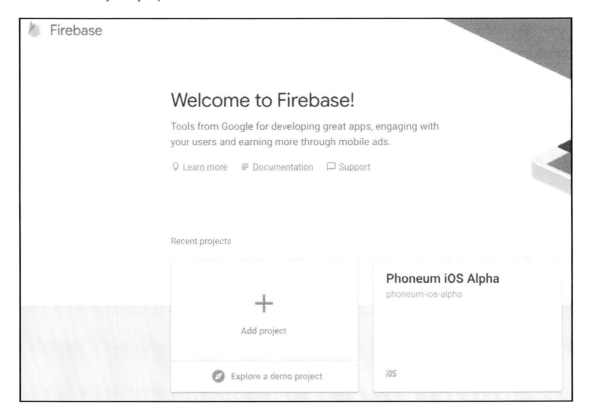

You need a Google account to be able to use Firebase.

Then, you have to create a new project. Simply give it a name: `InstagramLikeApp`. Pick a location that will be used to define the currency in which you will be working with Firebase and this particular project:

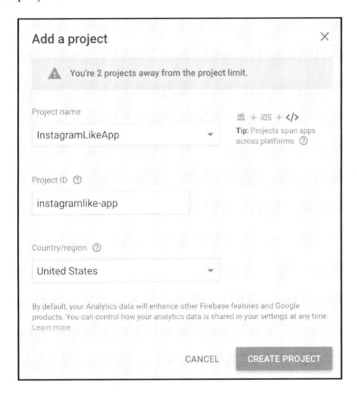

Once we have a valid project, then we should add an iOS app. Start the process with the + button at the top left.

First, you have to enter your application identifier. You can use something like `com.packtpublishing.swift4.InstagramLikeApp`. This is the same app bundle identifier (app ID) that we will use when creating the iOS project. Then, you can change the project name. Firebase only allows unique names for projects. This will be used later.

In the next step, you have to download `GoogleService-Info.plist`. This file should be added to the tabbed app project we created in the previous section.
The final step to finish Firebase's initial integration is to add the following code in `AppDelegate.swift`: `import Firebase` and `FirebaseApp.configure()` in the following function:

```
func application(_ application: UIApplication,
    didFinishLaunchingWithOptions launchOptions:
[UIApplicationLaunchOptionsKey: Any]?)
    -> Bool
```

If everything is correct, then once you run your app, it will start up like before. You will see the following information in the console:

```
2018-02-10 22:32:20.930944+0200 InstagramLikeApp[75045:4638997] 4.8.1 - [Firebase/Analytics][I-
ACS023007] Firebase Analytics v.40009000 started
2018-02-10 22:32:20.931509+0200 InstagramLikeApp[75045:4638997] 4.8.1 - [Firebase/Analytics][I-
ACS023008] To enable debug logging set the following application argument: -FIRAnalyticsDebugEnabled
(see http://goo.gl/RfcP7r)
2018-02-10 22:32:21.556512+0200 InstagramLikeApp[75045:4638997] TIC Read Status [1:0x0]: 1:57
2018-02-10 22:32:21.556660+0200 InstagramLikeApp[75045:4638997] TIC Read Status [1:0x0]: 1:57
2018-02-10 22:32:35.940931+0200 InstagramLikeApp[75045:4638997] TIC Read Status [2:0x0]: 1:57
2018-02-10 22:32:35.941138+0200 InstagramLikeApp[75045:4638997] TIC Read Status [2:0x0]: 1:57
```

In the next section, we will implement an authentication screen. This is the first step every user should take when starting *InstagramLikeApp*.

# Login

Every user should identify him/herself when using the mobile app to the server and other users. To achieve this, Firebase creates a user account. Each user should have at least one account to be able to use the *InstagramLike* service. Unauthorized access is not allowed through the mobile app.

There is no limitation on how many accounts can be created by a single user in Firebase. The only requirement is to have a  valid email or a valid mobile number. Linking virtual accounts (users) with unique items/services from the real world is a good technique to reduce the number of fake accounts in a system.

We will use the default account creation service provided by Firebase.

Firebase supports integration of the most popular social networks, *Facebook* and *Twitter*. LinkedIn is not supported, but there are open source projects that support it. Also, there is a way to use a phone number for login, similar to the real Instagram.

Let's create our sign-in screen. This will be a brand new view controller. At the moment, we have a single option to log in using email and password.

 If you want to use the Instagram logo or resources, you will have to visit the following site: `https://en.instagram-brand.com/`.

Here is our *Sign In* screen:

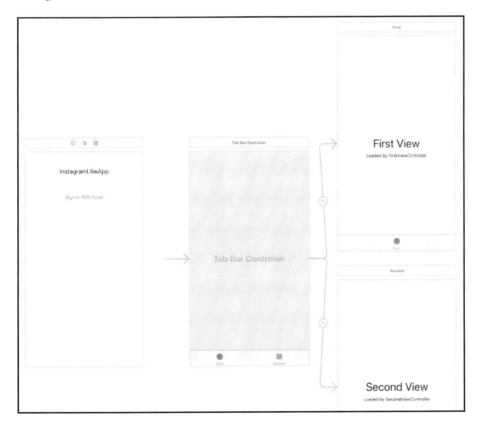

Sign In screen

It has a label and a single button. This button will start the sign in process, which is handled by Firebase. You have to make the **Sign in With Email** screen a main entry point of the app. Simply move the arrow that is pointing to the tabbed view controller so that it is pointing to the new view controller:

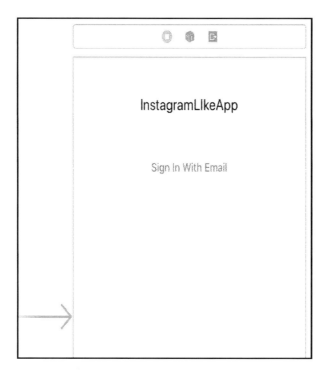

Don't forget to give a storyboard ID to the new view controller. You can use `SignInViewController`. Give a name to the main tab view controller, `TabbarViewController`:

Now, we should add the following pod to the Podfile:

```
pod 'FirebaseUI/Auth', '~> 4.0'
```

Don't forget the whole procedure of installing the pod and re-opening the workspace. You have to create SignInViewController.swift. In that file, we will create a SignInViewController class, which extends UIViewController. Here is the code of this new class:

```
import UIKit
import FirebaseAuthUI
class SignInViewController: UIViewController {
    override func viewDidLoad() {
        super.viewDidLoad()
        // Do any additional setup after loading the view.
    }

    @IBAction func signInWithEmail(_ sender: Any) {
        let authUI = FUIAuth.defaultAuthUI()
        if let authViewController = authUI?.authViewController() {
            present(authViewController, animated: true, completion: nil)
        }
    }
}
```

Don't forget to link the class with the view controller in the main storyboard. Also, add an action to the **Sign In With Email** button. This action uses the default Firebase flow, which handles the user sign in process. If the user already has an account, then it prompts for a password; otherwise, it creates a new account associated with the user's email.

We have to add some extra logic to our AppDelegate so that it can switch the starting screens based on user authentication. If the user has been authenticated (logged in successfully), he/she should see the app's home screen. If not, the SignInViewController should be presented:

```
class AppDelegate: UIResponder, UIApplicationDelegate, FUIAuthDelegate {
    //....
    func application(_ application: UIApplication,
didFinishLaunchingWithOptions launchOptions:
[UIApplicationLaunchOptionsKey: Any]?) -> Bool {
        // Override point for customization after application launch.
        FirebaseApp.configure()
        let nc = NotificationCenter.default
        nc.addObserver(forName: Notification.Name(
          rawValue: "userSignedOut"),
                       object: nil, queue: nil) { [weak self]
                       notification in
```

```
                        //TODO: remove the stored user information
                        self?.openSingInScreen()
            }
            // handle the successful sign in
            let authUI = FUIAuth.defaultAuthUI()
            authUI?.delegate = self
            let user = Auth.auth().currentUser
            if let user = user {
                save(user: user)
                self.openMainViewController()
            }
            return true
        }
    //continue ...
```

In the following code snippet, we add the helper functions that do the heavy lifting:

```
        //MARK:- helper functions
        func save(user: User) {
            //TODO: save the user in memory
        }
        func openSingInScreen() {
            if let signInViewController = self.window?
             .rootViewController?.storyboard?.instantiateViewController(
             withIdentifier: "SignInViewController") as?
             SignInViewController {
                signInViewController.view.frame = (
                  self.window?.rootViewController?.view.frame)!
                signInViewController.view.layoutIfNeeded()
                UIView.transition(with: window!, duration: 0.3,
                  options: .transitionCrossDissolve, animations: {
                    self.window?.rootViewController = signInViewController
                }, completion: { completed in
                    // nothing to do here
                })
            }
        }
    //continue ...
```

The preceding code can be used to present the `SignInViewController` class. Don't forget to add the same ID in the storyboard, because the iOS should find it to initialize it:

```
        func openMainViewController() {
            if let rootViewController = self.window?
             .rootViewController?.storyboard?.instantiateViewController(
             withIdentifier: "TabbarViewController") {
                rootViewController.view.frame = (self.window?
                  .rootViewController?.view.frame)!
```

```
            rootViewController.view.layoutIfNeeded()
            //nice transition between views
            UIView.transition(with: window!, duration: 0.3,
              options: .transitionCrossDissolve, animations: {
                self.window?.rootViewController = rootViewController
            }, completion: { completed in
                // maybe do something here
            })
        }
    }
//continue ...
```

The preceding function handles the case where we want to start the default application flow. In our case, this is the initial `TabBarViewController`. Don't forget to use the same ID for that view controller, so that we can instantiate it using code:

```
    //MARK:- FUIAuthDelegate
    func authUI(_ authUI: FUIAuth, didSignInWith user: User?,
      error: Error?) {
        // handle user and error as necessary
        if let user = user {
            save(user: user)
            self.openMainViewController()
        }
    }
//continue from above
}
```

The code in the preceding snippet will be triggered every time Firebase reports that the user has been successfully authenticated. This will happen automatically on every subsequent application start if the user has logged in once.

To recap, you implement `FUIAuthDelegate`. Then, you add some extra actions in the main function, which is called `func application(_ application: UIApplication,` `didFinishLaunchingWithOptions launchOptions:` `[UIApplicationLaunchOptionsKey: Any]?) -> Bool`. We added a notification to listen when the user logs out and opens the *Sign in* screen. The actual log out action will be implemented later. Then, we set the delegate of the authorization provider. Next, we check whether there is an active user; if there is we open the tab bar, otherwise the app will show the default screen.

We have a couple of help functions that are doing the heavy lifting in presenting the correct screen when the user logs in or logs out.

There is one really important step that we should take in the Firebase console, before checking the implementation. You have to activate email/password sign in. This can be done from the Firebase console. Select the project you created. Next, open the Authentication screen:

You have to click on **Sign-in method**, then you have to edit the first option. Set it to **Enabled**:

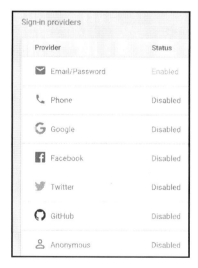

Everything should work. Start the app and verify that you can sign in with your email. Later on, we can include other providers, but for now email is just fine.

 If you develop an app that contains only being able to log in through social networks such as Facebook or Twitter, Apple will reject your app. Every app should be user-friendly and allow users to log in through email/username and password.

In the next section, we will do a rough design of the whole app. All missing view controllers will be created and hooked together.

# The different screens

Before moving onto the details, we should design the overall experience in our app. We will use a tab bar with five different sections. They are as follows:

- **Home screen**: This screen will contain the main feed of photos. It will show all the new photos from the users you follow.

- **Search screen**: Here, the user will be able to look for different content.

- **Create a post**: This screen will allow the user to take a photo and apply different filters. Once the whole process is finished, the photo will be published and visible on the home screen for all users to see.

- **Favorites screen**: This screen will show favorite posts.

- **User's profile screen**: This is your profile screen, where you can see all of your posts.

Open the storyboard and create three new empty view controllers. You should have two already generated from the previous steps. Add a single label in the center of each view controller and give it a nice descriptive name. Hook those view controllers to the main tab bar. Don't forget to add icons. This will make our app stand out and look nice.

Here is what the *InstragramLike* app looks like. Only UI screens define the whole app's basic structure. We will make them interactive and complete this step-by-step:

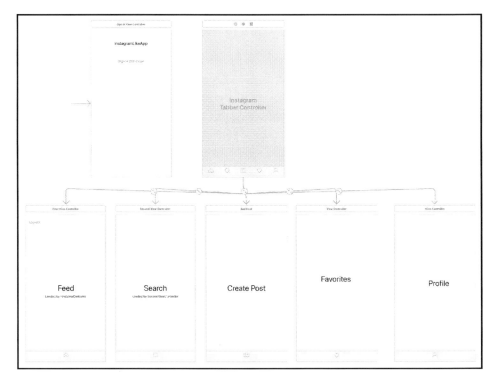

InstragramLike app

In the next section, we will discuss how to customize the tab bar so that it looks more like Instagram. The original app uses a toolbar that is customized, similar to one you can see in other applications such as Safari. We will take another approach that simulates this behavior pretty well.

# Custom buttons on the tab bar

The buttons on the default status bar can be customized in several ways. You can set custom icons, change the text below each icon, and add nice animations. The color can be changed as well, but we will need something slightly fancier here. We want to draw the users' attention to one specific button: the camera button that will trigger the create post flow. This is what we want to achieve:

To achieve that, we will be using an external open source library, ESTabBarController-swift. We should add the following row to the pod file:

```
pod 'ESTabBarController-swift'
```

Then, we have to change the class associated with the tab bar view controller in our storyboard. Let's create a custom class that inherits from ESTabbarController and name it InstagramTabbarController. This class will play a key role in our app, because it will be responsible for handling the tab bar buttons:

```swift
import UIKit
import ESTabBarController_swift

class InstagramTabbarController: ESTabBarController {
    override func viewDidLoad() {
        super.viewDidLoad()
        self.shouldHijackHandler = {
            tabbarController, viewController, index in
            if index == 2 {
                return true
            }
            return false
        }
        self.didHijackHandler = {
            [weak self] tabbarController, viewController, index in
            DispatchQueue.main.async {
                self?.pesentPicker()
            }
        }
        //update the middle icon
        if let viewController = self.viewControllers?[2] {
            viewController.tabBarItem = ESTabBarItem.init(
            AnimatedContentView(), title: nil, image:
            UIImage(named: "create_post"), selectedImage:
            UIImage(named: "create_post"))
        }
    }
    func pesentPicker() {
```

```
            //...
        }
    }
```

First, let's first explain what this class does. It redefines the behavior of the third icon (or the one with index 2, because those are zero index-based). The default behavior is to present a view controller that is linked to the tab bar view controller. This is not the desired behavior. We need to present an image picker and if the user doesn't pick an image to be part of their post, they should return immediately to where they were. In short, we don't need the view controller linked with the button; we want to present a new modal view controller. We should alter the default behavior.

In shouldHijackHandler, we should return true for all the indices we want to customize. In our case, it's only index 2. Then, the actual code that will be fired once the exact icon is pressed should be placed in didHijackHandler. (If you do this hijacking for more than one index, then you have to use the index argument. It is not needed now.)

We should present a picker window, which helps the user pick an image from the device image gallery. We need a new look and feel for the third icon. To achieve a fancy look, we are using a custom ContentView class.

AnimatedContentView defines the new middle icon (there are five buttons—the same number as the linked view controllers). Here are the key details:

```
class AnimatedContentView: ESTabBarItemContentView {
    override init(frame: CGRect) {
        super.init(frame: frame)
        iconColor = .black
        highlightIconColor = .white
    }
    public required init?(coder aDecoder: NSCoder) {
        fatalError("init(coder:) has not been implemented")
    }
}
```

In this code, we customized the button's color.

We can override the following two functions in our AnimatedContentView to add a nice effect when the button is pressed. Here is the code:

```
    public override func highlightAnimation(animated: Bool, completion: (()
-> ())?) {
        UIView.beginAnimations("small", context: nil)
        UIView.setAnimationDuration(0.2)
        let transform = self.imageView.transform.scaledBy(x: 0.8, y: 0.8)
```

```
        self.imageView.transform = transform
        UIView.commitAnimations()
        completion?()
    }

    public override func dehighlightAnimation(animated: Bool,
        completion: (() -> ())?) {
        UIView.beginAnimations("big", context: nil)
        UIView.setAnimationDuration(0.2)
        let transform = CGAffineTransform.identity
        self.imageView.transform = transform
        UIView.commitAnimations()
        completion?()
    }
```

The `highlightAnimation` scales down the whole image, which creates the illusion that the button is pressed down. The other function restores its initial size and position. By tweaking the numbers in this function, you can change the current behavior.

Next, we will implement the create post user flow. It starts picking the correct photo. That photo can then be modified by applying a filter, and then the user can add caption text before sharing it. All shared posts are stored on the Firebase server.

# Creating a post

We are going to use an external library to handle the complex process of rendering all the user's media, picking an image, and applying a filter for us. The name of the library is `YPImagePicker`. This is an open source library that implements an Instagram-like photo and video picker in Swift. Instead of spending too much time in this book developing such a component, we are going to use one off the shelf and focus on implementing the rest of the application. Add the library to the Podfile, by inserting the `pod 'YPImagePicker'` line to the file. Then install the new pod like we have done before.

If you are interested in how to implement such a picker, you can take a look at the `YPImagePicker` source code here:
https://github.com/Yummypets/YPImagePicker/tree/master/Source

We are hijacking the middle tabbar button action. The `pesentPicker` function is called once we detect that the button is clicked. The following code shows the custom image picker view controller:

```
func pesentPicker() {
    var config = YPImagePickerConfiguration()
    config.onlySquareImagesFromLibrary = false
    config.onlySquareImagesFromCamera = true
    config.libraryTargetImageSize = .original
    config.usesFrontCamera = true
    config.showsFilters = true
    config.shouldSaveNewPicturesToAlbum = !true
    config.albumName = "IstagramLikeApp"
    config.startOnScreen = .library

    let picker = YPImagePicker(configuration: config)
    picker.didSelectImage = {
            img in
            //TODO: ...
    }
    present(picker, animated: true, completion: nil)
}
```

If we try to run the app, it will crash. iOS has to ask the user for appropriate permissions to access the user's photos. To do so, it needs special keys to be defined in the `Info.plist` file and associated with short description texts. The problem is that we should let the user know why the app needs access to the Photos library, device camera, and microphone. Thus, we have to add a description of why the app needs those. A system alert will be displayed and the user should agree before moving forward. If the user declines, then we should handle this case and let them know that this is a critical part of our app, without which it can't function properly.

To add these descriptions, you have to open the `Info.plist` file. Then, start adding the following keys and values:

```
<key>NSCameraUsageDescription</key>
<string>InstagramLike app needs access to your camera.</string>
<key>NSPhotoLibraryUsageDescription</key>
<string>InstagramLike app needs access to your photos.</string>
<key>NSMicrophoneUsageDescription</key>
<string>InstagramLike app needs access to your microphone.</string>
```

You can start typing the key and Xcode will help you. Another option is to enter the keys in the `.plist` file if you have opened it like a regular text file. Here is the final result:

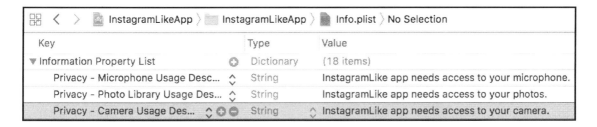

The new permissions are added at the top of the main `.plist` file.

When the descriptions are added, the application should function, but once we pick a nice image and apply a filter, we can't leave the picker. The problem lies in the `picker.didSelectImage` closure. We have to dismiss the screen manually when an image is picked. If you start the app and press the camera button, you will see screens that show your photo gallery images in a grid layout. Here is what it looks like on a simulator of iPhone 6s:

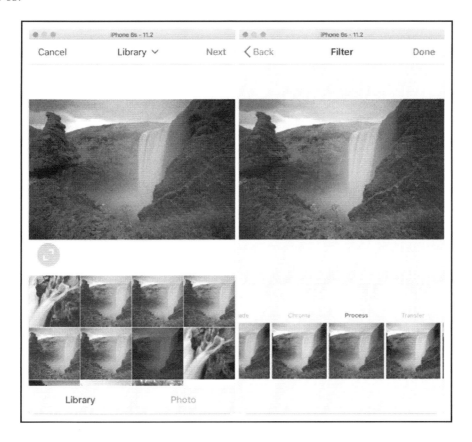

The powerful picker component doesn't implement the last step, which is adding a caption and the actual post sharing when you press **Done**. We have to create a new screen to do that. Let's start with the UI first. Open the storyboard and create a new view controller:

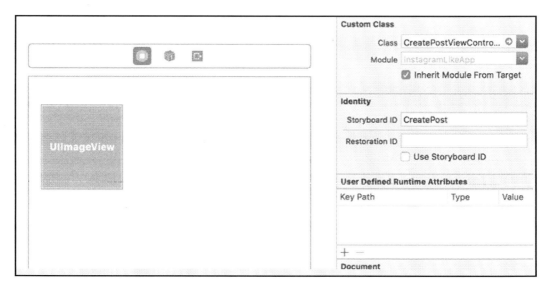

Then, add a `UIImageView` with a width and height equal to 110 points. Next to it, place a `TextView`, which will allow the user to add a short description to the images.

Points are mapped to different numbers of pixels on each device, based on the device screen density  (pixels per inch). On some old devices, 1 point was 1 pixel, but on the retina ones, 1 point could be 4  pixels or more.

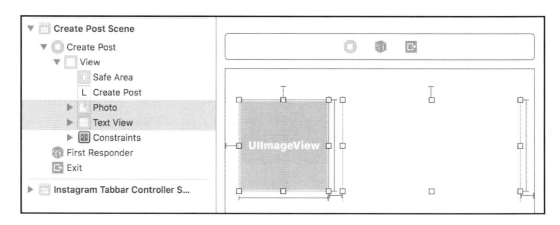

Here are the constraints that should be added so that the `UIImageView` has a fixed size and the `TextView` is filling the rest of the screen. You can use 15 points or more. You need a new Swift file, `CreatePostViewController.swift`, and a new class, `CreatePostViewController`, which should be associated with the new view controller. Don't forget to set the storyboard ID of that controller, similar to what we did at the beginning of this chapter for a couple of other controllers:

```swift
class CreatePostViewController: UIViewController {
    override var prefersStatusBarHidden: Bool { return true }
    private let placeholderText = "Write a caption..."
    public var image:UIImage?
    @IBOutlet weak var photo: UIImageView!
    @IBOutlet weak var textView: UITextView! {
        didSet {
            textView.textColor = .gray
            textView.text = placeholderText
            textView.selectedRange = NSRange()
        }
    }
    override func viewDidLoad() {
        super.viewDidLoad()
        textView.delegate = self
        photo.image = image
        navigationItem.rightBarButtonItem = UIBarButtonItem(
          title: "Share", style: .done, target: self,
          action: #selector(createPost))
    }
    @objc func createPost() {
        self.dismiss(animated: true, completion: nil)
    }
}
```

The view controller adds a **Share** button navigation item at the top right. The button should create the new post and close the picker, bringing the user back to their previous activity.

 The actual code that creates the post and saves it on the Firebase server will be added later.

To add a placeholder text to the `TextView` competent, we have to add the following extension to our view controller. It's a pretty simple and short workaround that makes the `TextView` behave more like `TextInput`.

This is an extension to the `CreatePostViewController` and we can add it to the bottom of `CreatePostViewController.swift`. The `placeholder` property is part of the main class, because it can't be part of the extension. Only read-only properties can be part of extensions. We define the functions that will present the placeholder on the screen in the following code snippet:

```
extension CreatePostViewController: UITextViewDelegate {
    func textViewDidChangeSelection(_ textView: UITextView) {
        // Move cursor to beginning on first tap
        if textView.text == placeholderText {
            textView.selectedRange = NSRange()
        }
    }
    func textView(_ textView: UITextView, shouldChangeTextIn range:
NSRange, replacementText text: String) -> Bool {
        if textVicw.tcxt == placccholderText && !text.isEmpty {
            textView.text = nil
            textView.textColor = .black
            textView.selectedRange = NSRange()
        }
        return true
    }
    func textViewDidChange(_ textView: UITextView) {
        if textView.text.isEmpty {
            textView.textColor = .gray
            textView.text = placeholderText
        }
    }
}
```

`TextView` decides what text to render based on what has been entered by the user. If the text is empty, the placeholder text is rendered. If the user enters any text, then that text is displayed. The selection is managed accordingly.

Now, let's try to hook our new `CreatePostViewController` to the picker. This will be done in `InstagramTabbarController`. We have to handle that in the `didSelectImage` closure:

```
picker.didSclcctImage = {
    [unowned picker, weak self] img in
    if let viewController = self?.storyboard?
      .instantiateViewController(withIdentifier: "CreatePost")
      as? CreatePostViewController {
        viewController.image = img
        // Use Fade transition instead of default push animation
        let transition = CATransition()
        transition.duration = 0.3
```

```
         transition.timingFunction = CAMediaTimingFunction(
            name: kCAMediaTimingFunctionEaseInEaseOut)
         transition.type = kCATransitionFade
         picker.view.layer.add(transition, forKey: nil)
         picker.pushViewController(viewController, animated: false)
      }
   }
```

In the closer, the picker is `unowned` because it will be *initialized* and we don't want to create a memory leak (reference cycle). The `self` should be weak, because we use it and we don't want to create another memory leak.

In many closures, you have to use `[weak self]` to prevent memory leaks.

We will create an instance of the controller using its ID, `CreatePost`. Then, we will use it to pass the selected *image* to that instance, which will be responsible for sending the image to Firebase. Then, a nice transition effect is created and applied.

In the next section, we will discuss why creating a model of the data is important. What are the benefits of using an abstract model compared to storing the data directly on the server?

# Models

We need the model abstraction layer to keep the data structured and organized. We can omit the model layer and store everything in dictionary objects, but this will come and bite us in the long run. When we define a hierarchy of classes that structures the data, we can use it later in different scenarios and we can solve more complex problems with ease. Good models help us to model real processes easily. Without such a layer, our app becomes too dependent on the Firebase database structure. If in the future, Firebase stops working (which is not too likely), it will be hard to migrate our app to other backend services and servers. Then, the easiest step will be to create a model and try to use that model with a new backend.

Usually, it's much easier to think about an application where you have small functional blocks and they are pretty close to the real world. Also, the model layer is used to abstract the actual data representation on the server. This means that if the backend is changed, then we should just fix the communication with the server and keep our model the same. This way, the rest of the application will function as expected without extra changes. If that layer is missing, every change on the server will result in a huge update in the app, which will cost extra time and money.

Here is our model, which is compact, but it does the job for this early stage of the app:

```
class PostModel {
    var photoURL:String
    var description:String
    var author:String
    var width:Int = 0
    var height:Int = 0
    init(photoURL: String, description: String, author:String,
      width: Int, height: Int) {
        self.photoURL = photoURL
        self.description = description
        self.author = author
        self.width = width
        self.height = height
    }
    var toDict:[String:Any] {
        var dict:[String:Any] = [:]
        dict["description"] = description
        dict["author"] = author
        dict["width"] = width
        dict["height"] = height
        if let photoURL = self.photoURL {
            dict["photo"] = photoURL
        }
        return dict
    }
}
```

This class is part of `DataManager.swift`, in which we define our data manager layer:

```
final class DataManager {
    //private constructor
    private init() {
        databaseRef = Database.database().reference()
    }
    //single instance
    static let shared = DataManager()
    var databaseRef: DatabaseReference!
```

```
var userUID: String?
func createPost(post:PostModel, image:UIImage, progress:
    @escaping (Double)->(),callback: @escaping (Bool) -> () ) {
      //...
}
}
```

In the next section, we will discuss how to configure the Firebase backend so that we can use the database and storage to upload posts there.

# Firebase

First of all, we have to install two new libraries, which are responsible for two Firebase services. Update the Podfile by adding these modules:

```
pod 'Firebase/Database'
pod 'Firebase/Storage'
```

Then, install the new libraries. Before developing the code, we should enable the database and storage in our Firebase application. To do that, you have to open the Firebase console and activate the **Database** tab:

You have to use the real-time database, not the Firestore, which is a new service.
Let's update the rules applied to database access. Open the **RULES** tab and replace the old rules with the following:

```
{
    "rules": {
        ".read": "false",
        ".write": "false",
        "myposts": {
            ".read": "false",
            ".write": "false",
            "$uid": {
                ".read": "auth != null",
                ".write": "$uid === auth.uid"
            }
        },
        "posts":{
```

```
        ".read": "auth != null",
        ".write": "auth != null"
    }
  }
}
```

These rules restrict unauthorized access to the database. It's really important to add correct rules, otherwise someone could gain access to data that should be secured.
We have to add Firebase store rules to limit the upload files. Open the **Storage** service:

Then, click on the **RULES** tab and replace the current rules with the following:

```
service firebase.storage {
    match /b/{bucket}/o {
        match /posts/{userId}/{allPaths=**} {
        allow read
        allow write: if request.auth.uid == userId;
      }
    }
  }
```

The rules limit the user to writing only in the /posts/<user-id> location. Let's write some code that uses these two new services:

```
func createPost(post:PostModel, image:UIImage, progress: @escaping
(Double)->(),callback: @escaping (Bool) -> () ) {
    guard let userID = userUID else {
        callback(false)
        return
    }
    // key for the data
    let key = databaseRef.child("posts").childByAutoId().key
    let storageRef = Storage.storage().reference()
    // location of the image for a particular post
    let photoPath = "posts/\(userID)/\(key)/photo.jpg"
    let imageRef = storageRef.child(photoPath)
    // Create file metadata including the content type
    let metadata = StorageMetadata()
    metadata.contentType = "image/jpeg"
    metadata.customMetadata = ["userId": userID]
    //continue ...
```

Next, we have to convert the image to a JPEG representation to be able to save it on the Firebase server:

```
let data = UIImageJPEGRepresentation(image, 0.9)
// Upload data and metadata
let uploadTask = imageRef.putData(data!, metadata: metadata)
//continue ...
```

The `uploadTask` object reports different messages that we can interpret, and then we can update the app's UI accordingly:

```
uploadTask.observe(.progress) { snapshot in
    // Upload reported progress
    let complete = 100.0 * Double(snapshot.progress!
      .completedUnitCount) / Double(snapshot.progress!
      .totalUnitCount)
    progress(complete)
}
//continue ...
```

In the preceding code, we are observing the progress and we are calling the progress closure with the exact percentage:

```
uploadTask.observe(.success) { [unowned uploadTask, weak self]
  snapshot in
    // Upload completed successfully
    uploadTask.removeAllObservers()
    post.photoURL = photoPath
    post.width = Int(image.size.width)
    post.height = Int(image.size.height)
    //save the post object
    var postData = post.toDict
    let childUpdates = ["/posts/\(key)": postData,
                        "/myposts/\(userID)/\(key)/": postData]
    self?.databaseRef.updateChildValues(childUpdates)
    callback(true)
}
//continue ...
```

In the preceding code, we handle the case where the `uploadTask` finishes with success. A post object is saved in the Firebase database and then the callback function is called. In the following code snippet, we illustrate the case in which the `uploadTask` fails:

```
uploadTask.observe(.failure) { [unowned uploadTask] snapshot in
    uploadTask.removeAllObservers()
    callback(false)
    if let error = snapshot.error as NSError? {
```

```
            switch (StorageErrorCode(rawValue: error.code)!) {
                case .objectNotFound:
                    // File doesn't exist
                    print("object not found")
                    break
                case .unauthorized:
                    // User doesn't have permission to access file
                    print("user has no permissions")
                    break
                case .cancelled:
                    // User canceled the upload
                    print("upload was cancelled")
                    break
                case .unknown:
                    // Unknown error occurred, inspect the server response
                    break
                default:
                    // A separate error occurred. This is a good place to
    retry the upload.
                    break
            }
        }
    }
}
```

In this case, we call the `callback` function, reporting false, which means that post creation has failed. It's really important to remove all observers in all cases to be sure that there will be no memory leak. Thus, we use the following call:

```
uploadTask.removeAllObservers()
```

The actual post creation happens on the following lines:

```
var postData = post.toDict
let childUpdates = ["/posts/\(key)": postData,
"/myposts/\(userID)/\(key)/": postData]
//create new records
self?.databaseRef.updateChildValues(childUpdates)
```

Our `PostModel` is converted to a dictionary object, `[String:Any]`. Then, it is used to update the values of concrete places in the database.

The `createPost` function does a couple of things. Let's discuss them one by one:

1. Generate a unique ID for the post and the image:

```
let key = databaseRef.child("posts").childByAutoId().key
let storageRef = Storage.storage().reference()
// location of the image for a particular post
let photoPath = "posts/\(userID)/\(key)/photo.jpg"
let imageRef = storageRef.child(photoPath)
```

2. Convert the image to JPEG representation.
3. Create `uploadTask`, which will be responsible for the upload and the reporting.
4. Attach the different observers that will be fired.

> To prevent memory leaks you have to remove all observers when using Firebase.

5. The `uploadTask` object is created and will be fired automatically:

```
imageRef.putData(data!, metadata: metadata)
```

6. If the upload fails, then the callback is triggered with a `false` value.
7. If the upload is successful, then the corresponding `PostModel` object is stored on the server and the callback is triggered with a `true` value.
8. Progress is reported using a closure with a single value, which contains the upload progress.

We have to use this function in our `CreatePostViewController` class, in its `createPost` method:

```
@objc func createPost() {
    guard let image = self.image else {
        return
    }
    let description = (textView.text != placeholder ?
      textView.text : "") ?? ""
    var post = PostModel(description: description, author:
DataManager.shared.userUID ?? "no user id" )
    DataManager.shared.createPost(post: post, image: image, progress: {
(progress) in
        print("Upload \(progress)")
    }) { (success) in
        if success {
```

```
        print("Successful upload.")
    } else {
        print("unable to create the post.")
    }
    self.dismiss(animated: true, completion: nil)
}
}
```

We call the function and pass two closures (blocks of code) that will be triggered. One is to update a future progress bar, if we add any, and the other one is to close the picker window. We can display different messages based on the outcome of the function. In the next section, we will discuss how easy it is to apply a filter to an image. This is helpful if we want to add extra filters in our app.

# Filters

We can use **CoreImage** or **CI** to manipulate images. Applying a filter is a breeze. Here is a function that can be used to generate a filtered version of an image, simply by passing a valid filter name.

 Many filters have extra arguments (data) that can be passed, which will affect the final result.
For example, a blur filter applies a level of blurriness.

In the following code snippet, we show how a filter can be applied to an image:

```
func filter(_ image: UIImage, filter name:String) -> UIImage {
    //no filter
    if name == "" {
        return image
    }
    //create a context, to draw on
    if let eaContext = EAGLContext(api: .openGLES2) {
        let context = CIContext(eaglContext: eaContext)
        let ciImage = CIImage(image: image)
        if let filter = CIFilter(name: name) {
            //pass the input image
            filter.setValue(ciImage, forKey: kCIInputImageKey)
            if let outputImage = filter.outputImage,
            let cgImg = context.createCGImage(outputImage,
              from: outputImage.extent) {
                //create new image
                return UIImage(cgImage: cgImg, scale: image.scale,
```

```
                orientation: image.imageOrientation)
        } else {
            return UIImage()
        }
    }
  }
  return UIImage()
}
```

This code creates a context and a filter. Then, the filter receives the input image. Next, the code checks the output result from the filter.

 All CI filters are executed on the GPU.

You can combine several filters and implement really complex image manipulations.

 CoreImage is smart enough to optimize and merge several filters, which reduces the time to apply them.

The output data is used to create a CGImage and then UIImage, which can be used anywhere in the app.
Here are the names of some popular filters:

- CIPhotoEffectMono
- CIPhotoEffectTonal
- CIPhotoEffectNoir
- CIPhotoEffectFade
- CIPhotoEffectChrome
- CIPhotoEffectProcess
- CIPhotoEffectTransfer
- CIPhotoEffectInstant
- CISepiaTone
- CIGaussianBlur

A full list of filters separated into sections can be found here: `https://developer.apple.com/library/content/documentation/GraphicsImaging/Reference/CoreImageFilterReference/index.html`. You can achieve pretty interesting effects when you combine filters or when you pass different values, but you have to experiment. Our app is using a default filter and if we want to add new ones, then we have to modify the code of the `YPImagePicker` component.

# Summary

Let's try to recap what we have learned in this chapter so far. We started with an introduction to Firebase. Then, we integrated a basic login to our app using Firebase. We built the general structure of the app with stubbed screens. Next, the tab bar was customized using an external library, so it functions slightly differently and looks cool. We implemented a Create Post screen, which is used to upload images to Firebase storage and save data in the real-time database on Firebase servers. The user flow was a nice mix of an external library and a view controller developed in the app. Finally, we discussed how easy it is to apply a `CoreImage` filter to an image.

In the last chapter of the book, we will continue our work on the Instagram-like app. We will create a nice-looking home screen and we will implement a Search screen. Then we will finish the profile screen where the user can set his username and he can upload an avatar.

# Instagram-Like App Continued **11**

We are going to continue working on our *InstagramLike* app to make it complete and functional. In this chapter, we will implement all the main screens, including the home screen, favorites screen, profile screen, and search screen. The app will start using content stored on Firebase. We will save some extra data in the database and will present it on some screens.

## Home screen

The home screen will display a list of all recent posts published by other users. The list is created by combining all the published posts. We have to design it from scratch using our knowledge about `UIViewCollection`s. We will need a function that loads the data from Firebase. Here are the steps that we should perform to implement the new home screen View Controller.

First, start with the UI of the home screen. Try to recreate the following layout:

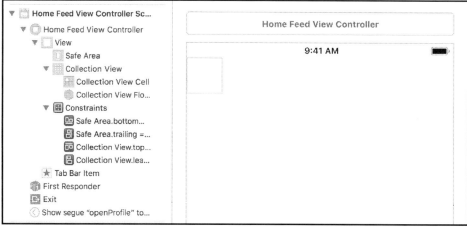

It has `UICollectionView`, which is stretched so it takes the whole screen estate and reaches the **Safe Area**.

 The **Safe Area** is the recommended rectangle in which your app should fit to look the same way on the regular iPhones and the new iPhone X.

You have to create a file called `HomeFeedViewController.swift`. It will contain our implementation of `HomeFeedViewController`. Then, you should add a `UICollectionView` property to `HomeFeedViewController`. Afterwards, you have to connect that class with the View Controller in the storyboard. Don't forget to stretch the collection view from edge to edge using constraints. Add the View Controller as `dataSource` to `UICollectionView`:

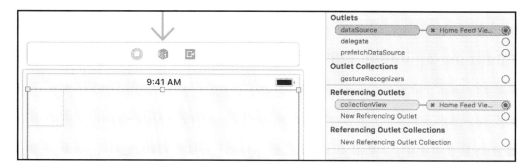

You can see this being done using the Interface Builder, but it can be achieved with the code. You have to pick the way that suits you best and stick to it. In our application, we use more than one approach to show the different possible ways to do this.

Here is what `HomeFeedViewController` might look like:

```
class HomeFeedViewController: UIViewController {
    private let reuseIdentifier = "FeedCell"
    var model:[PostModel]?
    @IBOutlet weak var collectionView: UICollectionView!
    override func viewDidLoad() {
        super.viewDidLoad()
        loadData()
    }
    func loadData() {
        model = []
    }
}
```

The preceding code shows the basic structure. We will continue adding details throughout the chapter.

Next, we have to create a separate class with `.xib` to present a single cell from the feed. You can do this from the **File** | **New File...** (*cmd* + *N*). Then, you have to select **Cocoa Touch Class**:

Click on the **Next** button. Enter the subclass—`UICollectionViewCell`. Give the following class name—`FeedViewCell`. Tick the checkbox, **Also create XIB file**. Stick to the Swift language:

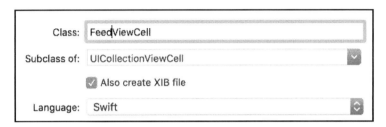

Then, finish the creation of the class. It will appear in the file browser on the left. In the .xib file, we will define the UI of a single cell. The collection view will be using this exact template to render all the items, based on the data passed to it from `dataSource`.

Let's focus on the layout of the cell. An idea of how to lay out the cell is presented in the following screenshot. You can experiment with different layouts. It won't affect the application's logic:

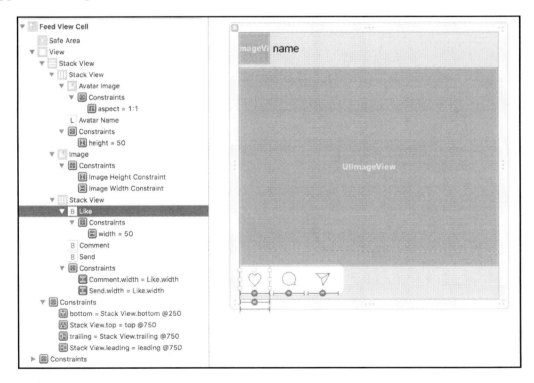

We are using stack views to arrange the items vertically and horizontally. At the top, we've placed the author's avatar image and a label next to it, which is going to display his/her name. Then, there is UIImageView, which will render the photo in the post. At the bottom, we add a list of actions, which we will keep inactive in this first version of our app. They can be easily extended to act appropriately—the heart icon to favorite a photo, the comment icon to add a comment to a post, and the arrow icon to send a direct message to the photo's author.

Now, let's define FeedViewCell.swift:

```
class FeedViewCell: UICollectionViewCell {
    override func awakeFromNib() {
        super.awakeFromNib()
        contentView.translatesAutoresizingMaskIntoConstraints = false
        avatarImage.layer.cornerRadius = avatarImage.frame.height / 2
        avatarImage.clipsToBounds = true
    }
    @IBOutlet weak var avatarImage: UIImageView!
    @IBOutlet weak var avatarName: UILabel!
    @IBOutlet weak var image: UIImageView!
    @IBOutlet private weak var imageHeightConstraint: NSLayoutConstraint!
    @IBOutlet private weak var imageWidthConstraint: NSLayoutConstraint!
    var imageDimentions: CGSize = .zero {
        didSet {
            let imageWidth = UIScreen.main.bounds.width
            let scaleRatio = imageDimentions.width/imageWidth
            let scaledHeigth = imageDimentions.height/scaleRatio
            imageWidthConstraint.constant = imageWidth
            imageHeightConstraint.constant = scaledHeigth
        }
    }
}
```

You have to connect all outlets. Don't forget to connect the constraints—imageHeightConstraint and imageWidthConstraint.

These good-looking cells should be filled with real data. We have to load all published posts from the Firebase database. The loading can be done in our DataManager class. We have defined PostModel, which is our core data object. Here is the function that loads all posts that will be displayed on the home screen:

```
func fetchHomeFeed( callback: @escaping ([PostModel])->()) {
    let ref = databaseRef.child("posts")
    ref.observeSingleEvent(of: .value, with: { snapshot in
        let items: [PostModel] = snapshot.children.compactMap { child in
            guard let child = child as? DataSnapshot else {
```

```
                return nil
            }
            return PostModel.init(snapshot: child)
        }
        DispatchQueue.main.async {
            callback(items.reversed())
        }
    })
}
```

In the preceding code, we load all items from the `/posts` section of our database. Then, we convert each item to a `PostModel`. Once we have all the items, we are ready to report the result using the callback. Because Firebase doesn't guarantee that all fetches are done on the UI thread, we have to use `DispatchQueue` to report the result on the UI thread. The final collection is reversed so the latest posts appear at the top—they are the newest and most relevant.

We have to call this function in the `loadData()` function, which is triggered once the view is loaded:

```
func loadData() {
    model = []
    DataManager.shared.fetchHomeFeed {[weak self] items in
        if items.count > 0 {
            self?.model? += items
            self?.collectionView.reloadData()
        }
    }
}
```

The callback function updates the model once it's triggered. Then, it reloads the collection view and the whole UI is refreshed.

Now, when the app is started and the user logs in, the home screen will display all the posts that have been published from all the users.

 The current app and DB will handle 1,000 or even more records without any problem, but the app should be optimized when the data grows.

In the next section, we will work on the profile screen. We will add some buttons and a UI that will display a user's profile data. Not all of it will be fetched from the server.

# Profile screen

We have to open the storyboard and update the profile screen. Here is the desired result. Don't forget to use constraints:

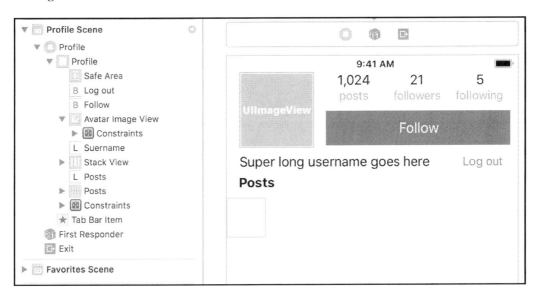

On the layout, you can see different visual items, which we have to connect with their respective outlets in the `ProfileViewController` class. We start with the user avatar, `UIImageView`, then `UILabel`, which will store the username. This is pretty similar to what we did in `FeedCellView` earlier. Next, we connect `UICollectionView`, which will show all the user's posts. The rest of the UIs will be inactive, storing some mock data, such as how many posts were created, how many followers the user has, and how many he/she is following. There is a **Log out** button that can be used to sign out from the app.

 Don't put the **Log out** button on the front row. When designing an app, you want to keep the user in the app. Just decide what's the best place for such a button. It should be there but not that easy to find, because it won't be used in every session.

Here is the view controller class in `ProfileViewController.swift`:

```
class ProfileViewController: UIViewController {
    var userUDID:String? = nil
    var listOfPosts:[PostModel]?
    @IBOutlet weak var avatarImageView: UIImageView!
    @IBOutlet weak var username: UILabel!
```

```
@IBOutlet weak var posts: UICollectionView!
@IBOutlet weak var followButton: UIButton!
@IBOutlet weak var logoutButton: UIButton!
@IBOutlet var avatarGestureRecogniser: UITapGestureRecognizer!
@IBOutlet var usernameTapGestureRecogniser: UITapGestureRecognizer!
private let photoCellReuseIdentifier = "PhotoCell"
private var pickedImage:UIImage?
    ...
}
```

The class defines a couple of outlets. Before connecting them, don't forget to associate the `ProfileViewController` class with our view controller in the storyboard.

Here is an implementation of the logout action, which should be triggered once the **Log out** button is tapped:

```
@IBAction func logoutHandler(_ sender: Any) {
    let authUI = FUIAuth.defaultAuthUI()
    do {
        try authUI?.signOut()
        let nc = NotificationCenter.default
        nc.post(name: Notification.Name(rawValue: "userSignedOut"),
                object: nil,
                userInfo: nil)
        //remove the active user
        DataManager.shared.user = nil
        DataManager.shared.userUID = nil
    } catch let error {
        print("Error: \(error)")
    }
}
```

In the preceding code, we sign out the currently logged in user and remove the reference, which we store in the shared `DataManager` instance.

When the view controller is loaded, it should adjust the UI, because it's not relevant to all profiles. We will reuse this view controller later in this chapter; that's why we make it a bit smarter:

```
override func viewDidLoad() {
    super.viewDidLoad()
    let cellNib = UINib(nibName: "PhotoViewCell", bundle: nil)
    posts.register(cellNib, forCellWithReuseIdentifier:
      photoCellReuseIdentifier)
    posts.dataSource = self
    //default avatar icon
    avatarImageView.image = #imageLiteral(resourceName: "user")
```

```
        username.text = userUDID ?? DataManager.shared.userUID
        if let layout = posts.collectionViewLayout as?
          UICollectionViewFlowLayout {
            let imageWidth = (UIScreen.main.bounds.width - 10) / 3
            layout.itemSize = CGSize(width: imageWidth, height: imageWidth)
        }
        //you can't follow yourself
        if userUDID == nil {
            followButton.isHidden = true
        } else {
            //disable change of avatar photo
            avatarGestureRecogniser.isEnabled = false
            //disable change of the username
            usernameTapGestureRecogniser.isEnabled = false
            logoutButton.isHidden = true
            //hide follow button
            if userUDID == DataManager.shared.userUID {
                followButton.isHidden = true
            }
        }
        loadData()
    }
```

First, we register a cell of type, `PhotoViewCell`, to `UICollectionView`. Then, we set the view controller as `dataSource` (we need an extra extension which implements `UICollectionViewDataSource`). The avatar is set to a default asset, `user`, and the username is set to the the auto-generated identifier. Next, we configure the layout to show exactly three items per row. Finally, we hide some part of the

UI components if `userUDID` is set. Later in the chapter, it will become clear why this code is needed.

We will have to create a new Cocoa component, similar to `FeedViewCell`. It should be called `PhotoViewCell`. The class is a one-liner:

```
class PhotoViewCell: UICollectionViewCell {
    @IBOutlet weak var image: UIImageView!
}
```

We define a single outlet. The view `.xib` is not complex either. Here is what it should look like:

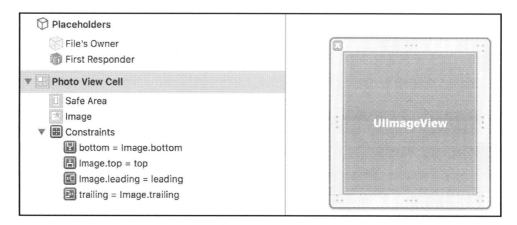

We have to add a single `UIImageView` that stretches and takes the whole cell screen estate. You can add to the **User Defined Runtime Attributes** section of `CellView` the `layer.cornerRadius` key, with value 5. This will add nice rounded corners of each cell:

We can specify different properties of a view from the Interface Builder, using the **User Defined Runtime Attributes** section of each item.

Don't forget to add **UITapGestures** to their respective components—`avatarImage` and `username`. The UI components should have **User Interaction Enabled** activated from the Xcode or via the following code:

```
avatarImageView.isUserInteractionEnabled = true
username.isUserInteractionEnabled = true
```

We will add the following feature—when the user is exploring his/her own profile, he/she can change his/her avatar photo, which will be saved on Firebase. He/she will be able to change his/her username to something more meaningful, replacing the default unique identifier assigned by Firebase.

Before adding the code that handles these neat features, we have to add new rules to the Firebase database rules. Here are the new rules that should be added to the current ones:

```
"profile":{
    ".read": "auth != null",
    ".write": "false",
```

```
        "$uid": {
            ".read": "auth != null",
            ".write": "$uid === auth.uid"
        }
    }
```

The extra rules allow every logged in user to read all the profiles. Writing is restricted and only the profile owner can update his/her own profile (to change the username and avatar photo).

The upload of an avatar image user flow can be triggered by tapping on the image at the top. We should add `UITapGestureRecogniser`, which is associated with `UIImageView` (`avatarImage`). The action that will be triggered will be:

```
func pickAvatarImage(_ sender: Any)
```

The name for this function is not fixed and you can pick another name in your code. Just link the correct one with `UIGestureRecognizer`.

 If your `GestureRecognizer` is not working, `UIView` might be the non-interactive one. You can verify that using the properties inspector in the Interface Builder.

We are going to use `UIImagePickerController` to present an image picker interface to the user. The picker allows you to crop and position the selected image. Once the image is picked, it will be scaled-down and uploaded on the Firebase store. The code that does this is logically separated from the rest of the class, so we can define it in a new extension:

```
extension ProfileViewController: UIImagePickerControllerDelegate,
UINavigationControllerDelegate {
    @IBAction func pickAvatarImage(_ sender: Any) {
        let pickerController = UIImagePickerController()
            pickerController.delegate = self
            pickerController.allowsEditing = true
            present(pickerController, animated: true, completion: nil)
    }
    func imagePickerControllerDidCancel(_ picker:
      UIImagePickerController) {
        picker.dismiss(animated: true, completion: nil)
    }
    func imagePickerController(_ picker:
      UIImagePickerController, didFinishPickingMediaWithInfo
      info: [String : Any]) {
        ...
    }
```

```
        }
```

In the preceding code, you can see that we are opening UIImagePickerController with extra editing configuration. We set self to be its delegate; thus ProfileViewController should implement UIImagePickerControllerDelegate and UINavigationControllerDelegate to present the UI and dismiss it.

The most interesting method is the handling of the selected image:

```
func imagePickerController(_ picker: UIImagePickerController,
didFinishPickingMediaWithInfo info: [String : Any]) {
    if let editedImage = info[UIImagePickerControllerEditedImage]
      as? UIImage{
        pickedImage = self.scale(image: editedImage, toSize:
          CGSize(width:100, height:100))
    } else if let chosenImage = info[UIImagePickerControllerOriginalImage]
        as? UIImage {
        pickedImage = self.scale(image: chosenImage,
          toSize: CGSize(width:100, height:100))
    }
    picker.dismiss(animated: true, completion: nil)
    //does the heavy lifting
    updateAvatar()
}
```

The code scales down the selected image and stores the result in a property called pickedImage. Then, the UI is dismissed and the function that uploads the image is triggered. The function is similar to the upload of a photo from Chapter 10, *Building an Instagram-Like App*, but this time the file has a predefined name, avatar.jpg. A link to the avatar resource is stored in the database, once the upload finishes:

```
func updateAvatar() {
    if pickedImage != nil {
        self.avatarImageView.image = pickedImage
    }
    DataManager.shared.updateProfile(avatar: pickedImage, progress: {
      progress in
        print("Upload avatar progress: \(progress)")
    }) { result in
        if !result {
            print("something went wrong")
        }
    }
}
```

The `updateProfile` function uploads the image to `/posts/\(userID)/avatar.jpg` and then saves this path to the `/profile/\(userID)/avatar` key in the database. (For more details, you can check the source code, which is similar to the one discussed in `Chapter 10`, *Building an Instagram-Like App*.)

The scale-down function keeps the aspect ratio of the image and resizes the source image. Its implementation can be found in the following block:

```
func scale(image: UIImage, toSize size:CGSize) -> UIImage? {
    let imageSize = image.size
    let widthRatio  = size.width  / image.size.width
    let heightRatio = size.height / image.size.height
    var newSize: CGSize
    if(widthRatio > heightRatio) {
        newSize = CGSize(width:imageSize.width * heightRatio, height:
imageSize.height * heightRatio)
    } else {
        newSize = CGSize(width: imageSize.width * widthRatio,  height:
imageSize.height * widthRatio)
    }
    UIGraphicsBeginImageContextWithOptions(newSize, false, 0)
    image.draw(in: CGRect(origin: CGPoint.zero, size: newSize))
    let newImage = UIGraphicsGetImageFromCurrentImageContext()
    UIGraphicsEndImageContext()
    return newImage
}
```

It depends on the device's density. If you want to use a specific density, then you should change the last argument of the following call:

```
UIGraphicsBeginImageContextWithOptions(newSize, false, 0)
```

With a similar interaction, the user will be able to change his/her username. He/she has to tap on the label, which displays the current username. This action will open an alert box with a text input where the new username can be entered. If the user taps on the **Update** button, then the new username will be saved in the database. The code that does this is shown here:

```
@IBAction func changeUsername(_ sender: Any) {
    let alertController   = UIAlertController(title: "Change your username",
      message: "Please, enter a new username.", preferredStyle: .alert)
    alertController.addTextField { (textField) in
        //do some textFiled customization
    }
    alertController.addAction(UIAlertAction(title: "Update",
      style: .default, handler: { [weak alertController, weak self]
```

```
       (action) in
         if let textFields = alertController?.textFields! {
            if textFields.count > 0 {
               let textFiled = textFields[0]
               //update the ui
               self?.username.text = textFiled.text
               //update the server data
               self?.updateUsername(username: textFiled.text)
            }
         }
      }))
      alertController.addAction(UIAlertAction(title: "Cancel", style:
   .default, handler: nil))
      self.present(alertController, animated: true, completion: nil)
   }
```

The UI is updated immediately and then the change is sent to the server. In general, this order is a bit misleading, because the save in the database might fail. It's better to reflect the change in the UI once it's confirmed by the server. But before that, you have to update the UI to show the user that the change is about to be applied:

```
func updateUsername(username:String?) {
    DataManager.shared.updateProfileUsername(username: username) {
      result in
        if !result {
           print("something went wrong")
        }
    }
}
```

In the preceding code, the callback logs the result from the Firebase. The actual heavy lifting is done by `DataManager`. Here is the method that implements the actual update in the remote database:

```
func updateProfileUsername(username newUsername:String?, callback:
@escaping (Bool) -> () ) {
   guard let userID = userUID else {
      callback(false)
      return
   }
   guard let username = newUsername else {
      callback(false)
      return
   }
   let dbKey = "profile/\(userID)/username"
   let childUpdates = [dbKey: username]
   databaseRef.updateChildValues(childUpdates)
```

```
        callback(true)
    }
```

In this function, we update the username field with the new value. We don't check if the username is already taken, because every user has a unique identifier and this username is more like an alias.

The next section presents the search screen, which renders all the photos that are fitting the search criteria in a grid.

# Search screen

The search screen has a search field at the top. This `UISearchBar` is a standard component that is used to allow the user to search through the data displayed on the screen. The UI component doesn't do the actual searching. It handles the user's interactions, and `UISearchBarDelegate` is responsible for taking action:

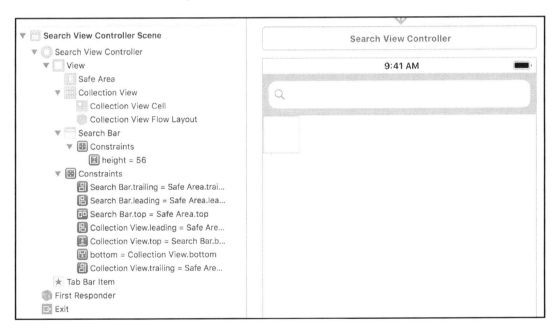

This is the layout of the screen, with a search bar at the top and a collection view below it. They are using constraints to fill the whole screen.

We need a new `SearchViewController.swift` file. It will store the logic of the view controller. The following code shows the initial implementation of the `SearchViewController` class:

```
class SearchViewController: UIViewController {
    private let photoCellReuseIdentifier = "PhotoCell"
    var model:[PostModel]?
    @IBOutlet weak var collectionView: UICollectionView!
    @IBOutlet weak var searchBar: UISearchBar!
    override func viewDidLoad() {
        super.viewDidLoad()
        let cellNib = UINib(nibName: "PhotoViewCell", bundle: nil)
        collectionView.register(cellNib, forCellWithReuseIdentifier:
          photoCellReuseIdentifier)
        let gridLayout = GridLayout()
        gridLayout.fixedDivisionCount = 3
        gridLayout.scrollDirection = .vertical
        gridLayout.delegate = self
        collectionView.collectionViewLayout = gridLayout
        collectionView.dataSource = self
        searchBar.delegate = self
        loadData()
    }
}
```

In `viewDidLoad()`, we are registering the same `CellView` that we used on the profile screen.

The `loadData()` function loads all photos from the home screen. Its code is pretty familiar to us being already from `HomeFeedViewController`. Here is our implementation, which loads all posts from the home view:

```
func loadData() {
    model = []
    DataManager.shared.fetchHomeFeed {[weak self] items in
        if items.count > 0 {
            self?.model? += items
            self?.collectionView.reloadData()
        }
    }
}
```

The `GridLayout` class is an external class that can be used to render the cells of `UICollectionView` in a grid with a predefined number of columns or rows. It defines a delegate, which can be used to stress on some cells in the collection.

The `GridLayout` class, an open source class, can be used in our app and can be found in **Github-gist** at `https://gist.github.com/heitara/9d3a3c2dccf5805b69d3d90cf6d24ac1`. The implementation of `GridLayoutDelegate` scales up every ninth item and it takes four virtual tiles from the layout. Every other item takes only a single virtual tile. The following code block shows the details:

```
extension SearchViewController: GridLayoutDelegate {
    func scaleForItem(inCollectionView collectionView: UICollectionView,
        withLayout layout: UICollectionViewLayout, atIndexPath
        indexPath: IndexPath) -> UInt {
        if indexPath.row % 9 == 0 {
            return 2
        }
        return 1
    }
}
```

We have to implement the `UICollectionViewDataSource` protocol in a separate extension. The following snippet reveals the details:

```
extension SearchViewController: UICollectionViewDataSource {
    func collectionView(_ collectionView: UICollectionView,
        numberOfItemsInSection section: Int) -> Int {
        return model?.count ?? 0
    }
    func collectionView(_ collectionView: UICollectionView,
        cellForItemAt indexPath: IndexPath) -> UICollectionViewCell {
        guard let cell = collectionView.dequeueReusableCell(
            withReuseIdentifier: photoCellReuseIdentifier,
            for: indexPath) as? PhotoViewCell else {
            return UICollectionViewCell()
        }
        guard let post = model?[indexPath.row] else {
            return cell
        }
        if let image = post.photoURL {
            let imgRef = Storage.storage().reference().child(image)
            cell.image.sd_setImage(with: imgRef)
        }
        return cell
    }
}
```

The preceding implementation is already something that we faced earlier in this chapter and many times in our book.

To communicate with the search component, `SearchViewController` has to implement `UISearchBarDelegate`, as shown in the following code:

```
extension SearchViewController: UISearchBarDelegate {
    func searchBarSearchButtonClicked(_ searchBar: UISearchBar) {
        if let searchText = searchBar.text {
            if !searchText.isEmpty {
                DataManager.shared.search(for: searchText) {
                    [weak self] items in
                    self?.model? = items
                    self?.collectionView.reloadData()
                }
                searchBar.text = ""
                //hide the keyboard
                searchBar.resignFirstResponder()
            }
        }
    }
}
```

We check the text that is entered in the search box. If it's not empty text, then we initiate a search. Then, the text is removed and the keyboard is hidden. Unfortunately, Firebase doesn't support a full-text search. We can implement a specific search behavior using the default functions available and a pretty powerful search if we use third-party APIs.

The search function returns all photo posts with a *description* that starts the same way as the passed search text.

Here is the actual search function that is part of the `DataManage` class:

```
func search(for searchText:String, callback: @escaping ([PostModel]) -> ()
) {
    let key = "description"
    databaseRef
        .child("posts")
        .queryOrdered(byChild: key)
        .queryStarting(atValue: searchText, childKey: key)
        .queryEnding(atValue: searchText + "\u{f8ff}", childKey: key)
        .observeSingleEvent(of: .value, with: { snapshot in
        let items: [PostModel] = snapshot.children.compactMap { child in
            guard let child = child as? DataSnapshot else {
                return nil
            }
            return PostModel.init(snapshot: child)
        }
        DispatchQueue.main.async {
            callback(items)
```

```
        }
    })
}
```

The search function looks for all posts with a description starting with the specific text. \u{f8ff} is a special UTF-8 character code that is greater than all other UTF-8 symbols. This special ending rule is added to filter out all items that have a  different beginning. The next section discusses the favorites screen. This is the last missing piece of our app.

# Favorites screen

The favorites screen should present the all favorite posts. The home screen provides a favorites icon, but we haven't attached any functionality. This means that there are no favorite posts stored on Firebase. We will develop the favorites screen to render a list of all of the user's favorite posts. If the list of posts is empty, then the app will show a prompt to the user (not an empty screen) to suggest there are no favorite posts:

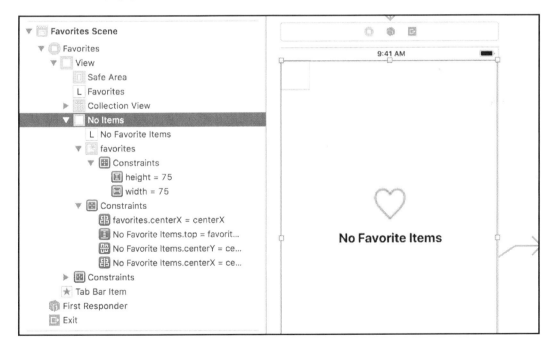

The UI has a collection view that can render all posts, similar to the one on the search screen. The more interesting part is the regular view, which contains a `UIImageView` and a `UILable` position in the middle. This view should be visible only when the collection is empty, to inform the user of the app.

The `FavoritesViewController` class is shown in the following code:

```
class FavoritesViewController: UIViewController {
    @IBOutlet weak var collectionView: UICollectionView!
    @IBOutlet weak var noItems: UIView!
    override func viewDidLoad() {
        super.viewDidLoad()
        showEmptyView()
        loadData()
    }
    func loadData() {
        //TODO: load all favorite posts
    }
}
```

The code is pretty short and simple. We show the information view and initiate the loading. Once the loading is done, the information view should be hidden and the collection view will be presented. We know that there are no favorites on Firebase, thus the `loadData` function is left empty. To make the whole picture complete, we have to define the `showEmptyView()` function. Let's design this piece of code so that we can reuse it on all other screens where we display a list of items.
First, we can start with a contract or a `protocol`:

```
protocol EmptyCollectionView {
    func showCollectionView()
    func showEmptyView()
    var collectionView: UICollectionView! { get }
    var emptyView: UIView? { get }
}
```

We need a function to show the collection view, one to show the empty view, and two properties to access the actual views. Let's define the default behavior of the two functions:

```
extension EmptyCollectionView {
    func showCollectionView() {
        self.emptyView?.isHidden = true
        self.collectionView.isHidden = false
    }
    func showEmptyView() {
        if self.emptyView != nil {
```

```
                self.emptyView?.isHidden = false
                self.collectionView.isHidden = true
        }
    }
}
```

The preceding functions are simple and short. They toggle between the two views. The extension of the protocol is used to provide a default implementation of the functions. We can redefine those once we implement the protocol. If there is no implementation, then the default one will be used.

And here is the final piece of the puzzle; how we can use `showEmptyView()` in our view controller:

```
extension FavoritesViewController: EmptyCollectionView {
    var emptyView: UIView? {
        return noItems
    }
}
```

The only missing bit is to extend the `EmptyCollectionView` protocol and to return the correct views. In our case, the collection has the same `collectionView` property and we only have to do it for the `emptyView`.

The next section discusses some improvements related to the home screen, such as loading user profiles, displaying the user's photo, and opening the profile screen when the avatar or the username is tapped.

# Polishing the home screen

We have the UI developed and we won't add any new visual elements. Each cell contains an avatar image and an avatar name. Our only task is to fetch all user profiles and load the information in each cell. This is not a trivial task.

We will use a dictionary to store the profiles of all the different users. Then, we can start the loading and, once we have all the profiles, we can refresh `UIViewCollection`:

```
var users = [String: UserModel?]()
```

This is the only new property which we will add to `HomeFeedViewController`. Then we have to add a new model to the DataManager.swift—`UserModel`:

```
class UserModel {
    var avatarPhoto:String?
```

```
    var username:String?
    init() {
        //nothing
    }
    init?(snapshot:DataSnapshot) {
        if let dict = snapshot.value as? [String:Any] {
            if dict["avatar"] != nil {
                self.avatarPhoto = dict["avatar"] as? String
            }
            if dict["username"] != nil {
                self.username = dict["username"] as? String
            }
        } else {
            return nil
        }
    }
}
```

We can define a function which loads `UserModel` based on an identifier. Here is what it should look like:

```
func loadUserInfo(userId:String, callback: @escaping (UserModel?) -> () ) {
    databaseRef
        .child("profile/\(userId)")
        .observeSingleEvent(of: .value, with: { snapshot in
        var userModel:UserModel? = UserModel.init(snapshot:snapshot)
        DispatchQueue.main.async {
            callback(userModel)
        }
    })
}
```

The function loads the user's profile and uses `callback` to report the result back. Let's dive into the details on how to load all profiles in `HomeFeedViewController`. We will need a new function for this:

```
func loadAllUsers() {
    var usersInfoToLoad = 0
    var usersInfoLoaded = 0
    if let model = self.model {
        for item in model {
            let userId = item.author
            if users[userId] == nil {
                usersInfoToLoad += 1
                users[userId] = UserModel()
            }
        }
```

```
//a function
let reloadView = { [weak self] in
    if usersInfoLoaded == usersInfoToLoad {
        self?.collectionView.reloadData()
    }
}

for author in users.keys {
    let userId = author
    DataManager.shared.loadUserInfo(userId: userId) {
      [weak self] userModel in
        if let userModel = userModel {
            self?.users[userId] = userModel
            usersInfoLoaded += 1
            //update the UI if we loaded everything
            reloadView()
        }
    }
}
```

This function has to be called from `loadData`. Here is the new version of that function:

```
func loadData() {
    model = []
    DataManager.shared.fetchHomeFeed {[weak self] items in
        if items.count > 0 {
            self?.model? += items
            self?.loadAllUsers()
            self?.collectionView.reloadData()
        }
    }
}
```

We have to update the method which fills each cell with data. We just have to add the following lines at the bottom before the `return` clause:

```
cell.avatarImage.image = #imageLiteral(resourceName: "user")
    //update the user info
    if let user = self.users[post.author] {
        cell.avatarName.text = user?.username ?? post.author
        if let avatarPath = user?.avatarPhoto {
            let imgRef = Storage.storage().reference().child(avatarPath)
            cell.avatarImage.sd_setImage(with: imgRef, placeholderImage:
                #imageLiteral(resourceName: "user"), completion: nil)
        }
    }
```

Here, we set a default icon, which will be replaced with a new one, once the profiles are fetched. The username is updated as well.

The next change handles a tap gesture, which is done on the first horizontal view stack in each cell. The new functions that we add to the `FeedViewCell` class are:

```
protocol ProfileHandler {
    func openProfile(cell: UICollectionViewCell)
}
class FeedViewCell: UICollectionViewCell {
    // old code is here ... except awakeFromNib
    var tapGestureRecogniser: UITapGestureRecognizer!
    var delegate: ProfileHandler?
    override func awakeFromNib() {
        super.awakeFromNib()
        translatesAutoresizingMaskIntoConstraints = false
        self.contentView.translatesAutoresizingMaskIntoConstraints = false
        avatarImage.layer.cornerRadius = avatarImage.frame.height / 2
        avatarImage.clipsToBounds = true
        //new lines
        tapGestureRecogniser = UITapGestureRecognizer(target: self,
          action: #selector(onProfileTap))
        avatarName.superview?.addGestureRecognizer(tapGestureRecogniser)
    }
    @objc func onProfileTap(sender: Any) {
        delegate?.openProfile(cell: self)
    }
}
```

The structure of the cell is defined by us; thus, we can add the gesture recognizer to the exact place:

If the structure of `FeedViewCell` is changed, then the code should be updated, because it's tightly coupled with the current layout. A better implementation is to add `UITapGestureRecognizer` using the Interface Builder.

`HomeFeedViewController` should implement the new protocol. In this implementation, it should start a segue, which will open a new instance of `ProfileViewController`:

```
extension HomeFeedViewController: ProfileHandler {
    func openProfile(cell: UICollectionViewCell) {
        guard let indexPath = self.collectionView.indexPath(for: cell),
        let post = model?[indexPath.row] else {
            return
        }
        performSegue(withIdentifier: "openProfile", sender: post.author
    }
}
```

We extract the identifier of the user and pass it to the segue. The actual handling is done in the `prepare` function:

```
override func prepare(for segue: UIStoryboardSegue, sender: Any?) {
    if segue.identifier == "openProfile"  {
        if let navController = segue.destination as? UINavigationController
{
            if let profileVC = navController.topViewController
                as? ProfileViewController {
                profileVC.userUDID = sender as? String
            }
        }
    }
}
```

We need one minor update in the rendered cell. We have to set the delegate to each cell to be the current instance:

```
cell.delegate = self
```

We have to create and give the correct identifier of the segue. We will add a new
`UINavigationController`, which has our `ProfileViewController` for a root view
controller. We have to add a segue called `openProfile`, which will be triggered when the
user clicks on the avatar:

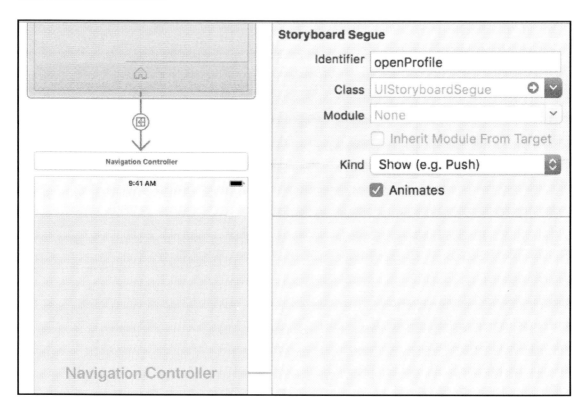

Here is the new **Navigation Controller**, which we will add to the storyboard:

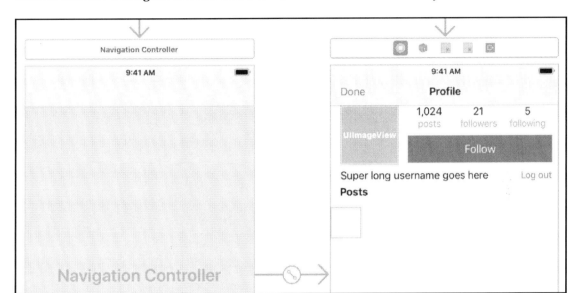

The **Done** button should trigger an action that dismisses the current view controller. UINavigationBar will appear only in cases when ProfileViewController is presented from a navigation controller. This will happen when a user taps on the avatar or the username. Also, the app has to handle all the different edge cases in ProfileViewController when an avatar is clicked—it could be a new avatar or the current user. In those two cases, we have to hide or show the **Log out** button and the **Follow** button, too.

We have developed the rest of the screens—home screen, profile screen, search screen, and favorites screen. Each screen is rendering real data from Firebase. We have applied knowledge from previous chapters mixed with the Firebase API. This helped us to create an application that looks close to our initial idea. Here are some screenshots of the working app on a simulator. This is the home screen on iPhone X:

This is the search screen in action:

This is the filter screen that's part of the **Create Post** user flow:

This is the favorites screen, showing that there are no favorite posts yet:

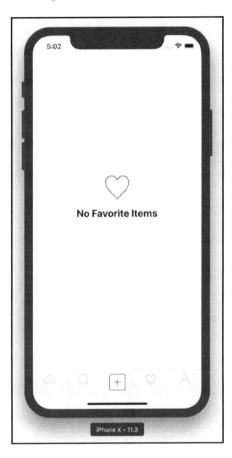

This is the screen that appears when an avatar is tapped from the home screen. It is slightly different from the regular profile screen:

# Summary

If you have followed the last chapters in this book, then you will probably have an app with similar screens. You can use these newly learned things to improve the app even more. Don't forget to use open source libraries when developing. This is a great boost and a time saver.

This was the last chapter, but we have a bonus one for you. It's about GitHub and how to contribute to a swift (open source) project hosted there. When we are using some open source libraries for free, not everything in them is working as we expect or how we would like. Thus, it's a nice thing to know how to extend such a library and how to bring the fixes back to the project. We will discuss the whole process for this in the bonus chapter.

# 12
# Contributing to an Open Source Project

In this chapter, we will discuss the basics of contributing to an open source project. We will start with getting familiar with GitHub, then how to **fork** an existing project in our account. Next, we will create a contribution (we will add something to the project), and the chapter will end with a guide on how to create a **pull request** so that our contribution can be added to the original project, making it a better one.

## Your account at GitHub

We have been using open source projects, some of which are hosted on GitHub. But we don't need an account on GitHub to do that. Unfortunately, when we want to contribute to a project (not only open source) hosted on GitHub, we will need an account. You can sign up using the `http://github.com/` page. Once you are registered, you have to log in and open the following project: `https://github.com/Yummypets/YPImagePicker`.

This is the project that we are going to be using to pick an image from the gallery in our *InstalikeApp*. We will try to add the ability to modify the filters that are displayed on the filter page. At the moment, there is no way to change them easily. One option is to change the code in the `Pods` project, but this can't be easily shared with other developers working with this component.

Now, you have an account at GitHub, which can be used to create a fork of a repository. This allows you to create your own version of every forked project and share it easily with the community. In the following sections, we will understand more about forks and why we need them.

# Forking a repository

You will have to open a web browser and open `https://github.com`. Then, open the project that you want to fork. To create a fork, you have to click on the **Fork** button at the top:

This will initiate the process of forking, which means that a special copy of the project will be created and you will have the rights to change its code in that very copy:

Now, you can see that the project exists at the following address: `https://github.com/{user-name}/YPImagePicker/`.

`{user-name}` will be replaced with your GitHub username.

 We have to check if the project has some rules or policies when we want to make a contribution. This is individual for each project.

You have to checkout the project to make your changes. You can use the Terminal and execute the following command:

```
git clone https://github.com/{user-name}/YPImagePicker/
```

Here is how you can fetch the source code of the forked repository using the Terminal:

```
Terminal — git ‹ git clone https://github.com/heitara/YPImagePicker — 80×9
emil@Emils-MacBook-Pro:~/Documents/Swift 4/Chapter 12$ git clone https://github.
com/heitara/YPImagePicker
Cloning into 'YPImagePicker'...
remote: Counting objects: 2341, done.
Receiving objects:  21% (502/2341), 8.18 MiB | 1.72 MiB/s
```

An alternative way is to clone the project using Xcode. Open Xcode, select the **SourceControl** menu, and then the **Clone** option. You have to enter the address of the repository that we mentioned previously:
`https://github.com/{user-name}/YPImagePicker/`.

In the next section, we will extend the project, so the list of filters can be easily customized. The improvement is not huge, but it will make the library really usable in custom scenarios, when we do need a special set of filters to be available on the filter screen.

# Let's contribute

Once we have downloaded the source code of the project, we can start exploring it in detail. You can use the project and open it in Xcode. This step is important, so we can decide what changes are best to implement the desired new behavior of the library.

We already know how we can use the `YPImagePicker` and what's missing. There is no easy way to change the list of filters that are available once an image is selected.

We will extend the configuration that is passed to the `YPImagePickerController` to contain the list of filters. This way, the developer who is using the library will be in control of the collection of filters. First, let's create a simple class that will define a filter.

A filter has a name and actual **CIFilter** that is used to transform the `UIImage`. Here is the class that we should add to the library – `YPFilterDescriptor.swift`:

```
public class YPFilterDescriptor {
    let name:String
    let filterName:String
```

```
        public init(name: String, filterName: String ) {
            self.name = name
            self.filterName = filterName
        }
    }
```

Then, we have to add a property in the `configuration`, which will contain all available filters. Based on this list of `descriptor` objects, the library will create the actual list of all filters, once an image is selected. This way, the configuration contains only light dummy objects.

Here is what the new property looks like:

```
public var filters:[YPFilterDescriptor] = [
  YPFilterDescriptor(name: "Normal", filterName: ""),
  YPFilterDescriptor(name: "Mono", filterName: "CIPhotoEffectMono"),
  YPFilterDescriptor(name: "Tonal", filterName: "CIPhotoEffectTonal"),
  YPFilterDescriptor(name: "Noir", filterName: "CIPhotoEffectNoir"),
  YPFilterDescriptor(name: "Fade", filterName: "CIPhotoEffectFade"),
  YPFilterDescriptor(name: "Chrome", filterName: "CIPhotoEffectChrome"),
  YPFilterDescriptor(name: "Process", filterName: "CIPhotoEffectProcess"),
  YPFilterDescriptor(name: "Transfer", filterName: "CIPhotoEffectTransfer"),
  YPFilterDescriptor(name: "Instant", filterName: "CIPhotoEffectInstant"),
  YPFilterDescriptor(name: "Sepia", filterName: "CISepiaTone")
  ]
```

The `configuration` object contains the default list of filters.

We need a slight change in the following class, `YPFiltersVC`, to start using the new configuration:

```
required init(image: UIImage, configuration: YPImagePickerConfiguration) {
        self.configuration = configuration
        super.init(nibName: nil, bundle: nil)
        title = configuration.wordings.filter
        self.originalImage = image
        filterPreviews = []
        //use the configuration to create all filters
        for filterDescriptor in configuration.filters {
            filterPreviews.append(YPFilterPreview(filterDescriptor.name))
            filters.append(YPFilter(filterDescriptor.filterName))
        }
    }
```

This is the new version of the `init` method. The preceding code updates the list of filters, taking into account what's in the configuration. If there is no change in the configuration, the library will have the same old behavior.

Our change extends the control, but keeps the current behavior. This is a well-designed feature, because after an update, without any change to the code, everything will work like before. Also, the developer will have better control and he/she might decide to use that in the future.

In the next section, we will discuss how to create a request and ask the maintainer of the project to bring your improvements back to the original project.

# Pull request

You have forked the repository so it knows its origins. This will allow us to use GitHub's special function to bundle all changes made. Then, we can easily send them in a special format to the original repository. Then, they can be easily applied to the original project. If approved, your contribution becomes part of the open source project and GitHub keeps that visible.

The maintainers of some projects keep a list of all contributors to their project on a visible place. This way, they acknowledge the contribution to the project and share that with the community.

The format that GitHub uses to send the changes back to the original project repository is called a **pull request**.

A pull request shows all the changes that you have made in your repository (a specific branch in it) compared to the origin. Once the request is opened, it tracks all the changes between two repositories. This means that you can do some extra commits and they will become part of the pull request if it's still opened.

The process of accepting (merging) a pull request might take extra time. Usually, the change is checked by the project maintainers; they comment and suggest improvements if there are any, and once everything is resolved and it matches the raised quality and project style, the request can be accepted.

It's possible to accept or reject a pull request.

Once your pull request is accepted, then your contribution will become part of the original project and who uses it in the future might use your feature.

Now, let's create your first pull request step by step.

First, confirm that you have committed the change and pushed the result to your repository. You can do that with the following command from the Terminal, if you are in the root folder of the project:

```
git add .
git commit -m "Extend the configuration to have a control over the list of
filters"
```

This will create a local commit, which should be pushed to GitHub. You can do this with the following command:

```
git push
```

Now, you have to open the project in a browser. It should be located at `https://github.com/{user-name}/YPImagePicker`. Don't forget to replace `{user-name}` with your GitHub username:

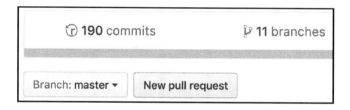

You have to click on the **New pull request** button. This will prepare the pull request and you will see its details:

pull request

You will see a lot of information about the new pull request that will be created. The page shows all the commits and all the changes:

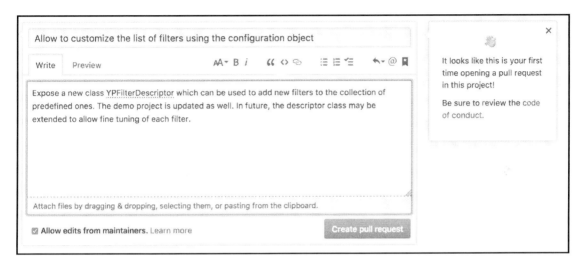

You can add a title and explain more about the actual pull request. We have entered some basic details about the implementation and possible improvements.

You can click on the **Create pull request** button at the bottom. This will create your pull request and a special thread where a discussion can be started with the maintainers.

You can verify that your pull request is opened. Just open the project's page and click on the **Pull requests** tab:

You can see the pull request that we created listed here. Once it's closed, you can find it in the closed section:

The changes that we have done here are already sent and are merged to the original project. You can decide to add something new to this library or to any other. The process should be clear and easy now that you have read this chapter.

Let's check what we have learned about GitHub and open source projects.

# Summary

In this chapter, we discussed the whole process of contribution to an open source project hosted on GitHub. The same technique can be applied to private projects as well. We started with a fork of a repository. Then, we created the changes and pushed those to our fork. By creating a pull request, we let the project's maintainers know about our improvements. Once the pull request is approved, our update will become part of the original project. The whole process might take a day or a month—it depends on the maintainers of the project—but in the end, the people who are using the project will benefit.

Through the process of writing mobile applications, you will use many open source projects. When you update one project, you can try to share your changes easily by applying what you have learned in this chapter. Don't forget that the open source projects are pushed by the developers, who are using them.

If you have reached this chapter, then you have already learned a lot about Swift. We started our journey with the very basics of Swift-like variables and functions. Then, we got familiar with Xcode IDE and the playgrounds where we can experiment with real code. After our first snippets, we created our first mobile app using Swift for iOS. Next, we discussed the details of structure, classes, and inheritance. At that point, we already knew a lot about Swift and iOS. We were ready to add some interactivity to our first mobile app. We continued discussing the basic data structures, which were object-oriented programming, extensions, and protocols.

With our growing knowledge about iOS, we built the first version of our *Weather* app, which had a couple of screens. Then, we learned more about how to integrate external libraries using CocoaPods and a little bit about some alternatives such as Swift Package Manager. Later, we discussed different ways to fetch data from web services and display them. This led to our refined version of the *Weather* app, which was our preparation for the final app—an Instagram cloning app which uses a real backend service, such as Firebase. Developing it from scratch took us a lot of time, but we used everything we learned in the previous chapters to develop one awesome working app.

In the last chapter of this book, we discussed how easy it is to contribute to an open source project host on GitHub. We made a minor contribution which is already part of a library that all other Swift developers can use.

Keep reading and practicing by developing your own ideas. Don't forget to share what you have developed with the other Swift developers, because they will help you to develop your libraries and make them stronger than ever.

If you have any questions, ideas, or just want to share something with the author of the book, you can get in touch using the information available on his GitHub profile.

# Other Books You May Enjoy

If you enjoyed this book, you may be interested in these other books by Packt:

**Learn iOS 11 Programming with Swift 4 - Second Edition**
Craig Clayton

ISBN: 978-1-78839-075-0

- Get to grips with Swift 4 and Xcode 9, the building blocks of Apple development
- Get to know the fundamentals of Swift 4 , including strings, variables, constants, and control flow
- Discover the distinctive design principles that define the iOS user experience
- Build a responsive UI and add privacy to your custom-rich notifications
- Preserve the data and manipulate the image with filters and effects
- Bring in SiriKit to create payment requests inside your app
- Collect valuable feedback with TestFlight before you release your apps on the App Store

## Mastering Swift 4 - Fourth Edition
Jon Hoffman

ISBN: 978-1-78847-780-2

- Delve into the core components of Swift 4.0, including operators, collections, control flows, and functions
- Create and use classes, structures, and enumerations
- Understand protocol-oriented design and see how it can help you write better code
- Develop a practical understanding of subscripts and extensions
- Add concurrency to your applications using Grand Central Dispatch and Operation Queues
- Implement generics and closures to write very flexible and reusable code
- Make use of Swift's error handling and availability features to write safer code

# Leave a review - let other readers know what you think

Please share your thoughts on this book with others by leaving a review on the site that you bought it from. If you purchased the book from Amazon, please leave us an honest review on this book's Amazon page. This is vital so that other potential readers can see and use your unbiased opinion to make purchasing decisions, we can understand what our customers think about our products, and our authors can see your feedback on the title that they have worked with Packt to create. It will only take a few minutes of your time, but is valuable to other potential customers, our authors, and Packt. Thank you!

# Index

Made in the USA
Lexington, KY
25 July 2018

AUG - - 2018
3843554